A HISTORY TODAY BOOK

CONFRONTING THE NAZI PAST

New Debates on Modern German History

———

A HISTORY TODAY BOOK

CONFRONTING THE NAZI PAST

New Debates on Modern German History

Edited by

MICHAEL BURLEIGH

COLLINS & BROWN

First published in Great Britain in 1996
by Collins & Brown Limited
London House
Great Eastern Wharf
Parkgate Road
London SW11 4NQ

A CIP catalogue record for this book
is available from the British Library

ISBN 1 85585 183 0

Commissioning Editor: Juliet Gardiner
Typeset by Falcon Oast Graphic Art
Printed and bound in Great Britain

CONTENTS

INTRODUCTION   1
Michael Burleigh

CHAPTER I
'THE REAL MYSTERY IN GERMANY': THE GERMAN
WORKING CLASS DURING THE NAZI DICTATORSHIP   23
Ulrich Herbert

CHAPTER II
RACIAL DISCRIMINATION AT WORK: FORCED LABOUR IN
THE VOLKSWAGEN FACTORY, 1939–45   37
Klaus-Jörg Siegfried

CHAPTER III
NAZISM AND HIGH SOCIETY   51
Jeremy Noakes

CHAPTER IV
UNDERSTANDING NAZI RACISM: PRECURSORS AND
PERPETRATORS   66
Paul Weindling

CHAPTER V
THE GERMAN *VOLKSGEMEINSCHAFT* FROM THE
PERSECUTION OF THE JEWS TO THE 'FINAL
SOLUTION'   84
Avraham Barkai

CHAPTER VI
SAVING MONEY, SPENDING LIVES: PSYCHIATRY, SOCIETY
AND THE 'EUTHANASIA' PROGRAMME   98
Michael Burleigh

CHAPTER VII
CHRISTINE LEHMANN AND MAZURKA ROSE: TWO
'GYPSIES' IN THE GRIP OF GERMAN BUREAUCRACY,
1933–60   112
Wolfgang Wippermann

CHAPTER VIII
SAVAGE WAR 125
Omer Bartov

CHAPTER IX
THE PLANNING INTELLIGENTSIA AND THE 'FINAL SOLUTION' 140
Götz Aly

CHAPTER X
THE PERSECUTION OF HOMOSEXUALS IN NAZI GERMANY 154
Hans-Georg Stümke

CHAPTER XI
WOMEN, MOTHERHOOD AND THE FAMILY IN THE THIRD REICH 167
Jill Stephenson

GLOSSARY 184

LIST OF CONTRIBUTORS 188

INDEX 191

ILLUSTRATION ACKNOWLEDGEMENTS 199

INTRODUCTION

STUDIES OF MODERN GERMAN HISTORY have reached not so much a
crossroads, as one of those motorway junctions where the driver circles around aimlessly amidst the bewildering choice of exit routes. In the
1960s and 1970s conventional diplomatic or narrative political history
was challenged by the structural models developed by advocates of
history as social 'science'. In the 1980s these were themselves partially
displaced by a new generation of historians concerned with, for example,
gender or mentalities; with the local, and some would say the trivial,
rather than the general; or with the repressive potentialities of supposedly
'progressive' disciplines such as medicine or psychiatry, with there not
being very much to distinguish doctors from policemen. It is too early to
speak with much certainty concerning how recent events — the collapse
of Communism; the resurgence of ethnic nationalism across Eastern
Europe and the former Soviet Union; the reunification of Germany; or,
to be more parochial, the self-immolation of such gurus of the 1980s as
Althusser, de Man, or Foucault — will influence the future writing of the
subject. Judging from very recent trends, the big picture — as distinct
from the current penchant for the minute, the marginal or the quirky —
is going to be dominated by the revival of forms of 'discourse' akin to the
totalitarian theories that were modish in the 1950s. The writing on the
wall can be seen from a few recent developments. Recently, the German
Volkswagen Foundation invited tenders for a vast research project on
'European Dictatorships in the Twentieth Century'. Among the project's
major concerns will be the 'comparative' study of the 'two German dictatorships', as if there is some intellectually serious comparison to be
made between the regimes of Hitler and Honecker or between the Stasi
and the Gestapo. According to the new director of the authoritative
Institut für Zeitgeschichte in Munich, the Nazi period will gradually lose
its salience in the collective memory of contemporary Europeans, being
supplanted by the 'much longer lasting experience of suffering' under the
Communists. A rather sinister example of this gradual displacement of
emphasis can be seen in the spate of memorials established to remember
those former Nazis imprisoned, and in many cases killed, after the war
in the special camps which the Soviet secret police created in former

concentration camps. At Sachsenhausen a new memorial now commemorates those who 'after 1945 . . . sacrificed their freedom, health and life
in resistance' as well as those who died in the camp during the Nazi
period — a singularly distasteful aggregation of victims and persecutors.

Many of the broad developments described above have been reflected
in the ways in which historians treat the Nazi period which, because of
its unique character, has generated not only an enormous volume of
scholarship, but also a quasi-philosophical literature and, indeed, many
notable artistic products such as films, novels and paintings. Academic
historians do not enjoy a monopoly of this subject in the way they do
with other periods of history. Indeed, even among academic historians it
is far from agreed whether the period of the Third Reich is 'history' in
the sense that, to take an example often used, the religious conflicts of sixteenth-century France are, undoubtedly, 'history'.

During the 1980s, while the *Historikerstreit*, or 'historians' dispute' —
with its explicit attempt to relativise Nazi barbarities — occupied all and
sundry, the eminent German historian Martin Broszat suggested that
after forty years it was time to go beyond what had become a blandly
routine black and white condemnation of the evils of Nazism, and to
begin assembling a more complex picture giving due consideration to the
predominantly grey areas of human behaviour during that period as
revealed by new social history approaches, and to continuities between
the Third Reich and the post-war Federal Republic. Broszat explained his
plea for the 'historisation' of the Nazi period or, in other words, for the
recovery of conventional historical 'distance' in the following passage:

> As I see it, the danger of suppressing this period consists not only in the
> customary practice of forgetting, but rather, in this instance — almost in
> paradoxical fashion — likewise in the fact that one is too overtly 'con
> cerned' for didactic reasons, about this chapter in history. As a result, what
> happens is that an arsenal of lessons and frozen 'statuary' are pieced
> together from the original, authentic continuum of this era; these increas
> ingly take on an independent existence. Particularly in the second and third
> generation, they then intrude to place themselves in front of the original
> history — and are finally, in naive fashion, understood and misunderstood
> as being the actual history of the time.

Broszat's 'plea' provoked considerable criticism from a number of
Israeli scholars, not surprisingly alert at the time of the *Historikerstreit* to
any attempts to adjust perceptions of the Nazi period. Sustained criticism

came from Saul Friedländer, one of the most intellectually sophisticated historians of the Nazi period working anywhere. Friedländer drew attention to some unfortunate similarities between Broszat's apparent concern with conceptual 'taboos' and the no-holds-barred approach of Ernst Nolte and Andreas Hillgruber, wondering quite where the line lay between Broszat's desire to restore the grey areas and Hillgruber's 'empathetic' identification with German soldiers allegedly holding back barbaric Bolsheviks from the frontiers of a western civilisation, which included Auschwitz. He was sharply critical too of attempts to discover normal patterns of evolution in Nazi Germany through parallels between, say, the welfare schemes of the German Labour Front and the British Beveridge Report, a subject that we will return to. Most profoundly, Friedländer argues that, given the universal relevance of Nazi Germany, the questions German historians wish to pose in order to come to terms with their own history or present society, should not preclude the very different concerns of others also affected by Nazism. As Friedländer says, 'the same past may mean something else to the victims of Nazism, whoever they may be, and for them, there are other, no less legitimate, modes of historicising the era'.

The remainder of this introduction is devoted to showing how for many people the Nazi period is not 'history', still less a period they remember for its 'modernising' impact, its 'normality', or its similarity to the United States or Bolshevik Russia. Popular perceptions of the period may for once have greater veracity than the increasingly febrile constructions of some academic historians, whose writings have an unreality akin to that of some branches of theology. All of the essays in this book represent original contributions commissioned from leading researchers in the field, working in Britain, Germany, Israel and the United States. None of the contributors belongs to a self-conscious historical 'school', or self-styled 'new' generation of scholars, and some of them would, no doubt respectfully, agree only to differ regarding their interpretations of the subject.

The desire of some historians to treat the Nazi period as 'history' immediately encounters considerable resistance when it cuts across the experiences of people directly affected by Nazi policies. For the latter, Nazism is not a matter of academic contemplation; but rather something which explains why they have no relatives or children; why they are chronically ill or have severe psychological problems; or why they live in Britain, Canada, Israel or the USA rather than Central Europe. The argument that the Nazis were in the business of modernising German society or defending Western civilisation from an 'Asiatic' barbarism whose political system their own paradoxically resembled, cuts little ice among those whose lives were shattered during that period.

One very large category of such people is that of former 'foreign workers', some of the seven million people, for the most part forcibly removed to work in Germany during the war. Almost half of them came from Poland or the Soviet Union, there being about 600,000 survivors alive in Poland alone today. Their collective experience consisted of appalling maltreatment at the bottom of the Nazis racial hierarchy; wages (in so far as they were paid at all), deliberately pegged below the levels paid to Germans; no provision for insurance, health care or pensions; and discrimination by the German population at large. The story of their quest for compensation is complex, and several factors contributed to their neglect. Firstly, the enormity of the Holocaust and the priority given to compensation agreements with Israel and the Jewish Claims Conference, led to the *de facto* marginalisation of other groups of victims. Secondly, wholescale plundering by 'Displaced Persons' in Germany after the war, and the mass exodus of ethnic Germans from the Communist states of Eastern Europe in the late 1940s, were deemed to be either compensation enough or a commensurate crime by many sectors of the German population. Finally, in a calculated move designed to reduce the enormous sums likely to result from individual claims, the West German authorities insisted on purely inter-governmental reparations. Supported by the Western Allies, who feared the economic and political consequences of a defeated Germany drained of its meagre resources, the West German government thus successfully managed to exclude from compensation by far the largest group of persons affected. The Soviet Union's decision — 'in agreement with the government of the People's Republic of Poland' — in August 1953 to waive any further reparations from the German Democratic Republic was interpreted by the government in Bonn as applying to the whole of Germany.

A further legal fiction was introduced to insulate private sector concerns from former 'foreign workers' seeking compensation. Although many firms had clearly actively solicited 'foreign workers', they were now deemed to have been merely 'proxies of the Reich' with the State being the 'quasi employer'. Approximately one third of all those employed in the armaments industry in 1944 were 'foreign workers', and in many private concerns the number of 'foreign workers' was between

50 and 70 per cent of the total workforce. The argument against compensation was that these concerns would pay fewer taxes which, in turn, would diminish the capacity of the Federal Republic to take an active part in the NATO alliance, to pay Israel and the Jewish Claims Conference, to contribute development aid to the Third World, and so on. Pressed to pay by their Western European allies, the Federal government eventually concluded 'voluntary' bilateral compensation agreements with eleven West European states worth DM876 million. The interests of German Ostpolitik and Polish restrictions on ethnic German would-be migrants eventually led to an agreement with Poland. In 1975 a deal was struck by Helmut Schmidt and Edward Gierek which consisted of a loan at favourable rates of interest and a one-off payment to cover pension claims, albeit at Polish rather than West German levels. Schmidt sarcastically noted that claims were addressed solely to the Federal Republic, 'as if the Germans living today in the GDR had absolutely nothing to do with it'. No deals were done with the Soviet Union, partly because the level of repression directed against former prisoners of war and civilian workers deemed 'collaborators' by the Soviet state would have made such claims embarrassing. The Federal Republic continued to refuse compensation to individuals.

Some of Germany's vast industrial concerns also refuse such compensation, despite corporate profits exceeding the budgets of some Third World countries, and an EEC directive recommending that they compensate former 'foreign workers'. Only very recently has Volkswagen (annual turnover DM68,000 million) decided to pay DM12 million to set up cultural and youth exchange facilities in countries that once supplied 'foreign workers'. It refuses to compensate individuals. The manner in which the concern recruited 'foreign workers', prisoners of war and concentration camp inmates and the conditions in which they lived, worked and in some cases died, are discussed in the chapter by the Wolfsburg historian Klaus-Jörg Siegfried. Like many major businesses, Volkswagen also invests in its own corporate history, commissioning the widely regarded contemporary historian Hans Mommsen to write what – when it appears – will clearly be an important social history of a major manufacturing and armaments firm intimately involved with the Nazi regime, rather than just an exercise in corporate vanity publishing.

Unlike many business histories, which tend to be commissioned as part of the firm's public relations, and read perfunctorily for references to oneself or to the founding 'geniuses', Mommsen's book is going to receive a very close reading, at least judging by the public furore that accompanied the recent publication of an interim report on the findings of his team, which was like an action replay of the scandal that in 1986 ensued after the publication of an official 'business history' to mark the centenary of the rival automotive giant Daimler-Benz. Alternative and radical journalists accused Mommsen of whitewashing Ferdinand Porsche, Volkswagen's founder, and suggested that the three million Deutschmarks which the project has so far cost, could have been better spent compensating some of the surviving 'foreign workers'. His attempts to present a balanced interpretation of Porsche's wartime record were oddly at variance with the willingness of Volkswagen executives to damn Porsche as an 'amoral technocrat'. Indeed, one of the more ironic aspects of the affair was the way in which the Porsche family was reduced to citing the firm's official historian to defend Ferdinand Porsche from criticisms being made by members of Volkswagen's present board of directors.

Although the charge of whitewashing the concern's history can be dismissed out of hand, it is not so easy to explain to many outraged former 'foreign workers', and concerned citizens of Wolfsburg, Mommsen's claim that during the war the Volkswagen workforce was 'a multicultural society', or his rejection of compensation to individuals because of (his) anxieties about 'manifestations of secondary corruption'. In an almost classic illustration of the difficulties that 'historicisation' can encounter when it collides with experience and memory, Joseph Rovan, an emeritus professor of German history at the Sorbonne and a former inmate of Dachau observed in a letter to *Die Zeit* regarding Mommsen:

> That a 'respected' historian could still defend his insensitive blunder despite the anger which his use of the words 'multicultural society' to describe the emaciated, starving, demoralised mass of foreign workers, Soviet POWs, and concentration camp inmates occasioned, is further proof of the inability of the historian to grasp what happened.

Volkswagen continues to reimburse those Germans who in the 1930s regularly saved in anticipation of one day owning a 'people's car'.

Sinti and Roma are a further group of victims of the Nazi regime who still experience considerable difficulties obtaining any form of compensation. An estimated five hundred thousand Sinti and Roma (or 'Gypsies', to use the word they keenly resent) perished in the *Porajmos*, the Roma word for the Nazi Holocaust. Persecuted under the Communist regimes of Eastern Europe, they have become one of the principal targets for aggression both in the 'democratic' successor states, and as refugees in Western Europe, most recently in the disgraceful occurrences in Rostock's Lichtenhagen a few years ago where two hundred of them were hounded out by a mob of alienated and murderous working-class bootboys with the encouragement of many of the ordinary inhabitants. They have experienced great difficulties in securing compensation for their suffering under the Nazis. The dice have been loaded against them for several reasons. Compensation claims tend to be acknowledged in cases where there was material loss or deliberate retardation of educational and professional prospects. Such a system clearly does not favour the propertyless; people without conventionally structured careers; or those who learn their 'life-skills' — whether as craftsmen or entertainers — within the family rather than in schools or colleges.

More significantly, compensation was withheld from Sinti and Roma because of the continuation of 'anti-Gypsy' prejudices after the war. In January 1956 the West German Federal Supreme Court decided that 'Gypsies' were fundamentally 'asocial' because of their nomadic way of life and allegedly 'criminal' inclinations. The court based this decision on the observation that Nazi laws against Sinti and Roma were not substantially different from similar legislation in both Imperial and Weimar Germany. Instead of concluding that the legislation from earlier periods was also inherently discriminatory because of its collective character, the Supreme Court used its existence to prove the normality of measures introduced by the Nazis. Following the logic of its decision as to what constituted legitimate police measures, the court also decided that Sinti and Roma had only become victims of racial persecution following the issuing of the so-called 'Auschwitz Decree' on 1 March 1943 which dispatched them to the extermination camp. These were far from being merely academic or jurisprudential matters. In 1957 a 'Gypsy' woman who had emigrated to Belgium in 1939 was denied compensation because the courts could not determine whether her flight had been provoked by Nazi persecution. A year later another 'Gypsy' was refused redress for false arrest by the Nazis, because neither his sedentary way of life nor regular employment allowed the courts to deduce racial persecution as the only logical explanation remaining. Most disgracefully, in 1961 a 'Gypsy' falsely imprisoned in 1938 for being 'asocial' — he owned two properties and had no criminal record — was denied compensation on the extraordinary grounds that his arrest might have been mistaken. The

courts also exhibited in-built prejudices against Sinti and Roma as witnesses, with lawyers and judges making off-the-cuff comments which,
had they been directed against Jews in the officially philosemitic climate
of the Federal Republic, would have resulted in universal outrage. By
contrast, considerable indulgence was shown to the very few men and
women prosecuted for crimes against Sinti and Roma, as is evidenced by
the fact that not a single individual has ever been convicted for acts of
genocide against them, and that the perpetrators of yesterday frequently
seem to have become today's 'experts on Gypsies'. It is literally a case of
'no perpetrator, no victims, no compensation'.

Because of a change in climate in the 1960s, in 1965 the Supreme Court
decided to revise its arbitrary date for the onset of racial persecution of
'Gypsies', backdating this to 1938 and the mass arrests and confinement
of the 'asocial'. Although this led to a reconsideration of compensation
claims hitherto rejected, it still did not include those Sinti and Roma persecuted under laws in which they were not explicitly mentioned — such
as the 1933 Law for the Prevention of Hereditarily Diseased Progeny or
the 1935 Nuremberg Laws — or who had been detained in the *ad hoc*
'Gypsy' camps that were established throughout Germany in the mid-
1930s. The Berlin historian Wolfgang Wippermann is a leading authority
on the Nazi persecution of Sinti and Roma, and the author of an official
report, which established the coercive and racist character of camps set up
in Berlin in 1936 to 'sanitise' the image of the Olympic Games host city.
In his chapter Wippermann highlights continuities between treatment of
Sinti and Roma in the Nazi and post-war periods by telling the story of
two individuals. The chapter also provides disquieting insights into the
workings of a particularly inhuman type of bureaucracy and courts
where the odds are firmly stacked against the victims.

The issue of individual compensation is not the only way in which the
legacy of the Third Reich continues to haunt the European and German
present, although it is often lost from view amidst the academic and pub-
licistic handwringing about 'national identity'. Hundreds of thousands of
Germans were compulsorily sterilised or killed because the Nazis
deemed them to be of 'lesser racial value'. This fact gives a particular
intensity to discussions about broad ethical issues, over and above the
sort of passions aroused by abortion or euthanasia in other countries. In
Germany, the experience of the Third Reich affects the words one uses,
or indeed the questions one can pose, in ways that outsiders find per-
plexing, and in the following case, uncongenial.

During the 1980s, 'euthanasia' once again became a major issue especially in Germany, but also in Britain, the Netherlands and parts of the USA, where 'right to die' enthusiasts managed to put it back on the popular agenda and university centres of bioethics lent it academic credibility. Manuals on how to kill oneself apparently did rather well in London bookshops. A recent Dutch film chronicling the last days of a terminally-ill man showed the effects of recent legislation in moving detail. In Germany, much of the debate centred upon the controversial views of the philosopher Peter Singer, who teaches bioethics at Monash University in Australia, which also happens to include a Centre for Molecular Biology and Medicine heavily engaged in test-tube fertilisation. Singer was hitherto best known for his impassioned advocacy of 'animal liberation' and antipathy to factory farming; however in the summer of 1989, he was invited to speak at a European Symposium on 'Bioengineering, Ethics, and Mental Disability' held in Marburg. Singer wished to argue that 'the parents of severely disabled newborn infants should be able to decide, together with their physicians, whether their infant should live or die'. This would be so in the case of, for example, infants born with anencephaly (literally 'no brain'), major chromosomal disorders, or severe forms of Down's Syndrome and spina bifida.

In the event, Singer was abruptly 'disinvited' as the conference organisers baulked at the anticipated scale of public protest. In the end they cancelled the entire conference. Undeterred, Singer took up an invitation to speak at the University of Saarbrücken. Despite whistles and shouts, Singer endeavoured to convince his critics that he was not a spokesman of the far Right, and that since three of his Austrian-Jewish grandparents had died in Nazi concentration camps he could hardly be described as a 'fascist'. Singer obviously found his confrontations with people who wanted to debate whether there should be a debate about 'euthanasia' deeply unsettling, so much so that he converted his experiences into a full-blown defence of free speech in a New York literary journal given over to grand issues. Still reeling from the shock, Singer noted that Franz Christoph, leader of the self-styled 'Cripples Movement' had chained his wheelchair to the doors of *Die Zeit* when the weekly tried to hold a debate on the subject, while an audience in Zurich had chanted 'Singer raus' ('Singer out') in a manner that had unfortunate associations with an earlier era. Singer wrote 'there is . . . a peculiar tone of fanaticism about some sections of the German debate over euthanasia that goes beyond normal opposition to Nazism, and instead begins to seem like the very

mentality that made Nazism possible', in a pointed allusion to the phenomenon of 'Left-wing fascism'. He concluded, 'Germans and Austrians,
both in academic life and in the press, have shown themselves sadly lack-
ing in the commitment exemplified by the celebrated utterance attributed
to Voltaire: "I disapprove of what you say, but I will defend to the death
your right to say it."'

One key theme in Singer's thinking is that our present attitudes
towards the sanctity of human life stem from the coming of Christianity
and would have been alien to the Greeks and Romans. He writes, 'Today
the doctrines are no longer generally accepted, but the ethical attitudes to
which they gave rise fit in with the deep-seated Western belief in the
uniqueness and special privileges of our species, and have survived.'
Secondly, he rejects what he calls anthropocentric or 'speciesist' distinctions between persons and non-human animals. Pointing to the conceptual capacities of chimpanzees and dolphins, which he feels give them
claims to 'personhood', Singer says, 'Some members of other species are
persons: some members of our own species are not . . . So it seems that
killing, say, a chimpanzee is worse than the killing of a gravely defective
human who is not a person.' Given the limited scope of amniocentesis,
Singer suggests controlled infanticide, which would also reduce the number of healthy foetuses aborted because of suspected defects. He concludes,

> We do not doubt that it is right to shoot a badly injured or sick animal . . .
> To 'allow nature to take its course', withholding treatment but refusing to
> kill, would obviously be wrong. It is only our misplaced respect for the
> doctrine of the sanctity of human life that prevents us from seeing that what
> it is obviously wrong to do to a horse it is equally wrong to do to a defec-
> tive infant.

How does Singer distinguish between these arguments and those used
by the Nazis to justify their campaign of mass murder? He attempts to
refute the slippery slope argument with the observation that 'The Nazis
committed horrendous crimes; but this does not mean that everything the
Nazis did was horrendous. We cannot condemn euthanasia just because
the Nazis did it, any more than we can condemn the building of new
roads for this reason', an argument which, as we shall see is enjoying
some currency among younger German historians. He is noticeably silent
on the Nazis' Weimar antecedents. Correctly pointing out that many
rational people would consider that a life of suffering could be construed

as not being worth living, Singer overlooks the fact that this description would not apply to most of the Nazis' victims. Rightly regarding racism and crude utilitarian calculations as the primary motivating forces behind the Nazi 'euthanasia' programme, Singer omits to mention that one of the essential elements of their propaganda was the denial of personality to the victims, who are referred to as 'beings', 'ballast existences', 'creatures' or 'useless eaters'. Suffering animals, like a blind old hunting dog or a lame laboratory mouse, were also frequently used in books and films of the Nazi period deliberately to sow precisely the sort of moral uncertainties which Singer so unselfconsciously then avails himself of. Displaying a remarkable naïveté regarding the perpetrators of the Nazi 'euthanasia' programme, who were of course leading academic psychiatrists and doctors, Singer counters the argument propounding the danger of an ever-widening circle of victims with the far from comforting observation, 'If acts of euthanasia could only be carried out by a member of the medical profession, with the concurrence of a second doctor, it is not likely that the propensity to kill would spread unchecked throughout the community', and states that the ancient Greeks and traditional Inuit were restrained and circumspect in their killing of, respectively, their sickly infants and elderly parents. Leaving the Inuit to one side, critics have pointed out that Singer's grasp of ancient history is as slight as his awareness of the Nazi period, and that the practices he regards as exemplary belong to the earliest period of Spartan history and were regarded as barbaric and unusual by the few Greek authors who bothered to describe them. Perhaps Singer's German critics were more incensed by his lack of historical awareness than by his utilitarian philosophy?

My own chapter describes the origins of the Nazi 'euthanasia' programme during the liberal Weimar Republic and its extension into the mass murder of the Holocaust. It includes discussion of the arguments used by Nazi propagandists to legitimise medicalised mass murder. Most of these arguments had been inherited from the Weimar period, when the moral brutalisation resulting from the First World War combined to deadly effect with economic crisis and questions of cost.

So far we have been considering the tensions between attempts to 'historicise' the Third Reich and its place in many people's memories. The argument is that direct experience of the period is still too raw for it to be amenable to treatment in the same way as any other historical 'subject', and that what historians regard as important about it may actually miss its universal message and significance. It is nice to know that life went on as normal in villages in the Hunsrück; that Nazi Germany shared certain characteristics with Stalin's Russia; that German psychiatrists and social planners believed they could 'modernise' health provision by killing their own patients; or that Hitler was an egalitarian, keen to implement his version of North American society, but what does this tell us about a society responsible for Auschwitz, the most abiding image of the entire Nazi period?

Academic debate on the Nazi period is itself often conducted with a passion and intensity, well beyond the usual rancour found amongst academics. Gradually the dust settles, as the debates are rehearsed in countless textbook surveys for regurgitation in student essays and exam papers. An almost 'textbook' case of this process is the debate between 'intentionalists' and 'structure-functionalists' over the origins of the 'Final Solution'. Eventually the simple restatement of what was once blindingly obvious, for example the centrality of racism to Nazism, takes on the character of a novel interpretation. The chapter by Paul Weindling, a medical historian, is a detailed attempt to reveal the complex and competing intellectual, scientific and social strands that informed the Nazis' racial vision, which, as his work shows, cannot be reduced to the simple implementation of the simple-minded *obiter dicta* of Adolf Hitler, but rather represented a specifically German solution to the medicalisation of the 'social question'.

Four chapters in this book represent some of the areas where historians are most in disagreement and where much interesting research is currently being done. They concern the putatively 'modernising' impact and intentions of the Nazi regime; the complicity of the *Wehrmacht* in ideologically-motivated atrocities on the Eastern Front; and, finally, the involvement and responses of the German people to the persecution of the Jews. The authors, Götz Aly, Omer Bartov, Avraham Barkai and Jeremy Noakes, have each made major contributions in these areas.

One does not have to go very far in Germany today to hear the opinion that the Third Reich had its good as well as bad sides. In the past it was possible to console oneself with the view that this was a product of an evasive and partial treatment of the subject in official discourse and the nation's schools, of the kind revealed in Michael Verhoeven's film *The Nasty Girl*, the story of a not so innocent schoolgirl who decided to write a prize essay about her own town's murky history, and paid the price in terms of social ostracism and acts of violence ever after. Sooner or later, the findings of recent research would filter through into popular consciousness through such 'multipliers' as teaching or television, or indeed through the widespread writing of *Alltagsgeschichte* (the history of 'everyday life') by laymen. None of this, of course, will have the slightest influence on those self-styled neo-Fascists for whom the facts of the period are so many fictions. As we saw at the beginning, recent trends in academic research have begun to undermine this last assumption. In the mid-1960s, Ralf Dahrendorf and David Schoenbaum drew attention to the real or imagined impact of the Nazi 'national community' upon traditional German society, the ways in which it destroyed older class, confessional or regional loyalties and thus paved the way for post-war liberal democracy, at least in that half of Germany not ruled by the Communists. Detailed studies of particular social classes have not on the whole confirmed Schoenbaum's vision of the 'triumph of egalitarianism'.

In a ground-breaking chapter on the highest echelons of German society, Jeremy Noakes charts the failure of Nazi attempts to fashion a new social élite and of their efforts to infiltrate the existing one. Although individual scions of the aristocracy may have fallen for the chic-cum-kitsch glamour of the SS black uniform, the Europeanised high aristocracy were 'more or less totally detached from the regime and regarded it with a mixture of contempt and disgust'. Parvenu Nazi officials were still consigned to meals alongside the servants. These subtle social realities continue to elude historians fashionably (and remotely) sensitive towards such colourfully marginal groupings as juvenile delinquents or prostitutes. By contrast, Schoenbaum's views upon the extent of working-class integration into the Nazi 'national community' seem to be being endorsed by recent research, despite the gallant attempts of some on the Left, such as the late Tim Mason, to sustain a picture of working-class solidarity in alienation. In his chapter, Ulrich Herbert, the author of the definitive account of 'foreign workers' in the Third Reich, takes a much more sceptical view of working-class reactions to the blandishments of the Nazi regime and deals honestly with the subject of working-class racism, something curiously absent from most histories of German labour. It is to be hoped that this lack will be remedied as the ranks of those writing about German history become more politically pluralistic than has been the case since the 1960s.

In the last decade modernisation theories have undergone a renaissance among younger historians of Nazi Germany writing from both ends of the political spectrum. If on the Left this is part of the ongoing project of discrediting the liberal capitalist Federal Republic by stressing its Nazi antecedents, motivation on the neo-Conservative Right seems obscurer. Adding their voices to Martin Broszat's plea for a 'demoralising' history of National Socialism, a group of scholars associated with Rainer Zitelmann, has recently put together a body of work which stresses the intentionally 'modernising' impact of National Socialism. Zitelmann argues that Hitler's principal aim was the creation of an egalitarian, per- formance-oriented society, and that his models were the Soviet Union and the United States of America, rather than retrograde visions of a medieval social order. This will come as something of a surprise to any- one who has even glanced through the Declaration of Independence or Lincoln's Gettysburg Address. Echoing Martin Broszat's plea for 'his- toricisation', Zitelmann writes:

> Historical writing, in which moral and political intentions will play at least
> a more limited role and in which popular pedagogical motives make way
> for detached points of view, will find it easier to recognise the modernising
> function of National Socialism.

This modernising function is illustrated with the by-now-familiar analogies between, say, the welfare plans for the post-war era of Robert Ley's German Labour Front and the Beveridge Report, although how the latter sits with Hitler's admiration for the USA is never made explicit. But leaving America aside, to regard Robert Ley as an equal of William Beveridge seems as ridiculous as it would be to equate the calculated phil- anthropic activities of the Mafia or the Colombian drug cartels among the poor of their respective milieux with the work of Roman Catholic missionaries.

During the 1980s, attempts to interpret the Third Reich with the aid of a variety of modernisation theories were augmented by groups of German 'alternative' historians, or researchers working outside a conventional academic framework to which they evince considerable, and sometimes quite understandable, hostility. It would not be doing violence to reality by associating these groups — sometimes misleadingly known as the 'Hamburg school' — with the far Left of the political spectrum. Some of the most interesting research on the 'euthanasia' programme, 'foreign labour', health and social policy in recent years has come from Götz Aly, Matthias Hamann, Susanne Heim and Karl-Heinz Roth. Much of their work concentrates upon the role of 'intellectuals', by which they mean the academics, psychiatrists and scientists churned out by German universities, rather than thinkers with independence of mind or creativity. Like similar extremely sectoral perspectives, for example that of the bureaucracy or indeed history 'from below', this approach has its merits and demerits. Recently, Götz Aly and Susanne Heim have developed their earlier work on one obscure population planner into a comprehensive account of the 'Final Solution'. They begin by rejecting both catastrophist and nihilistic explanations of the 'Holocaust', that is to say the idea that this was an event beyond human comprehension or an unparalleled instance of 'destruction for destruction's sake' which flew in the face of even economic rationality. They posit the existence of a group of academic experts — economists, agronomists, demographers, statisticians and so on, working under the aegis of the Four Year Plan apparatus and in the Generalgouvernement in Poland — who decided to modernise and rationalise the backward and overpopulated societies of Central and Eastern Europe by eliminating 'surplus' people, a task then carried out on their behalf by the SS Reich Main Security Head Office. This would have led to capital formation, the mechanisation of agriculture and the creation of a further industrial base subordinate to Germany. Killing the Jews of Eastern Europe would at once remove one of the most visible manifestations of urban poverty and create opportunities for social mobility for the 'surplus' non-Jewish rural proletariat, while facilitating the rationalisation of urban commerce through the removal of artisans and penny-capitalists.

Not that the Jews were the sole or primary objects of these policies. In the more grandiose versions, the 'Final Solution of the Jewish Question' became a detail amidst plans to 'evacuate', or in other words murder, thirty million people. Rational planning and racial fanaticism fused to terrible effect in this broadly conceived attempt to engineer a new social order. Not surprisingly, these ideas — elaborated here in Götz Aly's own contribution — have given rise to controversy, without, it should be said, managing to displace some of the more familiar academic debates about the origins of the 'Final Solution'. The importance of Aly and Heim's work lies in the light it sheds on the involvement of a previously unknown group in the 'Holocaust', and more importantly, in the element of deliberation it restores to a chain of events which some historians are inclined to view as almost the by-product of competing bureaucratic structures. Critics of their thesis have pointed to the lack of consensus evident among middle-ranking functionaries responsible for, for example, policy towards the inmates of ghettos in Poland, as well as to the obvious fact that the economic circumstances that the experts described did not fit Amsterdam, Paris or Rome, whose Jewish populations also perished. Aly and Heim also fail to connect the cogitations of their experts with what is known about the origins of the 'Final Solution' — Himmler, Heydrich and the Reich Main Security Office were not merely executants for Goering — and more seriously, run the risk of confusing the legitimisation and rationalisation of policy with the factors — notably race hatred or the transference of the ethics of colonial wars to Europe — that motivated it. Sanitation, military and security experts also provided 'cogent' grounds for mass murder, but no one has bothered so far to take them seriously.

In contrast to this rather localised, would-be historical controversy, the *Historikerstreit* or 'historians' debate' of the mid-1980s assumed almost global dimensions, spawning a vast and often highly acrimonious literature in the form of books and articles in journals and newspapers. The bull elephants of the historical profession (few women historians took part) roared at one another across continents. Several people who had never previously published a line on Nazi Germany now felt compelled to air their views on the Holocaust, Idi Amin, Pol Pot, Stalin and other mass murderers. The controversy began on 11 July 1986 when the philosopher and sociologist Jürgen Habermas published a coruscating attack upon what he deemed 'the apologetic tendencies in the writing of German contemporary history', evident, for example, in the recent work of Andreas Hillgruber and Ernst Nolte. Nolte, whose work utilises the outré products of the 'revisionist' far-Right, insinuated a causal relationship between Bolshevik and Nazi barbarities, with the latter taking on the character of 'preventive murder'. Hillgruber, an internationally respected authority on German diplomatic history, had just published a slim book entitled *Two Forms of Downfall: The Smashing of the German Reich and the End of European Jewry*, a title whose uneven emotional cargo deserves its own consideration. The book was widely criticised for its invitation to empathetic identification with German troops fighting on the Eastern Front, who, notwithstanding the resultant prolongation of the death camps, saved the eastern areas of the Reich from being overrun in an 'orgy of revenge' by the Red Army. This was a novel variant upon the pertinacious idea that the German Army had fought a normal war, and that relatively small units of the SS and SD had been responsible for all criminal enormities. This view obviously suited a society where virtually every family had a member who had been a soldier, and where the young soldiers were now workers and bureaucrats, professionals, teachers, novelists, industrialists and politicians.

The clichéd dichotomy between the decent German soldier and the ideological fanatics of the SS, served up incidentally in virtually every Anglo-American post-1945 war film, was first seriously challenged in the late 1970s with the publication of Christian Streit's *Keine Kamaraden*. This showed the ways in which the *Wehrmacht* moved from cognisance of, to complicity in, acts of brutality between the campaigns against Poland and Russia, culminating in the deliberate starvation and murder of three million Soviet prisoners of war and culpable involvement in the 'Final Solution'. Much of the research which ensued in the wake of Streit's work served to endorse his views concerning the high-level involvement of the military élite in National Socialist racial imperialism. Omer Bartov's book on *The Barbarisation of Warfare on the Eastern Front*, which appeared in 1986, was the first study to shift attention from élites to the everyday realities of combat as experienced by junior officers and their subordinates. A few years ago Bartov developed this work in an outstanding book entitled *Hitler's Army*. This reveals the degree of ideological saturation evident among ordinary soldiers, bereft of primary group loyalties because of the appalling casualty rates, and fighting under 'demodernised' conditions an enemy depicted as being racially 'subhuman'.

Bartov's account does not, of course, preclude the existence of decent dissenters and shirkers — the 'slipper soldiers' who opted out of the war — unearthed by Theo Schulte in his study of army rear areas in Russia. In line with much recent work on the social history of Nazi Germany, Schulte argues for the existence of pockets of normality in a highly abnormal situation. The American historian Christopher Browning has recently pushed this line a bit further with an outstanding study of the everyday life of an 'ordinary' police battalion engaged in mass murder. Bartov's chapter here outlines the unique character of the war in the East and relates this to debates about the social history of the Third Reich and on the comparability of *Wehrmacht* conduct with that of other armies. The final section of his contribution has bearings not only upon the revisionism of Ernst Nolte, but also upon facile and fashionable analogies between Auschwitz and the bombing of Dresden and Hiroshima.

In 1898, at the height of the Dreyfus affair in France, many European countries began to express reservations about whether to participate in the forthcoming 1900 Paris Universal Exposition. Influential circles in

Germany, apparently totally unaware of their own hypocrisy, were of the opinion that France 'was a country where all rights are violated, where only the anti-Semitic and chauvinist population makes the law, and where anyone who doesn't share their passions runs the risk of being hurled into the Seine'. If anyone at the turn of the century was to have predicted the probable location for eruptions of anti-Semitism, they would have alighted upon France, Poland, Rumania or Russia, rather than Germany.

The issue of German popular responses to, and involvement in, the Nazis' systematic persecution of the Jews has generated a considerable academic literature. Older studies which used a relatively narrow range of sources to substantiate quite sweeping generalisations about the Germans in general, have been superseded by careful and nuanced analyses of particular regions, confessional groups and social classes. Some of the most detailed and judicious work on this subject has been that of Ian Kershaw on Bavaria, which is conceived very much in the spirit of Broszat's plea for 'historicisation':

> Popular opinion on the 'Jewish Question' formed a wide spectrum running from the paranoid Jew-baiters at the one extreme, undoubtedly a tiny minority; through a wide section of the population whose existent prejudices and latent anti-Semitism, influenced in varying degrees by the virulence of Nazi propaganda, accepted legal restrictions on Jews amounting to economic exclusion and social ostracism whilst rejecting the blatant and overt inhumanity of the Jew-baiters; and finally including another minority imbued with a deeply Christian or liberal-humanitarian moral sense, whose value-system provided the most effective barrier to the Nazi doctrine of racial hatred.

In a memorable phrase, Kershaw remarked that 'the road to Auschwitz was built by hate, but paved with indifference'. Kershaw's views have not won universal acceptance, and would seem to be too cautious in the light of recent experiences in Rostock, where ordinary citizens enthusiastically egged on working-class neo-Nazi skinheads as they laid waste the block of flats occupied by asylum seekers. Michael Kater claims that Kershaw and others seriously underrate the durability and popular roots of German anti-Semitism and the extent to which manifestations of it were genuinely spontaneous rather than the product of state manipulation:

> Between 1933 and 1939, discrimination by Germans against Jews in the private sphere, without the involvement or sanction of state agencies and without heed to existing laws, was both spontaneous and calculated. It

spanned the entire spectrum from verbal humiliation to denunciation, depredation, and physical harm. It could be committed by individuals or by corporate bodies, who may have had formal connections with party or state, but were not under their directive at the time of the transgressions.

Israeli scholar, Otto Dov Kulka and American scholar, Aron Rodrigue, who have also extensively studied the sources on this issue, have questioned the typicality of Kershaw's rural Bavarian examples, and suggested the substitution of the term 'passive complicity' for his more neutral 'indifference'. They conclude:

> The concept of 'indifference', suggesting as it does only a lack of concern, is too limited in scope, and does not convey the full complexity of popular opinion. For example, it cannot account for the widely reported attitude that something, one way or another, had to be done to 'solve the Jewish Question'. This 'Question' might not have been high on the list of priorities for the population at large. Nevertheless, the attitude that measures had to be initiated to reach a solution of this problem was as much in evidence when the issue did come up, as the attitude of not caring one way or the other.

Discussing the period of deportations and extermination, Kershaw concludes that the former 'were apparently unaccompanied by much attention from the German population' and that the response to the killings in the East was 'that the Jews were out of sight and literally out of mind'.

Recent studies, notably by Willy Dressen, Ernst Klee and Völker Ullrich, present a much bleaker picture of avaricious neighbours squabbling over the household goods of Jews yet to be deported, and of housewives, reminiscent of the Polish peasant women interviewed in Claude Lanzmann's film *Shoah*, knowingly remarking, in their Berlin working-class argot, of a Jewish family being transported, 'They'll be gassed too.' Passengers on trains passing through the major rail-junction at Auschwitz were engulfed in a sweet-smelling fog and could see flames shooting up from the crematoria in the camp — a distance of fifteen to twenty kilometres. Many people were more or less directly involved in the 'Final Solution'; for example the local authorities, railway officials, diplomats, bank employees and the manufacturers of exterminatory technology, as well as ordinary soldiers, police and SS men. The photographer Joe Heydecker noted:

There were always soldiers, railwaymen, men from the Organisation Todt, civilians, sometimes in bathing trunks and frequently equipped with cameras who spectated at the dreadful scenes which were enacted at the mass graves where in place after place the Jewish inhabitants were bloodily butchered without regard to age or gender.

Letters home from the Front again and again registered considerable animosity towards the Jewish populations of Eastern Europe and the Soviet Union — 'The deeper we advance into Russia, the more Jews we encounter. The fellows are just as cheeky as they are in time of peace. One should shove many more of these monsters up against a wall than has been done so far' — and described the murder of thousands of people in terms of the utmost inhumanity. However, as Hans Mommsen has remarked in a careful study of these issues, it remains an open question as to how far knowledge of individual episodes of barbarity coalesced into an awareness of the terrible scale of the 'Final Solution'; knowledge of the depredations of the *Einsatzgruppen* killing squads did not mean awareness of Auschwitz.

Avraham Barkai is a leading authority on the German economy and on the economic exclusion and ruin of Germany's Jews in the Nazi period. In his chapter Barkai addresses himself to the relationship between the Nazis' 'national community' and the persecution of Germany's Jewish minority, exploring the long- and short-range aspects of both phenomena. He argues that a deep-seated tradition of Christian anti-Semitism — recycled in the secular terms of Nazi propaganda — as well as such perennial motives as sheer greed combined in powerful response to the open season on Jews licensed by the Nazi leadership. A constant barrage of propaganda and a steady extension of what was possible — stretching from the early boycott through informal and formal discrimination, 'aryanisation' of economic concerns, to the violence of *Kristallnacht* — gradually engendered a climate in which the murderous obsessions of the Nazis could become practicable. As Barkai remarks, 'the persecution of the Jews seems the necessary, although not sufficient precondition, for the murder of European Jews'. These things would not, and did not, occur in any other historical context.

The two final chapters in this book are concerned with questions of sexuality and gender. Hans-Georg Stümke's account of the Nazis' persecution of homosexuals is a timely reminder of the biologistic and collectivist thinking which determined the Nazis' treatment of all minorities. Homosexuals were not persecuted because they subverted the Nazis' notions of masculinity, still less because Nazi homophobia was driven by anxieties about the allegedly latent homosexuality in the ranks of an aggressively masculine Party, but because they considered homosexuality to be an 'illness' which was undermining the nation's racial–demographic vitality. The 'threat' posed by homosexuals was thus closely akin to that posed by Jews, who were held to be peculiarly responsible for the spread of syphilis and later typhus, or that represented by people with allegedly hereditary illnesses and psychiatric disorders who were compulsorily sterilised or murdered. Although, as Stümke shows, homosexuals suffered terribly under the Nazis, very few of them have ever received any form of compensation. Apart from the Federal government's refusal to regard Nazi legislation against homosexuals as 'abnormal', this also reflects the reluctance of older homosexuals to 'come out' in a hostile climate in order to qualify for compensation. People sterilised for allegedly hereditary illnesses or psychiatric problems often experience similar, and quite understandable, inhibitions.

Women's history has become a thriving area in modern German historiography. Jill Stephenson has made distinguished contributions both to the study of specific issues and by surveying the position of women in society as a whole. In her chapter, Jill Stephenson, takes a critical view of the degree to which women were successfully integrated. She notes, for example, that there were few alternatives to the associational life that the Nazi dictatorship had on offer, and rightly questions whether Nazi policy merely represented 'more of the same' by drawing attention to the regime's philogenerative fixations and its ruthless persecution of the 'racially unfit' through compulsory sterilisation and 'euthanasia', or indeed 'valuable' women who had liaisons with foreigners deemed to be 'racially inferior'. Other scholars are beginning to explore such issues as indirect female complicity in the crimes committed by their perpetrator husbands.

These essays are a coherent and representative cross section of work by some of the most active international researchers in the field. No one is here by dint of something they wrote twenty years ago, or the frequency or loudness with which they repeat the same old views about, say, the origins of the 'Final Solution'. Our authors do not represent the view of any self-conscious 'School' since it is unlikely that they would agree with one another. This approach, which leaves the reader to draw his or her own conclusions, seems more satisfactory than some dubious consensual 'evaluation' of arguments that sometimes remain obstinately irreconcilable.

Apart from introducing them to a body of work often published in German, the book is explicitly designed to stimulate sixth-formers and undergraduates to consider a range of issues that are sometimes encompassed by, but which more often go beyond, conventional historiographical debates about the period. Broadly speaking, these essays reflect the major currents of the 1980s and 1990s, that is an 'essentialist' emphasis upon biological politics and a rejection of neo-Marxism and sub-Weberism, the dominant intellectual fashions in many of our universities, if nowhere else. The issues discussed here include the pathologies of racial prejudice; the role of scientific 'experts'; the relationship between calculations of social utility and Nazi exterminism; why soldiers behaved barbarously on the Eastern Front; and how different social classes conducted themselves under a dictatorship, including that relatively understudied group — the German upper classes. Readers will at least have a good idea of how historians conceptualise these subjects, sharing the adventure of finding solutions to very difficult questions.

CHAPTER I

'THE REAL MYSTERY IN GERMANY'. THE GERMAN WORKING CLASS DURING THE NAZI DICTATORSHIP

Ulrich Herbert

How did the German working class conduct itself in the Third Reich? Almost no other question was so crucial during the early years of the National Socialist dictatorship. It was widely assumed that if any power in society was capable of endangering the Nazi regime and its partners among the traditional élites in industry, the military or civil service, then this would inevitably be the working class. The hopes of the exiled leadership of the working-class parties, as well as the fears of Germany's National Socialist rulers, hinged upon the working class. However, the picture of working-class behaviour under the Nazi dictatorship, relayed by the correspondents of the Social Democratic Party in exile (Sopade) through the 'Sopade' reports, was so diverse and contradictory that the analysts in the Party's makeshift headquarters in Prague were hardly in a position to offer accurate prognoses. In December 1935, a Sopade commentator described the response of the working class to the Nazi dictatorship as being 'the real mystery in Germany'. As well as references to labour stoppages and the almost universal rejection of the Nazi dictatorship by the workers, there was also talk of depression and humiliation; depoliticisation and opportunism; and even loud complaints about 'deserters', or assent and 'enthusiasm' for Hitler's regime. But a considered judgement was equally difficult in the case of those reports which provided a more coherent picture; for how and against what was one to measure the circumstances they described? Comparisons with conditions before 1933 were of limited value, because they neglected the peculiar circumstances of a dictatorship. Since there was no comparable experience in the entire history of the working-class movement, it was impossible to estimate the room for manoeuvre that the workers may or may not have had under the Nazi dictatorship. However, in general, the German workers' readiness to fight was over-estimated by the editors of the 'Sopade' reports from Germany, out-weighing the disappointment, or indeed bitterness, regarding 'the degree to which the Nazis' divide and rule tactics have already born fruit in the shape of class-betraying individualism'.

The obvious overestimation of the cohesion and strength of a working class schooled in the socialist labour movement was broadly endorsed by the National Socialists. The greatly expanded network of spies and informers established following the seizure of power in January 1933 thought that if domestic resistance to the Nazi regime should occur, then it would inevitably emanate from the working class. The panicky and pernickety investigation of even the most trivial occurrence attributable to working-class dissent can be attributed to this false assumption. The Nazi authorities breathed a sigh of relief a few years later as it became obvious that their initial apprehensions were exaggerated; however, the attitudes of the working class could never be taken entirely for granted.

The views expressed on this subject by later historians are equally con-fused by this difference between what people thought should happen and the actual course of events. The left-wing historian Tim Mason asked, 'Why were there only individual acts of protest or resistance? Why weren't there more mass protests from the working class?' This implied that, given the socio-political position before the Nazis came to power, another, more radical response might have been expected from the work-ing class to the Nazi dictatorship.

By way of an answer to these questions modern psephological research — reflecting the state of research in the early 1970s — came to the con-clusion that worker resistance was less strong than expected — in itself an interesting way of putting things — on the basis of the fact that in 1932 a mere quarter of workers voted for the National Socialist German Workers' Party (NSDAP), which went some way to explaining why 'there was a considerably greater level of working-class integration in the National Socialist national community than had commonly been assumed'. If this assumption, based as it was upon the expectations of contemporaries, had not existed, then the same findings could be inter-preted as indicating that in 1933 three-quarters of the working class was opposed to the Nazis, while only slightly more than a third of other social classes was similarly disposed. However, the period of exaggerated expectations among both contemporaries and contemporary historians was superseded by a phase — according to individual temperament — of relief or disappointment, in which the working class was now regarded as being the main social pillar of the Nazi regime. The particular attention paid to the conduct of the German working class during the Nazi dictatorship drew upon the image of the working-class and labour movement from the era before 1933. Behind this lay, on the one hand, an obvious concern to discover the genuine sources of opposition to the regime, and therewith a source of political legitimacy, and, on the other hand, concern with the question of how Nazi policies of control and integration functioned, with the extreme example of the working class assuming a particular saliency, while also promising a degree of moral unburdening for German society as a whole.

The widespread hope among many of the cadres of the labour movement that although the Nazis had smashed the workers' organisations and persecuted its leaders, nonetheless the semi-private network of social contacts in working-class housing districts or on the factory floor would endure, or that working-class solidarities might even be consolidated, as they had been at the time of Bismarck's 1878 anti-Socialist laws, proved illusory. The breaking-up of proletarian social milieux, including even leisure and sports clubs destroyed their sense of social identity. Certainly, the Nazis were unable completely to suppress worker solidarity within these milieux, but they did manage to largely depoliticise them. At the same time, the sense of being delivered up to an uncertain fate served to weaken worker self-confidence, while diminishing the attractions of the working-class movement and, above all, of the Communists, who a few weeks before the Nazis came to power in 1933 had been predicting the immanence of a proletarian revolution. Now, however, they were not even in a position to do anything about SA forays into working-class districts. The traditional division between a minority of political activists, who were determined to resist, and the mass of workers in the factories or working-class areas became deeper, resulting in a steady drift into two mutually incomprehensible realms of experience. But when in July 1933 Kurt Schumacher said that 'the process of conversion to fascism ... begins with the workers. One only has to listen to the conversations in working-class circles', this may be seen as somewhat exaggerated, at least in terms of the early years of the Nazi regime. Despite their sense of impotence and their exposure to Nazi terror, the workers also discovered that, notwithstanding the strident propaganda, nothing had changed as far as their economic circumstances were concerned. Thus, commentators agreed in describing the response of the workers during this phase as being characterised by surliness and a despondent form of acceptance. Only from 1935 onwards were their lives affected by new developments: the novel experience for many of having a stable job to go to, as well as the socio-political offensive of the National Socialist regime.

As far as the actual socio-economic position of the workers before the outbreak of war is concerned, two clear tendencies are evident, bearing in mind the differences in the various sectors of the economy.

First, real wages rose considerably in the wake of an armaments-led boom, achieving pre-war levels in certain sectors between 1936 and 1939. If one includes the number of hours worked per week and therefore the amount of overtime paid, one can see that before the war German workers probably achieved the highest rates of pay hitherto on offer in their entire history. The reasons for this were general economic recovery and a resulting labour shortage, with the regime's attempts to suppress wage rises — by, for example, the demand for expanding welfare provision in factories — being circumvented by lump sum payments. The regime's attempts to restrict labour mobility were also partially invalidated by aggressive recruitment or the widespread practice of informal or illicit changes of employment.

Second, these favourable developments for the workers were in part nullified by the acute food and housing shortages they experienced before 1936. In comparison with other social classes, who benefited more rapidly from the country's financial recovery, the workers continued to be at a disadvantage; their living standard remained at a low level. Since the middle of the First World War this had been a familiar experience for most workers. What was different now was that they had stable employment and at least the hope of a long-term improvement in their conditions. The politically crucial comparison with the situation before 1933 enabled the improvements achieved since then gradually to move to the foreground.

Any attempt to assess the impact of these developments upon the situation and political attitudes of the workers is complicated by the problem of identifying what was specifically National Socialist about them. Certainly, rationalisation, structural change and differential rates of pay would have accompanied recovery from a crisis in a non-National

Socialist Germany too. However, the terroristic marginalisation of representatives of organised labour meant that these developments could be introduced more radically, without having to pander to the demands of the working class.

However, it was also significant that links began to be forged between performance and eugenic criteria. The hierarchy no longer merely included those who worked well and thus reaped their rewards, but at the bottom end of the scale, those 'rejects' who failed or refused to perform were now not merely poorly rewarded, but rather actively punished and persecuted. One of the most important conceptual advances in recent research lies precisely in examining the relationship between, on the one hand, labour and social policy and, on the other, racism and extermination, two areas hitherto treated separately. The ideological foundation of National Socialist social policy was the conviction that a large part of social deviance, or phenomena that suggested social maladjustment had biological causes. This biologisation of the social — a core concern of racist thought — was based on the concept of the *Volk* as an autonomous, overarching supraindividual biological and cultural unity. Just as the various nations could be differentiated according to their biological substance, so the internal composition of a nation was determined by the biological worth of its individual members. According to this model, deviant behaviour could be attributed to the biological, inherited and heritable 'substance' of an individual, ranging from mental illness via physical abnormalities to criminality, alcoholism and 'asociality', all of which could be put down to his or her inherited constitution.

The aim of labour and social policies posited upon this model had to be to promote those 'valuable' members of the 'national community' (value was identified with social conformity and performance), by supporting their families and increasing their fertility in order to increase the proportion of 'valuable' substance in the body of the nation. At the same time, it was necessary to identify the 'less valuable' elements — who were regarded as being so many 'ballast existences' — who would then be deliberately disadvantaged, separated out or even 'eradicated'. The specifically National Socialist component of the labour and social policies developed during the Third Reich consists of this combination of promotion and separation, 'social policy' coupled with 'eradication'.

The working class was most affected by the National Socialists' racially informed social policies simply because they contributed the majority of those who were poor, inefficient and socially inadequate, as well as most

of the prostitutes and vagrants, even if one chooses to refrain from applying the problematic concept of *Lumpenproletariat* in the interests of
defining these groups out of the working class. This was particularly
apparent in connection with the campaign waged by the Gestapo and the
authorities running the Four Year Plan to boost the economy in 1937–8
against the 'workshy', a group that encompassed, among others, tramps,
beggars, 'Gypsies' and pimps. Such campaigns were used to exert pressure upon those working in factories, but also to 'cleanse' the 'body of the
nation' of those elements whose behaviour signalled their 'lesser value'.
The ruthless pursuit by the police and war economy bureaucracy of
'shirkers' and 'layabouts', which was stepped up following the outbreak
of war, reveals the close connection between social discipline and racially-
motivated 'eradication'.

Measures designed to separate and eradicate the 'less valuable' were
accompanied by various positive social policy measures which catered for
the 'valuable'; however, particularly in so far as they were directed at the
workers, these measures must be regarded as part of the regime's continuing attempts not merely to neutralise politically those who were distant
from or overtly opposed to the dictatorship, but actively to solicit their
acquiescence. These measures included the egalitarian rhetoric of the
regime, a form of propagandistic compensation for the repression of the
working class, which repeatedly referred to the 'honest worker' and
'German socialism', while mobilising resentments against 'reactionaries',
'bosses' and other putative privileged elements, including the Jews.
However, purely ideological compensation without social improvements
was insufficient reward for the loss of political rights. Many of the socio-
political offerings of the Nazis were little more than proof of a purpose-
less activism, which had no actual impact on the situation of the working
class.

Tangible social improvements were received much more positively,
and included family support and, above all, the leisure activities organised
by the regime — namely the introduction of a minimum annual holiday
period of, on average, six days — and the creation of an organisation,
called Strength through Joy, dedicated to mass tourism, which in 1938
organised some 10.3 million holidays. Naturally cruises to Madeira were
still virtually inaccessible to most workers, for whom organised short
trips to relatively close destinations were more usual. Nevertheless, the
cruises to Madeira signalled the arrival of fresh possibilities — symbolis-
ing not real, but at least prospective opportunities for social mobility, and

tangible proof of the hope of further improvements.

By contrast, the Nazi authorities' repeated insistence on the existence of a collective form of 'worker opposition', as evidenced in report after report, requires considerable qualification. For example, when in 1936–8 the Gestapo claimed it had detected 356 'strikes', this was no doubt, from the perspective of their self-styled totalitarianism, a scandalous alarm signal. It could also be taken to imply that the terror inaugurated after 1933 had simply failed to halt social conflict. On the other hand, in 1936–7 a 'strike' may have meant little more than fifteen unskilled building workers downing tools for three hours because of some disagreement about wages. Just as the economic recovery was, above all, an expression of a general economic upturn which was merely accelerated by Nazi rearmament, so the increase in inner-factory conflicts can mainly be attributed to a number of different factors whose extent and form were merely influenced or modified by the policies of the Nazi regime. What was crucial in terms of domestic stability and worker attitudes towards the political system was that inner-factory social conflicts were not directly related to the prevailing form of government, which meant that the Nazis' policy of intimidation and repression had been successful.

At the same time, the relationship of the overwhelming majority of the workers towards National Socialism was generally one of distance. However, it also appeared to be the case that the Nazis' economic and foreign policy successes resulted in a situation in which a fundamental antipathy to Nazism was accompanied by approval of some aspects of their policy. Explicit rejection of, or indifference to, the regime and its works, was superceded by a form of double-think, in which some policies were rejected while others won widespread approval; what Tim Mason called a 'disassociation of consciousness' ensued, a process which, by stifling exchanges of experience, prevented an overall analysis of individual experiences or occurrences. The main achievement of the working-class movement before 1933 lay precisely in this capacity to relate individual experiences to political outlook; this capacity did not arise from the relationships between workers themselves, but rather was a product of political analysis and the power of conviction. Bereft of this comparative political context, the individual was fully exposed to the suggestive power and dynamism of the socio-political developments which came into play before 1939. Thus it could be argued that it was less the heterogeneous nature of the experience that promoted working-class disassociation, than the individualisation of the process of analysis.

If the regime's leaders succeeded in at least politically neutralising the working class before 1939, by partially integrating at least part of it, they were also aware that this was largely due to economic recovery. Terror and threats were not enough to secure 'peace on the home front' in the event of war. It would be necessary to maintain the living standards of the pre-war period. However, the experience of the First World War suggested that a reduction in living standards was an inevitable result of sustained conflict. Upon the outbreak of war, the Nazi regime found itself precariously perched on the horns of this dilemma. When, in September 1939, the authorities began to try to implement wage reductions and increased working hours in order to finance the conflict, they did this in the hope that the impression made by the outbreak of war and its consequent appeals to patriotism would stifle ill-will among the workers. This calculation soon proved illusory: the number of people reporting sick increased, and reports of 'shirking' and other forms of discontent became more frequent.

The regime reacted tentatively and hesitantly to mounting worker discontent, because it still had vivid memories of the socio-political conflicts of the First World War. Rapid military successes made it possible to rescind the 'September decrees' by the Spring of 1940. The opposite of the wage reductions desired by the authorities ensued, with real weekly wages rising above average until 1942. Despite a considerable deficit in the supply of labour available, the overall number of women in employment fell by about 300,000 following the outbreak of war (only achieving pre-war levels again in 1943), with some six million German women capable of working being officially counted as not working in 1939. Generous separation allowances for the wives of soldiers meant that there was no pressure upon them to undertake paid employment. The fact that the Nazi leadership did little to reverse these trends was because of their fear that working-class discontent over the conscription of women would aggravate dissatisfaction with poor pay and inadequate rations to the point where the destabilising domestic experiences of the First World War would be repeated. On the other hand, following the defeat of Poland and the invasion of France, the arguments of the economic technocrats began to seem less convincing. Now, the Party in particular began to demand that as wartime economic constraints appeared to be at an end, priority should be given to labour and social policies of a *völkisch* type, which would benefit the German population. Nor did the industrial conscription of women accord with social policies posited upon racial criteria. Equally, of course, the fact that the number of working women in pre-war Germany was relatively high by European standards should be taken into account. Recently, Richard Overy has modified the picture of a 'peacetime-like war economy' between 1939 and 1941. In reality, the policies of the regime — tax increases, food rationing, cuts in consumer production, savings programmes designed to soak up purchasing power in the interests of financing the war — had considerable consequences for the standard of living of the population. An American observer found life in Berlin during the winter of 1939–40 'thoroughly spartanic', but since it had been like that for the working class before the war, they probably did not regard this as either novel or serious. In contrast with conditions in the First World War, food supplies remained at a high level. Large parts of the population, and in particular the workers, were obviously concerned to ensure that the living standard they had arduously achieved before the war was not going to be forfeited again.

Military successes also promoted working-class loyalty to the regime, and the victory over France was regarded as being the high-point of assent and enthusiasm among most sections of the population. If hitherto Hitler's foreign policy successes and approval of the Nazi regime had been two rather separate quantities, so now the boundaries became fluid and the discontent with this or that aspect of Nazi policy was superseded by basic acceptance of Hitler's regime among the workers. This was particularly so once there were no realistic political alternatives, especially after the pact between Hitler and Stalin of 1939 disoriented Communist support and isolated them from other opponents of Hitler.

Mounting working-class assent to the Nazi regime may also be ascribed to the success with which the authorities were able to shift the burdens of war on to the populations of countries occupied by the German military (*Wehrmacht*). The slogan went: 'First the Wehrmacht, then the German people, and only then the populations of occupied countries!' The extent to which this would be taken literally only became fully apparent with the economic preparations for the war against the Soviet Union. Domestically, a very tangible and immediate reminder of this principle of displacement were the mounting numbers of foreigners brought to Germany for 'labour deployment'. By the summer of 1941 some 3 million foreigners, mostly Poles and Frenchmen, were working in Germany; the use of foreign labour reached a peak in the autumn of 1944, with some 7.7 million foreign civilian workers and prisoners of war. The largest group were workers from the USSR, of whom there were 2.2

million (half of them women), including 630,000 prisoners of war. Until
the autumn of 1941 most of these foreign workers were deployed in the
agricultural sector; from the winter of 1941–2, when the fortunes of war
altered, more of them were employed in industry. By 1944 foreigners
comprised more than a quarter of all those employed in the German
economy: in armaments factories, in construction work, mining and agriculture the quota of foreigners was over 50 per cent. In the last stages of
the war, German workers were only active as foremen and mastercrafts-
men, with 80–90 per cent of the workforce being foreigners. Among the
workforce a strictly segmented racial and national hierarchy developed,
with German workers at the apex, followed by workers of 'Germanic'
origin such as the Danes or Dutch, and then down, via the Poles, to Soviet
civilian workers and finally prisoners of war. This hierarchy determined
the living and working conditions of workers. Germans were generally in
supervisory positions where workers from Eastern Europe were
deployed; and in large factories, Germans were usually there solely to
train or to control the others. Certainly, German workers were also subject to increased pressure, but foreigners were much more adversely
affected by the draconian punishments for 'shirking' or 'breach of contract' than their hosts. There was some potential for the development of
common interests between Germans and foreigners in the factories, and
the number of cases where people were ready to help 'foreign workers'
was not inconsiderable. However, most German workers, like the population in general, were neither ready to help nor ready actively to maltreat
foreigners, but rather regarded their presence with disinterest, an attitude
that hardened as the war progressed and as the Germans became preoccupied with their own problems. Gradually, an attitude developed
towards such foreigners which silently presupposed racial inequalities
and did not regard effective participation in racial policy as being anything worthy of much comment.

This had long-term consequences for the German working class.
Regardless of how individuals behaved towards foreigners, their presence
set in motion a form of social restructuring that provided unprecedented
prospects for social mobility. The conversion of the German economy
from one of *Blitzkrieg* to a long war of attrition as a result of the military
failure outside Moscow in the autumn of 1941, rapidly altered the living
and working conditions of the German workers. The composition of the
factory workforce altered. Although, apart from foremen and skilled
craftsmen, those remaining in factories were mostly over fifty, conscription

began to make inroads even into the workforce of armaments factories. An increasing proportion of German workers was called up, an event that dramatically and decisively altered their destinies, (although here we are entering the realm of supposition in the absence of hard evidence). What is certain is that, depending upon luck or otherwise, a couple of months or fifteen years in the army not only broadened a socially and geographically very narrow range of experience, but also profoundly influenced their political and moral values. In relation to this, squabbles about pay, socio-political improvements or the role of the German Labour Front — to take only a few subjects all too prevalent in recent historical literature — seem rather marginal.

The primary concern of those who stayed at home was to make sure they were categorised in reserved occupations or that their presence on the domestic front was essential. This became one of the most effective means of disciplining German workers. On the other hand, the working population was much preoccupied with erratic food supply and bombing raids. Given the decrease in available consumer goods, wage rates lost their significance and food became the primary subject of interest. The logical consequence of rationing and food shortages was a burgeoning second economy: panic buying, illicit slaughtering, hoarding and the black market quickly assumed great significance — an obvious, almost logical development, which certainly did not politically threaten the Nazi regime. However, it was an obvious challenge to that regime's totalitarian aspirations, because it threatened to puncture belief in the regime's administrative efficiency. Despite the brutal but obviously ineffectual intervention of the Gestapo, it was impossible to get rid of the black market; however, the Nazis were successful in limiting memories of its activities to the post-war era.

The decisive element in the disintegration of the pro-National Socialist consensus was undoubtedly the bombing campaign, which, because of the density of urban working-class residential districts, affected them worse than any other class. The concomitant burdens were considerable: the time and place of work frequently altered, and in many factories the workers had to work all day and then do air-raid service at night. The mood of the German population, especially in towns within bombing range, gradually switched to one of apathy and resignation; the reduction of social awareness to matters of day-to-day existence and the mounting disinterest in social or political questions, were all manifestations of this development. Nevertheless, there was no broadly based political opposition.

This political apathy was not merely a by-product of increased terror on the part of the security services, nor of a growing concern with individual survival. The air-raids themselves contributed not merely hopelessness and fear, but also, by promoting anger and bitterness towards a superior opponent, provided the National Socialist leadership with sentiments they could harness. Broad sections of the population, including the workers, were also afraid of a German defeat, particularly at the hands of the Soviet Union, which again provided Nazi propaganda with something to play upon in the last two years of the war.

It is, in fact, very difficult to separate the experiences of the working class from those of other groups during the third and final stage of the war. The reason for this lies not simply in the changes among the workforce brought about by conscription or the deployment of foreigners. Rather, as the effects of the war became more and more apparent, individual horizons narrowed and other criteria assumed vast importance: whether one was called up or not; whether one ended up on the Eastern or Western Front; whether one was wounded or not; whether one's family lived in a small country town or a major industrial region; in the suburbs or the town centre; whether they had been bombed out or not; whether the children had been evacuated; whether they had taken in refugees or had had to seek shelter themselves; whether one lived in eastern Germany and had had to flee, or in the west where the bombing raids were severer — these were the questions that primarily determined individual destinies and comprised people's experiences. Ties to the collective development of a class to which one once belonged lost their significance. Instead, people formed communities of destiny, whose fate was determined by geographical, military and political factors, and, last but not least, by luck. This was important for the German workers because, more than any other class, their lives had been focused upon a class-bound collectivity even though the cohesive power of the proletarian milieu had diminished in recent years.

The initial problem of how to interpret the development of the working class under Nazi rule has led to the stressing of consensus, integration and agreement rather than such factors as nonconformity, opposition and resistance. When looking at the pre-war years as a whole what seems striking in terms of the Nazis' assumption of power is the relative continuity of development in the context of favourable economic circumstances as well as the form assumed by social conflict. What was new was the changed political framework which favoured employers, following the destruction of organised labour and the terrorising of the working population, rather than any automatic material consequences for the workers themselves. The National Socialists' specific contribution in this phase consisted in introducing racial-hygienic principles into social policy: by excluding the 'unfit' or 'biologically burdened'. If one compares these developments with the corporatist social policies of the Italian Fascists, then the difference would seem to lie, above all, in the Nazis' more modern conception of not excluding the workers explicitly from a share in economic development, but rather attempting to include the 'valuable' elements among them in the 'national community', something achieved by promoting a vision of society in which the dividing lines were horizontal rather than vertical. In view of the miserable socio-economic condition of the German workers since the middle of the First World War this strategy was successful, because it gave the workers stability, albeit on a very modest level, while simultaneously opening up prospects of longer-term social mobility. The Nazis were therefore reacting to the workers' primary social concerns, against which political repression seemed quite secondary, especially since terror was limited to resistance activists, while the persecution of the 'racially' or 'biologically' inferior did not directly concern them. In any case, one could hardly say that many younger workers, including supporters of bourgeois and Right-wing groups and indeed the Communists, had a very profound acquaintance with the notion of democratic freedom before 1933. Thus, political criticism of the Nazi regime abated with improvements in personal circumstances, while the continuation of social conflict in the factories was not directly connected with the political rule of the National Socialists. Put differently, it was not a case of political consensus, but rather socio-economic improvements that neutralised and partly integrated the workers, with the regime going to considerable lengths until the last year of war to appease the German worker.

This occurred principally through the imposition of burdens upon the populations of occupied countries, which radicalised existing domestic racism while simultaneously turning it outwards. But while those elements excluded from the German population — Jews, the disabled, Gypsies, the asocial and others — were lost from view, the arrival of millions of foreign workers whose presence explicitly worked to the advantage of a German population deemed to be racially superior was a tangible everyday reality. At the same time, a considerable proportion of the working class became part of the Nazi war machine for such long periods that the effects and influence of this upon their own self-esteem and political outlook were probably extraordinary and considerable.

Nonetheless, neither experience — as privileged German workers or German soldiers — was sufficient to achieve political cohesion; working-class adherence to National Socialism was bound up with the regime's success. If there was no success, Nazism lost its attractions. The bombing war destroyed the preconditions for acceptance of the regime without, it should be said, resulting in active political opposition. The political ties to the regime that existed among the workers quickly lost their power and were replaced by a disillusioned pragmatism, with experience contradicting the regime's ideologically determined models of a perfect society. But at the same time, people's first experience during the late 1930s of the interplay of security of employment, relatively high wages, welfare provision, leisure activities and a focus upon family life left lasting and positive memories. In the light of these experiences, all future policy would be judged by German workers in accordance with these standards.

'The Real Mystery in Germany'
M. Burleigh and W. Wippermann, *The Racial State: Germany, 1933–1945* (Cambridge, 1991; 2nd edn. 1992); David F. Crew, *Nazism and German Society, 1933–1945* (London, 1994); N. Frei, *National Socialist Rule in Germany: The Führer State. 1933–1945* (Oxford, 1993); U. Herbert, *Fremdarbeiter, Politik und Praxis des 'Auslander-Einsatzes' in der Kriegswirtschaft des Dritten Reiches* (Berlin, 1985); ibid, *Arbeit, Volkstum, Wettanschauung* (Frankfurt au Main, 1995); L. Niethammer, 'Heimat und Front', in L. Niethammer (ed.), *Die Jahre Weiss Man Nicht, Wo Man die Heute Hinsetzen Soll* (Berlin, 1983); D. Peukert, *Inside Nazi Germany* (London, 1989); M.-L. Recker, *Nationalsozialistische Sozialpolitik im Zweiten Weltkrieg* (Munich, 1985); J. Stephenson, 'Triangle: Foreign Workers, German Civilians, and the Nazi Regime', *German Studies Review*, 15 (1992).

CHAPTER II

RACIAL DISCRIMINATION AT WORK: FORCED LABOUR IN THE VOLKSWAGEN FACTORY, 1939–45

Klaus-Jörg Siegfried

O N 26 MAY 1938 ADOLF HITLER laid the foundation-stone for the Volkswagen factory at Fallersleben which was being constructed under the auspices of Robert Ley's German Labour Front (DAF). The Volkswagen plant was built for the mass production of a cheap 'people's car' — costing a relatively modest RM990 — designed by the Stuttgart-based engineer Ferdinand Porsche, the only private sector car manufac-turer to regard such a vehicle as either feasible or desirable. Other manufacturers such as Opel had explored the idea, principally to offset the prospect of a Nazi takeover of the automobile industry. When they retired from the quest for a cheap popular vehicle, Porsche and a col-league from Daimler-Benz stayed on to run the whole project, which was essentially a state concern run by private sector managers. The factory was to be equipped with its own power plant, foundry, rolling-mills and facilities for the manufacture of glass and tyres, with assembly lines copied from the Ford factory at Rouge River. A 'model town' was to be built near Fallersleben, to be called 'the town of the Strength through Joy car', 'Strength through Joy' being the DAF subsidiary organisation ded-icated to shaping the leisure time of the working-classes. At a time when car ownership was still a luxury enjoyed by the middle classes, the Nazis wanted to demonstrate that their policies would benefit the working classes. Ley and the DAF took an interest in the scheme chiefly because involvement in one of the Führer's pet projects would counter the DAF's reputation for corruption, mismanagement and scandal. Paradoxically, the idea of approaching the DAF seems to have come from the chairman of Bayerische Motorwerke (BMW), who by linking ownership of a 'people's car' with DAF membership, was clearly hoping to preserve intact his own firm's share of the middle-class market.

In the event, following the outbreak of war the Fallersleben factory was gradually subsumed by the arms industry, becoming a regionally significant producer of arms for the duration. The plant produced military vehicles, such as the Kübelwagen or 'bucket car' (in 1943: 28 per cent of output); aircraft parts for Junkers 88 bombers (in 1942: *circa* 40 per cent of output; in 1944: *circa* 8 per cent of output); becoming from 1944 the largest manufacturer of V-1 flying bombs, of which between 13,000 and 14,000 were produced before the end of the war. The factory also turned out a range of smaller weapons, such as mines, bazookas, ammunition, tank tracks and stoves for the troops on the Eastern Front.

Although the initial transformation from civil to military production was accompanied by a number of setbacks, the factory became a flourishing part of the armaments sector as industrial capacity was mobilised for total war. However, this was only achieved through increasing resort to foreign forced labour, prisoners of war and inmates of concentration camps. Like most other armaments manufacturers, the Volkswagen plant made up the deficit of skilled workers lost to the armed forces by participating in the conscription and deportation of millions of people from countries under German occupation. Even as the plant was being established, management had had difficulties recruiting labour due to competition from other armaments manufacturers in the Brunswick area, notably the Hermann Göring-Werk at Salzgitter. Workers had to be recruited from Austria, the Saarland, Upper Silesia and the Sudentenland. A factory training school was established at Brunswick to provide future skilled workers. However, with the outbreak of war the management was faced with the loss to the armed forces of the nucleus of skilled workers they had carefully assembled. Many of the eager trainees at Brunswick enthusiastically volunteered for the *Waffen*-SS. Arms contracts, which were accompanied by allocations of forced labour, were one way of solving the firm's labour crisis. Initially, Volkswagen acquired foreign workers either on a voluntary basis, or through agreements with Allied or neutral countries. For example in 1938 the management could replace 3,000 construction workers drafted to the 'Westwall' fortification project with a corresponding contingent of Italians, under an agreement between the DAF and the Fascist Confederation of Industrial Labour. This element of voluntarism increasingly disappeared in the case of Germany's defeated opponents. In mid-1943, about 1,500 French workers arrived at the factory to perform labour service. Their number included members of the collaborationist Vichy youth organisation. They were followed shortly by 150 Belgian civilians, about 300 Dutch students and smaller contingents from other occupied countries.

The extent and method of labour recruitment were determined by political factors and by the Nazi regime's all-pervasive racial ideology. The main criterion was the racial proximity of any given nationality to the so-called 'Aryan master-race'. The Dutch, Flemings, Danes and Norwegians received better treatment because of their alleged racial affinity with the Germans. By contrast, workers from Poland and the Soviet Union were regarded as being of 'lesser racial value' or 'sub-human', and hence lived in conditions that were designed merely to keep them alive. Accordingly, in eastern Europe and the Soviet Union the Nazi regime rapidly resorted to conscription and deportation, with entire villages being ringed by the police, SS or army, and the inhabitants shipped to Germany in railway cars designed for freight or livestock. In this fashion, the Volkswagen plant acquired about 1,500 Poles, many of them under fifteen years of age, and four to five thousand so-called 'eastern workers' from the Soviet Union, the majority of whom were women aged between sixteen and twenty.

A further 1.9 million prisoners of war were also deployed in the armaments industry, although this was expressly prohibited by international law. Some 850 French and 850 Soviet prisoners of war worked in the Volkswagen factory, with their ranks eventually being augmented by 1,500 Italian 'military internees', that is soldiers loyal to Marshal Badoglio rather than Mussolini. These prisoners were subject to the discipline and orders of the German armed forces, lived behind barbed wire and were denied the freedom to move about outside their camps. Their allocation to armaments factories was carried out by the labour authorities.

In the case of concentration camp prisoners, compulsory labour was inseparable from the organised terror perpetrated by the SS. Industrialists applied directly to the SS department responsible for concentration camps in order to satisfy their labour requirements. As a result of this initiative by the management of the Volkswagen plant, about 600 prisoners were contracted to build a light metals foundry; in 1944 a satellite camp of Neuengamme concentration camp was established with about 860 prisoners who then constructed a camp for forced foreign labour there. In the same year, 650 Jewish women were transferred from Auschwitz to the Volkswagen plant to work on the manufacture of bazookas and mines. Finally, about 7,000 concentration camp inmates were distributed among a number of outlying or underground work-shops established as a consequence of worsening Allied air-raids. Concentration camp labour, both in the Volkswagen plant and in the armaments sector as a whole, contributed little to the regime's ever-growing production targets.

How did the management of the Volkswagen factory control this army of forced foreign workers, prisoners of war and concentration camp inmates? In the Nazi state armaments factories were areas where normal rights were suspended and the management could call on the SS to dis-cipline the workforce. In practice, this meant that the Volkswagen factory was organised according to the Führer principle; the workforce lost any form of independent representation (the 'works council' was a sham) and was subjected to the totalitarian control and propaganda of the German Labour Front. Surveillance of the workers, designed to obstruct any form of political activity, was carried out by informers who reported to the Gestapo and the representative of military intelligence. The factory guard or *Werkschutz*, consisting of SS men, patrolled the factory corridors and floor with guns and dogs, arresting workers for the slightest infraction of rules; they were then beaten, confined in the factory cellars and taken to a special works (punishment) camp, or in more serious cases for three weeks' detention in Labour Camp 21 at Hallendorf near Salzgitter. Those who were not killed there returned to their workplaces in a desolate con-dition or were sent to hospitals to recover from their injuries.

Foreign workers were particularly subject to these terror practices; they were entirely under the control of German master-craftsmen and foremen whose instructions had to be obeyed without demur. Much therefore hinged upon the character or political persuasion of individual German workers; whether they abused the foreign workers, making them work at a frenzied tempo or whether they treated them sympathetically when hunger and exhaustion meant that they could not fulfil their pro-duction quotas. Foreign workers were further subject to control and sur-veillance in the camps where they lived. The camps were under the direction of commandants from the German Labour Front who were also employees of the Volkswagen factory. They relied upon a subordinate hierarchy of camp spokesmen and auxiliary police to maintain control. Concentration camp prisoners, who were housed in total isolation from the rest of the workforce, were guarded exclusively by the SS.

It was characteristic of National Socialist rule that terror and violence were augmented by integrationary strategies so that consensus accompanied coercion. These included not only ideological and propagandistic conditioning or concessions of a socio-political type, but also cultural events and the organisation of leisure time. The Volkswagen factory had a vast leisure centre known as the Cianetti Hall. The eponymous Tullio Cianetti was the President of the Fascist Confederation of Industrial Labour who concluded the arrangement with Robert Ley to deploy thousands of Italian construction workers in order to build the 'town of the Strength through Joy car'. The Cianetti Hall was designed as a monument to Italo-German friendship, a fact suggestive of the political function of the various cultural activities — concerts, ballet, plays, films, exhibitions and sporting events — that took place there. These were primarily designed to influence German and Italian workers, although the Belgians, Dutch and French were allowed to participate too. The Poles and 'Eastern workers' and naturally prisoners of war and concentration camp inmates were excluded from the events held in the Cianetti Hall. Italian military internees were admitted or debarred from these events in accordance with the degree of submission and willingness to work they evinced. In other words, the official cultural offerings of the leisure organisation 'Strength through Joy' themselves reflected racial criteria in accordance with the patterns of discrimination which governed the working and living conditions of all 'foreign workers'. How did this work in practice?

Discriminatory racial criteria also determined living and working conditions. Foreign workers deemed to be racially akin to the Germans were to all intents and purposes treated like Germans. Political considerations also played a part. Workers from allied states, for example until 1943 the Italians, or workers from collaborationist Vichy France were regarded by the Germans as 'workmates' and enjoyed a relatively privileged position. This was particularly so in the case of members of a Vichy organisation who volunteered to work in the Volkswagen factory. These 'Western workers' were properly fed and received adequate medical attention. They could leave their barracks after work and could go about the town if they wished to. They were also allowed to organise their own cultural activities. The French seem to have been particularly active on the cultural front, organising concerts, exhibitions and Christmas festivities in the Cianetti Hall, and taking part in an orchestra and choir which were occasionally allowed to undertake outside engagements.

Matters were otherwise for Polish and Soviet 'eastern workers'. They had to wear discriminatory identificatory markings on their clothing, analogous to the Star of David worn by Jews: a 'P' for Poles and 'OST' for people from the Soviet Union. They were highly vulnerable to abuse by fanatical master-craftsmen, foremen, camp commanders and the factory guards, and were usually forbidden to leave the camps in which they were housed. There they were certainly permitted their own cultural activities, but it was highly unlikely that any of them were keen on taking part in amateur dramatics when they were starving and having to work ten or twelve hours a day. Any enthusiasm for cultural activities soon evaporated and they sank into the dull monotony of the camp's daily routine. While many of them sickened and died as a result of exhaustion and hunger at an unusually premature age, none of the Dutchmen or Frenchmen at Volkswagen died.

The weakest were worst affected. Inevitably, intimate relations developed which resulted in many Polish and Russian women becoming pregnant. The regime stipulated that female forced labourers had to part with their children two weeks after delivery in order to return the mothers to the productive process as rapidly as possible. The children were to be raised in a 'children's home of the simplest sort'. From the autumn of 1944 all newly born children taken to the Volkswagen children's home at Rühen died on account of this officially inspired neglect of basic hygiene. Because of this, after the war the British occupying forces tried and executed Dr Körbel, the doctor responsible for the home.

Living conditions of prisoners of war were also determined in accordance with racial criteria. They were subjected to greater control and more stringent discipline than civilians from the same countries. Conditions were especially atrocious for Soviet prisoners of war. Demonised as the 'Jewish Bolshevik enemy', many of them never survived the long treks into captivity or confinement in vast camps with nothing to shelter them from the harsh Russian winter. Millions of them simply lost the will to live and died. Those Soviet prisoners of war who arrived at the Volkswagen plant were often in a deplorable condition, with many of them suffering from typhus from which they soon died. Economic, rather than humanitarian, considerations led the management

to give these men food and medical attention so that they might be incorporated into the productive process. Notwithstanding this initial concern, most of them soon vegetated in lice-ridden rags at the margins of
human existence. The same fate awaited the Italian 'military internees' —
known colloquially as 'Badoglio swine' — or those Italian soldiers captured by German troops after the fall of Mussolini in 1943. They became
the special targets of the fury and frustration of German workers and
foremen, who regarded them as traitors and who blamed Germany's erst-
while ally for setbacks on the battlefields. Many of these Italians committed suicide or died of hunger and exhaustion. Soviet and Italian
prisoners of war were almost on the same level as concentration camp
prisoners. In the latter case, discrimination against foreign workers escal-
ated into the deadly maxim 'extermination through labour'. The SS were
not concerned to conserve the labour capacity of the prisoners —
although this sometimes happened in the interests of productivity — but
rather to 'exhaust' it (i.e. not to restore them from hunger and exhaustion). By the end of 1944, the Volkswagen plant and its outlying work-
shops had incorporated the deaths of these prisoners into their business
calculations.

How did the foreign forced workers and concentration camp prisoners
react to their fate? One of the objectives of the racially discriminatory
measures considered here, was to stimulate antagonism and resentment
between the various categories of foreign workers, thus making it impossible for them to unite in the interests of resistance to Nazi terror. By and
large this strategy failed. No durable enmities developed between
'Western' and 'Eastern' workers, or between civilian workers, prisoners
of war and concentration camp inmates. Even the policy of physically
isolating the various groups failed. Although they lived in separate camps,
the foreign workers mingled in the factory, with the sole exception of
concentration camp inmates who worked separately. This resulted in
numerous contacts and expressions of solidarity: French, Dutch, Belgian
and Italian men developed close personal relations with Polish or Russian
women; Dutchmen learned Russian, while Ukrainian girls acquired a
smattering of Dutch; French civilian workers shared their food with
starving Soviet prisoners of war; an Italian doctor secretly smuggled
medicines to women Jewish concentration camp prisoners; two unknown
Polish Jewish nurses cared for sick Dutch foreign workers in hospital.

Cultural activities were a means of counteracting the deleterious
psychological effects of forced labour. Even though the cultural activities

offered by the regime had a transparent ideological and political message, they nonetheless contributed to the inner stability of the individual in the comfortless milieu of the camps in which the workers lived. Autonomous cultural activities strengthened national group solidarities and hence powers of resistance. For example French forced labourers produced their own newspaper, which was tolerated by the camp commandant and factory management because of its supposedly non-political content. They and the Gestapo simply failed to note the hidden ironies of much of the content, which hence became a platform for the expression of French opposition.

All of the forced foreign workers were united in their rejection of the Nazi regime, regardless of differences in their conditions and treatment; for even the Dutch, Belgians and Frenchmen, including collaborationist Vichy workers, were victims of SS and Gestapo repression if they expressed undesirable political views, let alone participated in spontaneous demonstrations. This universal opposition to the regime did not result in every group of forced foreign workers participating in active resistance. Gestapo and factory militia control were far too tight and the punishments too draconian for this to happen. Accordingly, there was only passive resistance, consisting of innumerable minor acts of individual sabotage, which were difficult to detect: machinery was wrongly set, small parts were incorrectly assembled and so on. Moreover, individuals endeavoured to overcome hunger and exploitation by deliberately working at a slow pace, pretending to be sick or stupid, by smuggling food from the kitchens or by surreptitiously cooking stolen potatoes at the work-bench with the aid of buckets and electric cable. Many Dutchmen and Frenchmen took the opportunity of home leave to disappear entirely, before home leave was cancelled for all 'west workers'. Among those who stayed behind, a few had the courage to tune in to foreign radio stations to learn of Allied military advances.

Exploitation of foreign forced labour at the Volkswagen plant ceased when Fallersleben was occupied by American troops on 11 April 1945. The Nazi functionaries and SS men fled, and the machinery finally lay still. Soviet forced labourers and prisoners of war, who had suffered the most in the preceding years, armed themselves and went on a looting spree in the town, killing anyone who tried to stop them. Former 'west workers' supported the efforts of Allied forces and what remained of the German administration to restore law and order. Subsequently, all foreign workers were repatriated. The concentration camp inmates had been taken away by the SS before the town was liberated by the Allies. Many of them were so debilitated that they died before they too could be liberated.

What was the significance of armaments production and forced labour for the Volkswagen concern? While other firms were swiftly integrated into the armaments sector, the outbreak of war initially threatened the very existence of Volkswagen. Planned as a car factory and only partially completed, the factory could not immediately be converted to military production. It faced the real danger of being left incomplete and idle, or of being taken over by an existing arms manufacturer. This gave a certain urgency to the concern's quest for arms contracts and the forced labour that went with them. Since the Volkswagen factory had had considerable difficulties recruiting labour in the year of its foundation, and then had to relinquish many of those it managed to recruit to the armed forces, the firm felt obliged to bridge the labour shortage by resorting to foreign forced labour and concentration camp inmates. The problem was compounded by the management's attempts to expand its share of armaments manufacturing, a policy that was only possible by increasing the number of those foreign workers most subject to the Nazi regime's repression. Since these groups comprised the greater part of the army of forced labour in the Volkswagen factory (with about 8,000 Polish and Soviet civilian workers and prisoners of war as well as Italian 'military internees') it can be seen that the Volkswagen factory became a leading participant in the regime of terror that the Nazis created in the armaments sector. The result was massive dependence upon forced labour, consisting of 70 per cent of the total workforce in 1943, a figure that far outstripped the numbers employed in other factories.

Which of the directors and managers of the Volkswagen plant were responsible for these decisions? The Nazi war economy was dirigiste. Allocations to factories of raw materials and labour were in accordance with state production programmes established by the Ministry of Armaments in response to military priorities. The private sector itself was involved in allocating as well as implementing government contracts. This permitted businessmen from the more powerful concerns to exert influence upon state planning. The Volkswagen plant enjoyed this sort of influence, since the firm's foundation was intimately bound up with one of the regime's favoured social projects. Moreover in 1943 Volkswagen derived additional prestige from being designated a 'model wartime concern', a title augmented a year later into 'model National Socialist concern'. More important was the fact that the chief executive was Ferdinand Porsche, the designer of the 'people's car'. The other executive directors were the DAF functionary Dr Bodo Lafferentz and Jakob Werlin, a member of the board of Daimler Benz. Porsche was a confidant of Hitler, who used Porsche's reputation as a designer of genius to identify the regime with technological progress. In 1941 Hitler put Porsche in charge of a commission concerned with tank manufacture, the most important weapon on the eve of, and during, the invasion of the Soviet Union. Porsche's role was to act as a conduit for Hitler's own ideas on tank warfare. He used his contacts with the Führer to achieve the integration of Volkswagen into the armaments sector, but he also had a personal interest in doing so, since he was in charge of a firm in Stuttgart-Zuffenhausen which fulfilled contract work on behalf of the Volkswagen factory. What benefited Volkswagen benefited Porsche too. Ferdinand Porsche was thus responsible for Volkswagen's conversion to an armaments factory. He eagerly sought out fresh defence contracts, including one for the V-1 flying bombs which were used to destructive effect against London from 1944. A representative of Porsche roamed the occupied Soviet Union in search of 'eastern workers'. Engineers from the factory also had their pick of Soviet prisoners of war caged at Fallingbostel, as well as of hundreds of Jews from the extermination camp at Auschwitz. Porsche's keenness eventually ensured his ensnarement in the conflicts of competence and interest within the Nazi polyocracy. He crossed swords with the Minister of Munitions, Albert Speer, who eased Porsche from the chairmanship of the commission on tank production. In order to realise his ambitions in the armaments sector, Porsche sought for a powerful ally, finding one in the shape of Reichsführer-SS, Heinrich Himmler, who was interested in securing a share of the arms sector for his ramified concentration camp empire. In 1937 Porsche had already put out 'feelers' to Himmler by requesting SS men to test drive the Volkswagen Beetle (so-called because of its shape). Later, he availed himself of the SS to provide guards for the workers forced to toil in the Volkswagen factory. The Waffen-SS in turn backed his plans to convert the Beetle for military purposes. In 1942, Porsche used his connection with Himmler to secure from Hitler the authorisation to build a concentration camp at Volkswagen whose inmates would construct a foundry. In return, Porsche agreed to supply the SS with 4,000 'bucket' vehicles (jeep-type military vehicles). Porsche's aim was eventually to use the foundry for the production of civilian vehicles; whether he still harboured these ideas by the end of the war is doubtful, since he was still trying to secure military contracts in 1944, by which time they were much reduced in number. For example, he requested from Himmler 3,500 concentration camp inmates for the production of V-1 rockets and aircraft in a subterranean factory. Himmler rewarded his commitment and enthusiasm by granting him the honorary rank of SS-Oberführer and a death's-head ring for his finger.

The historian Hans Mommsen, who for some years has been producing a history of the Volkswagen plant during the Nazi period on behalf of Volkswagen AG, which has so far not appeared in print, has characterised the behaviour and personality of Porsche as follows. Porsche was 'tantalised by the technological opportunities which the regime made available to him' and did not shrink 'from exploiting the personal relationship which existed between him and Hitler in the interests of both his design bureau and then the plant'. Mommsen continues, 'Especially in the later stages of a war which was effectively already lost, Porsche revealed himself to be a champion of armaments production at any price', and 'as a supporter of a policy of soldiering on to the bitter end ... He himself never questioned the system of forced labour. He also proceeded relatively unscrupulously when it came to the implementation of his projects.'

However, it would be wrong to judge Porsche in isolation from the historical circumstances of his actions or to explain them solely through reference to the nature of his character. The biases of the car manufacturer were typical of German industrialists in the Nazi period, and many of his decisions could certainly also have been made by other entrepreneurs. It has already been noted that the German armaments industry was closely involved with the apparatus of the Nazi state. The regime wanted to direct arms production in accordance with its policies and military strategies and thereby availed itself of the private sector, upon which it was necessarily dependent. However, this dependence gave the most powerful concerns the chance to maintain themselves vis-à-vis the state, or indeed to use its institutions and organisations in their own interests. Without being necessarily convinced of the racial ideology of the Nazi regime, many industrialists colluded with the racially-motivated imperialist goals of the Nazis' war effort since arms production meant vast, state-guaranteed profits, while the regime's military expansionism promised a considerably enhanced sphere of economic activity and influence. Mommsen writes that 'In this respect the management of the Volkswagen factory was no different from any other large concern.' The political horizons and economic activities of industrialists such as Porsche progressively lost their moral dimension the more hopeless the war appeared and the more brutally the regime practised its policies of extermination during the phase of 'total war'. The cumulative desensitisation that accompanied this process saw a progressive loss of scruple regarding the employment of forced labour and concentration camp prisoners, and the ruthless exploitation of their labour, until only purely economic and technocratic aims counted. This may explain why, for example, Porsche intervened to improve the rations of half-starved Soviet prisoners of war, while doing nothing to prevent the mass demise of the children born to forced workers in the Volkswagen factory.

'Moral deadening, a professionalised loss of a sense of reality and National Socialist indoctrination, went hand in hand in the attitudes of functionaries at various levels' is how Mommsen characterises the behaviour of Porsche and other members of the management in the last phase of the war. But even though contemporary circumstances and the climate of the times may determine the behaviour of individuals, they do not exonerate them from responsibility. It remains the historian's task to distinguish and evaluate the degree to which the behaviour of an individual was influenced by social circumstances, or the result of individual decisions that also carry the burden of personal responsibility.

THE MASS DEATH OF THE CHILDREN OF POLISH AND SOVIET FORCED LABOURERS IN THE VOLKSWAGEN PLANT.

1942: The Nazi regime decides to halt the repatriation of pregnant foreign workers since it needs their labour capacity for armament production. The children are to be removed from their mothers and raised in children's homes 'of the simplest type'.

February 1943 to the end of 1943: The management of the Volkswagen factory establishes a maternity ward and a children's home within the camps for pregnant foreign workers. Ten children die of malnutrition.

October 1943 to May 1944: The children fall ill with scabies, boils and ulcers. Thirty-five of them die.

14 June 1944: The home is moved to Rühen (about 15 kilometres from the Volkswagen plant). The children contract gastroenteritis. The death rate rises to 100 per cent.

BIOGRAPHY OF A PERPETRATOR: DR HANS KÖRBEL

1909 born in Höchst. Attended a grammar school and then studied medicine.

1927 Membership of the Nazi Party.

1929 Joined the SA.

1934 Graduated with a doctorate from Heidelberg. Practical training in Darmstadt, Mainz and Heidelberg. Served as a factory doctor with Opel, I.G. Farben and other concerns. Promoted to SA *Obersturmführer* and awarded a golden Nazi Party decoration.

1935 Assistant physician in the university medical clinic at Heidelberg. Resigned from the SA and joined the SS. An *Untersturmführer* in the SS Security Service (SD), promoted to SS-*Obersturmführer* in September 1936.

1939 Promoted to SS-*Hauptsturmführer*. Became leading factory doctor in the Volkswagen plant, simultaneously assuming the following functions:

1940 Medical adviser to the factory health insurance scheme.

1941 Chief of the factory insurance scheme.

1943 Chief of the 'town of the Strength through Joy car' municipal hospital.

1946 Sentenced to death by a British military court for killing Polish and Russian children through deliberate neglect.

7 March 1947 Executed.

Forced Labour in the Volkswagen Factory

Bernard P. Bellon, *Mercedes in Peace and War: German Automobile Workers, 1903–1945* (New York, 1990); Ulrich Herbert, *A History of Foreign Labour in Germany* (London, 1990); ibid., *Fremdarbeiter. Politik und Praxis des Ausländereinsatzes in der Kriegswirtschaft des Dritten Reiches* (Berlin and Bonnn, 1985); Heinz Hohne, *The Order of the Death's Head* (London, 1972); Edward L. Homze, *Foreign Labor in Nazi Germany* (Princeton, 1967); Hans Mommsen, *Die Geschichte des Volkswagenwerks im Dritten Reich* (Bochum, 1991); Klaus-Jörg Siegfried, *Rüstungsproduktion und Zwangsarbeit im Volkswagenwerk,*

1939–1945 (Frankfurt am Main and New York, 1987); ibid., *Das Leben der Zwangsarbeiter im Volkswagenwerk, 1939–1945* (Frankfurt am Main and New York, 1988); Alfred Streim, *Die Behandlung Sowjetischer Kriegsgefangener im 'Fall Barbarossa'* (Karlsruhe, 1981); Christian Streit, *Keine Kamaraden* (Stuttgart, 1978).

CHAPTER III

NAZISM AND HIGH SOCIETY

Jeremy Noakes

'HIGH SOCIETY' IS NOT A TERM that has a respectable academic pedigree. Nevertheless, it expresses a social reality, namely the existence — at any rate from the 1920s to the 1940s — in the major capitals of Europe of an élite group whose basis was their social intercourse, their participation in an endless round of social engagements — dinners, balls, banquets, receptions, teas, soirées, concerts, theatre performances, race meetings and other social events of a similar nature. According to Martha Dodd, the daughter of the American ambassador to Berlin (1934–7), 'During the winter months most people got in two to four teas a day and a lunch or a dinner.' Membership of this group was determined by birth, official position or status, money, or — a trend that was beginning to develop during the 1920s — popular prestige as reflected in the mass media, or a combination of these attributes. High society was not identical with the political élite. Nevertheless, since it was widely regarded both by its own members and, through the influence of the media, by the population at large as the social élite, it invariably included a substantial proportion of the political élite.

At the centre of high society in Weimar Germany was the diplomatic corps. This marked a shift from the pre-war period when the central role had been performed by the Court and the diplomatic corps had formed simply a part of Court Society. During the first years of the Republic, much of the nobility associated with the Court had avoided social engagements with the despised new regime presided over by the ex-saddler, Friedrich Ebert, as President of the Reich. But, with the election of Field-Marshal von Hindenburg as President in 1925, they began to return to the capital and to play a role in high society. Until the outbreak of war, the Crown Prince continued to act as a focus for some members of the old aristocracy — retired generals and former ladies-in-waiting, who were known collectively and somewhat disparagingly as 'the

Potsdam Set' — entertaining at his 'stockbroker Tudor' mansion, the Cäcilienhof in Potsdam, or in his palace on Unter den Linden. In addition to the diplomatic corps and members of the former nobility, there were a number of wealthy businessmen who entertained on a grand scale. Some, such as the head of the Siemens electrical engineering combine, Werner von Siemens, were 'old money'; others had done well out of the war or the inflation and tried to make up for their lack of breeding by the lavishness of their entertainment. Then there were leading politicians, top civil servants, generals, artists and musicians, the occasional academic, film stars and the odd sports personality (tennis star, racing driver or flying ace).

Although most of the conversation that went on at these events was of a purely formal or conventional kind ('dull beyond belief' according to Martha Dodd), they did provide the opportunity for contacts and conversations of a more political nature — hence the intense involvement of the diplomatic corps. Moreover, acceptance within this circle implied social approval and so would confer a degree of legitimacy on any politician or political movement whose members could gain admittance. For the Nazi movement in the years before it came to power in 1933 the need to gain social acceptance among the élite was of considerable, indeed growing, importance. The abortive Munich Putsch of November 1923 had demonstrated that the Party could only come to power legally within the rules laid down by the Constitution. At the same time, it had tainted the movement with the reputation of being a group of violent revolutionaries. During the period 1925–9 the Party had to struggle against its image of being wild men on the political fringe. After the effective ending of parliamentary democracy with the appointment of Heinrich Brüning as Reich Chancellor in March 1930, political power became increasingly concentrated in the hands of the small group of men who had access to and influence over the Reich President. These men — Franz von Papen, Kurt von Schleicher, the young Hindenburg, Otto Meissner — were leading members of German high society. In these circumstances, the Nazis' need to transform their image, to convince the German élites that they were *salonfähig* (socially acceptable), formed an important part of the wider requirement to convince such groups that they were acceptable as a future government or at least as part of a future government.

Hitler was well aware of the political importance of social acceptability; he had owed his initial success in Munich to a significant extent to his ability to win friends and influence people within Munich high society. The post-war Munich high society suffered, like that of Berlin, from the loss of the Court. There was a small diplomatic corps in the shape of the foreign consuls — Munich was a relatively important posting after 1918 because of the importance and sensitivity of relations between Bavaria and the Reich, but its role in high society was not nearly so significant as that of Berlin. Munich high society was dominated by leading members of the upper middle class, particularly from the educated bourgeoisie — publishers, academics, artists, officials and professional men. Some of them were already associated with such extreme Right-wing *völkisch* organisations as the Thule Society and the Deutschvölkische Schutz und Trutzbund: men such as the publishers Julius Lehmann and Ernst Boepple, and the writer and translator, Dietrich Eckart. Others were impressed by Hitler's gifts as a demagogue, for example Munich University's Professor of Forestry, Karl Escherich, and the Professor of History, Karl Alexander von Müller.

Hitler had a particular appeal for upper-middle-class society ladies. With his shabby blue suit, long trench-coat, his dog whip and his revolver, Hitler was an exotic figure in the salons of Munich high society, either providing a frisson of radical chic or awakening the motherly instincts of his hostesses. Frau Erna Hanfstängl, the wife of 'Putzi' Hanfstängl, an early Nazi admirer whose family owned a prestigious international art publishing firm, sheltered Hitler after the abortive Munich Putsch. The Bechsteins, the famous piano manufacturers, invited Hitler to their suite in the Bayerischer Hof hotel and to their country house at Berchtesgaden. Frau Bechstein even loaned jewellery to the Party for use as collateral and gave Hitler advice on etiquette. But she had to compete for Hitler's attentions with Frau Bruckmann, the wife of the publisher of the works of Houston Stewart Chamberlain, the son-in-law of Richard Wagner. Hitler met Chamberlain when the Bechsteins introduced him to the Wagner household at Haus Wahnfried in Bayreuth in October 1923. Although this was not the most politically useful or financially lucrative of the numerous introductions provided by these society figures, it was undoubtedly the one that gave Hitler most personal satisfaction. Chamberlain's letter to Hitler, written following the meeting and shortly before his death, and praising him as the future saviour of Germany, not only boosted Hitler's self-esteem but impressed Winifred Wagner and laid the foundations for Hitler's long association with Haus Wahnfried.

More significant politically and, above all, financially were the contacts that were established through the Bavarian industrialist, Dr Emil Gansser, and the 'Baltic baron' Max Erwin Scheubner-Richter. Through Gansser's contacts, for example, Hitler spoke twice in the influential 1919 National Club in Berlin in May 1922 and received financial contributions from the two leading Berlin industrialists, Ernst von Borsig and Siemens, among others.

Although clearly Hitler's success during these early years depended primarily on his demagogic talents, nevertheless, it is difficult to see how he or his party could have survived, let alone prospered during 1922–3, years of hyperinflation and authoritarian government in Munich, without the protection of elements within Munich high society and among the Bavarian political and military establishment.

Following Hitler's abortive putsch in November 1923, the Nazi movement was obliged to spend several years in the political wilderness, a period in which, inevitably, it lost much of its appeal to high society in Munich or beyond. At the time of his trial in the spring of 1924, Hitler was still able to attract the favourable attention of some members of Munich society and, during the years 1925–8, he still had influential supporters, such as the coal magnate, Emil Kirdorf, who in 1926, for example, arranged for him to speak to Ruhr industrialists in Essen and to the élite 1919 Club in Hamburg.

However, the year 1929 was the turning-point in terms of the renewal of the attractiveness of the Nazi movement for high society. Moreover, this appeal was no longer largely confined to Munich but existed at national level. This development reflected both the changing electoral fortunes of the Nazi Party as apparent in the state and local government elections in the autumn of 1929 and, above all, the inclusion of the Party in the campaign against the Young Plan regulating German reparations payments organised by Alfred Hugenberg, the leader of the Right-wing German National People's Party. The fact that the Nazis were now officially allied to such socially respectable bodies as the Reichslandbund, the pressure group representing agriculture in general and the Prussian Junker landowners in particular, and the veterans' organisation, the Stahlhelm, of which Reich President von Hindenburg was the honorary president, removed from them the stigma of being a fringe group of wild men; the movement was now officially part of the right-wing anti-Republican establishment. This position was strengthened by the Party's massive gains in the Reichstag election of September 1930.

In fact, some members of the nobility had begun to gravitate towards the Nazi movement even before its electoral breakthrough in September 1930. Initially, the SA, the Stormtroopers' organisation, was the Nazi unit which proved most attractive, since its paramilitary style clearly appealed to the ex-officers and Free Corps leaders who were the first noble recruits. By August 1929, many of the leading positions within the SA were held by noble ex-officers. Its leader was Captain von Pfeffer; the deputy leader for West Germany was Lieutenant-Colonel Kurt von Ulrich and his adjutant was Werner von Fichte; the deputy leader for central Germany was Naval Commander, Manfred von Killinger, while the adjutant of the deputy leader for South Germany was Hanns Günter von Obernitz. Moreover, in that year a number of leading members of the German aristocracy joined the SA: Prince August-Wilhelm of Prussia, the fourth son of the Kaiser, Prince Friedrich-Christian of Schaumburg-Lippe and Prince Philipp of Hesse, who was the son-in-law of King Victor Emmanuel of Italy. The motorised division of the SA (the NSKK) was joined by Duke Eduard of Saxe-Coburg. Over the next four years, the higher ranks of the SA were full of members of noble families: Karl Friedrich Freiherr von Eberstein, Wolf Heinrich Count von Helldorf, Dietrich von Jagow, Hans von Tschammer und Osten, among others. However, although the SA had secured a head start in attracting members of the German nobility, in the event it was not the SA that was destined to become the élite Nazi formation but its rival, the SS.

Even before the appointment of Heinrich Himmler as its leader on 6 January 1929, the SS had the reputation of being an élite unit. In 1926 it was ordered that the SS 'must consist of specially selected, able, and circumspect human material' and, at the first Party rally in Weimar in the same year, Hitler entrusted it with the 'blood banner', the swastika flag that had survived from the Munich Putsch of 1923, a signal honour. However, it was Himmler who was primarily responsible for turning the SS into the élite corps of the Third Reich, a goal that he sought from the moment of his appointment.

Like Hitler, Himmler had no great respect for the German nobility, regarding it as substantially degenerate. However, he shrewdly recognised that one way of rapidly achieving élite status for his organisation was to attach to it the prestige of the existing high society, and so he deliberately set out to win them over. His success was impressive. Between 1930 and 1933, nobles began to join the Nazi movement in ever-increasing numbers and these new recruits tended to prefer the smart tailored black uniform of the SS to the more plebeian brown shirt of the

SA. Among the German aristocrats who joined the SS before 1933 were the Hereditary Grand Duke of Mecklenburg, the Hereditary Prince of Waldeck and Pyrmont and the Princes Christof and Wilhelm of Hesse, as well as a string of lesser nobles.

With its electoral gains of 1930, the Nazi Party had for the first time become a serious player on the national political stage. During the next two and a half years, the Nazis set about integrating themselves into Berlin high society. Many of the nobles who had been recruited hitherto — for example, most of the ex-Free Corps SA leaders — were not members of high society as such. The Party still needed to gain an entrée into the drawing-rooms of Berlin. Bella Fromm, the society correspondent for the *Vossische Zeitung*, who had remarkable social connections, particularly with the diplomatic corps, noted in her diary on 29 January 1932: 'Society slowly gets accustomed to the originally plebeian National Socialist movement. People from the upper crust are turning to Hitler.'

As in Munich during the early 1920s, an important role in this process was played by individual society hostesses, notably Helen ('Mammi') von Carnap, the ambitious wife of the Kaiser's last Chamberlain, Viktoria von Dirksen, wife of a wealthy monarchist, whose palace was a meeting place for the highest aristocracy and members of the royal family, and Manna von Winterfeld, wife of a general in the Imperial army. On 19 October 1932 Bella Fromm noted:

> They get in everywhere these National Socialists. They are patient, they bore from within and from without ... Frau von Dirksen, relic of the *Geheimrat* Willibald von Dirksen, always a monarchist, has for years been an eager hostess of the National Socialists in her magnificent palace ... She has acted as a mediator between the National Socialists and the old courtiers. Her brother, Karl August von Leffert, the German 'Jules Verne', attends his sister's receptions in the full splendour of his SS uniform. 'Auwi', Prince August Wilhelm, is generally to be found there in his brown uniform, and both the hostess and her youngest daughter wear the swastika pinned conspicuously on their bosoms.

In addition to these salon Nazis, there were one or two figures closer to Hitler who performed a key role in mediating between the Nazi movement and the German establishment, of whom the most important were Hermann Goering and Joachim von Ribbentrop. Both of them in their different ways were well-equipped to play the part. Goering's father had been a low-ranking diplomat, consul-general in Haiti, and Goering had been brought up in a castle in Bavaria owned by his mother's lover. During the First World War he had won Germany's highest military award, the Pour le Mérite, while leading the élite Richthofen squadron. Thus, although not a member of the social élite, Goering's background made him sufficiently *salonfähig* to move easily in high society and establish and maintain the right contacts. He was also an appropriate figure to take on the post of President of the Reichstag, the most prominent public position held by a Nazi before the takeover of power.

Ribbentrop lacked Goering's war record but made up for it with the wealth he had acquired from his marriage to Annette von Henckell, whose family owned the largest German champagne business. Ribbentrop, whose 'von' was acquired rather than inherited, had travelled widely abroad and, his excellent manners made an urbane impression. He entertained lavishly at his villa in the exclusive Berlin suburb of Dahlem, providing one of the best tables in the capital. His villa was the venue for the key negotiations that preceded Hitler's appointment as Reich Chancellor.

The recruitment of large numbers of nobles and other figures from German high society in the years 1929–33 ensured that the immediate impact of the Nazi takeover of power in this sphere was limited and was felt more as a stage in a transitional process. In the months before January 1933 brown and black Nazi uniforms were already part of the social scene; Magda Goebbels and Annette von Ribbentrop were already members of high society; by the autumn of 1932, much of the social élite was already coming to terms with the possibility if not the prospect of a Nazi victory, and some were already seeking a place in the new order.

After the Nazi takeover in January 1933, the stream of noble recruits to the Nazi movement became a flood as German nobles scrambled to position themselves advantageously for the opportunities offered by the new regime and to protect the positions they already had. Both the ex-Kaiser and the Crown Prince sounded out the prospects of a restoration of the monarchy and, for a few months, Hitler let them and their supporters keep their illusions — until his regime was well established. In this behaviour the nobility were of course no different from their bourgeois compatriots. However, whereas the mass of the 'March violets' or 'March casualties' (as those who had joined the NSDAP after March 1933 were called) joined the Party, the noble recruits preferred the SS. The result was that, as one author put it: 'the membership lists of the SS soon began to resemble pages from the Gotha [the official record of the German nobility]'.

Despite his contempt for what he regarded as the degeneracy of much of the nobility, Himmler approved of its two traditional foundations, namely careful breeding from approved stock and the ownership of land, and he urged his SS officers to try and win over the good blood in the nobility by seeking out their society. As he told a meeting of SS leaders in 1936:

> I refer, for example, to the horse-riding sports in which the Prussian landed nobility are heavily involved. If you take a look at the individuals involved, you have to admit there is some damned good blood among them; and you have to admit further that the Party has not won over this good blood. That is a sober statement of fact . . . We must try to fill the sons and daughters of those who are now opposed to us with our ideology, which after all is not so very far removed from the ideological principles of the nobility . . . Sometimes, when I was in the society of such people I commented maliciously: I expect you're surprised that we use a knife and fork, that we can do it too. At first, they found it in bad taste that one said something like that, but then one could talk to each other frankly about many things which one otherwise wouldn't have been able to discuss . . . But if we succeed in winning over one or two society people then they will gradually come to understand: that's right, they too have a shortage of leaders . . . And so I want you to have a word with your Gauleiter and other leaders of the movement and tell them: you must attend these social occasions. And if they refuse, saying that there's no point, that as old revolutionaries they're not going to meet this reactionary, then you must reply: we didn't carry out a revolution for the sake of carrying out a revolution. And that among those who move at this level there are a number who are worth winning over, just as there were a number among the workers who were worth winning over.

As part of this strategy, in 1933 the SS had succeeded in taking over the most important of the élite riding clubs in the most important horse-breeding areas of East Prussia, Holstein, Oldenburg, Hanover and Westphalia.

By 1938, the nobility made up 18.7 per cent of the SS *Obergruppenführer*, 9.8 per cent of the *Gruppenführer*, 14.3 per cent of the *Brigadeführer*, 8.8 per cent of the *Oberführer* and 8.4 per cent of the *Standartenführer*. However, it would be wrong to assume from this relatively high proportion of nobility in the upper ranks of the SS that the nobles as such had any significant impact on the goals and ethos of the SS.

The figures tell us more about the German nobility than about the SS. In the first place, some of these ranks were effectively honorary ones carrying no real influence. Secondly, the key positions in the SS were held by those, whether noble or not, who had joined relatively early and who were committed to its ideology.

Himmler's intention was to create a new synthetic élite based on 'good blood'. Some attempt was made to measure 'good blood' through pseudo-scientific techniques involving the assessment of alleged racial characteristics through physical examinations, most notoriously in the SS Marriage Order of 1931, which required the physical examination of both an SS man and his fiancée before marriage. However, in practice 'good blood' was generally assumed to be present in those who demonstrated loyalty, commitment and efficiency in the pursuit of SS goals. As the SS journal *Das Schwarze Korps*, put it on 13 May 1935:

> We have new standards, a new way of appraising. The little word 'von' no longer means to us the same thing as it once did. We believe that a nobility has the right to exist, not a nobility of class, not a nobility of birth or property, but a nobility of achievement . . . the best from all classes . . . that is the nobility of the Third Reich.

The fact that so many members of the German élites, including many among those elements who formed Berlin high society, had either joined the Nazi movement or were, at least, contemplating doing so before 30 January 1933 ensured then that there was a transition from the old to the new order rather than a sharp break. Nevertheless, the changes became increasingly noticeable. Bella Fromm, who as a Jewess felt the changes particularly acutely, noted in her diary on 16 March 1933: 'We had our fourth charity tea. I can't put my heart into the work any longer. A Nazi "lady" at every table. Mrs Meissner [wife of the State Secretary of the Reich President's office] basked in the presence of so many Brown stars. She just loves to raise her arm in the Hitler salute. She is not aware of how unbecoming the gesture is to her.' A year later, on 2 February 1934, she commented on the Foreign Minister, von Neurath's, ball on the eve of his sixty-first birthday:

> A very formal affair . . . Uniforms of all shades and designs were prominent. The Nazi officials felt uneasy in the crowd of nobility. They function best when braced by quantities of alcohol. It is not very becoming. They lost control over their heads and feet and were soon unable to conduct any kind of lucid conversation. Impressively towering Frau von Neurath was

escorted by one of the younger members of her husband's staff who introduced 'that crowd', as she called them, to her.

Strange that, in spite of their behaviour, they gain social ground steadily.
I think the reason is the curiosity, the thrill, which the foreigners find in
associating with the Brown hordes. Also, perhaps their naive pleasure in
gathering uniforms at their parties, if only brown uniforms . . .

The fact and form of social entertaining in German life has changed considerably during the last twelve months, Rolf [an anonymous noble friend]
and I concluded, as we sat in the corner of the Ballroom. The contrast
between what was before us and what we had known all our lives was so
strong that we could not help commenting on it.

'The old elegance has gone,' said Rolf sadly.

The reference to the diplomatic corps is significant. It continued to be
at the heart of Berlin high society and, since one of the main functions of
diplomats is to gain information, it was inevitable that they would be
obliged to engage in social intercourse with the new political leadership.
At the same time, however, the indigenous section of Berlin high society,
now with a substantial injection of 'new men' to replace those members
of the old order who for various reasons were no longer acceptable or —
fewer in number — who found the new order unacceptable to them, continued to flourish with the usual round of receptions, dinners, balls and
gala performances. Thus, whereas previously there had been gala performances in aid of the Winter Aid Programme for disadvantaged 'National
Comrades' sponsored by President von Hindenburg, now Gigli sang for
the new Nazi Winter Aid Programme. And society ladies now attended
charity teas for the Nazi welfare organisation, the NSV (or National
Socialist Peoples Welfare).

The leading members of the regime varied in the extent to which they
— and most importantly — their wives played a role in high society.
Hitler himself was well aware of the importance of representational
obligations and he fulfilled them when necessary. He purported to
despise the nobility. In *Mein Kampf* he referred to its 'degeneracy'. In
practice, however, he was prepared to make individual exceptions of
those who had demonstrated their fitness by joining his movement.
Indeed, initially at any rate, he displayed an Austrian petty-bourgeois
awe of the nobility. Thus, at his first formal social appearance at a large
party after his appointment as Reich Chancellor — a reception given by
Vice-Chancellor von Papen, Bella Fromm reported that

Hitler's eagerness to obtain the good graces of the princes present was subject to much comment. He bowed and clicked and all but knelt in his zeal to please oversized ugly Princess Luise von Sachsen-Meiningen, her brother, hereditary Prince George, and their sister, the Grand Duchess of Sachsen-Weimar. Beaming in his servile attitude, he dashed personally to bring the princesses refreshments from the buffet. He almost slid off the edge of his chair after they had offered him a seat in their most gracious company ... Upon the arrival of the immensely rich Prince Ratibor-Corvey and his two daughters, Hitler was again overwhelmed.

In fact, however, although convinced of the need for an élite, Hitler, like Himmler, believed it should no longer be based on birth or inherited wealth but rather should become a meritocracy based on achievement in the service of the national community. But he recognised that this could only develop gradually and, in the meantime, was prepared to pay lip-service to the traditional German high society.

Of the other leading Nazis, Goering, Goebbels, Ribbentrop, and — until his murder in July 1934 — the SA leader, Ernst Röhm, were the main participants in Berlin high society. The other leaders — Hess, Himmler, Frick and Rosenberg made only occasional appearances. This was partly because they and/or their wives lacked social flair and partly because their political roles within the regime made it unnecessary for them to play a significant part in high society. Robert Ley, although uncouth himself, had an elegant and sophisticated wife and they participated to some extent.

The outbreak of war soon put an end to the form in which high society had operated hitherto. Apart from the restrictions created by wartime exigencies, much of the diplomatic corps, which had provided the core of high society, had left within the first nine months. There were still opportunities for high living. For example, Horchers, the exclusive restaurant in Berlin's Lutherstrasse, which was effectively not subject to rationing regulation, continued to do good business throughout most of the war. But high living was not the same as high society.

The war years demonstrated above all that the regime had failed in its goal of integrating the old upper class of birth and property with the new Nazi élite. For, although, on the one hand, the Nazis had succeeded in recruiting members of the nobility while, on the other hand, individual Nazi leaders successfully asserted their claim to membership of high society on the basis of their official positions, and although the two groups mingled at the various social engagements that they attended, there was never a true integration. In particular, the traditional nobility had never been wholly won over to the new regime, despite the large numbers who had joined various Nazi organisations at the beginning. Some of its members had regarded the new order with greater or lesser hostility from the start and, by the end of the 1930s, the numbers of those who were distancing themselves from it was growing. In some cases the motive was disappointed hopes for personal advancement; others became increasingly aware of the contempt of the Nazis for their values and disgusted by the regime's mendaciousness and widespread corruption. As their concern at its totalitarian and revolutionary policies — for example, *vis-à-vis* the Churches — grew, so their disillusionment increased. In some cases, as for example with Count Gottfried von Bismarck-Schönhausen, a grandson of Otto von Bismarck, who was an early enthusiast, becoming an SS *Standartenführer* and District Civil Governor of Potsdam, this disillusionment led to active participation in the Resistance and eventual death, others merely distanced themselves from the regime as best they could.

As this process of disillusionment increased so the networks of family and friendship which bound the nobility together began to create a sphere that the totalitarian thrust of the regime found difficult to penetrate. This sphere acquired a semi-institutional basis in certain ministries, or certain departments within ministries, and within sections of the officer corps — for example, in the Foreign Office or, more particularly in its Indian Special Department under Adam von Trott zu Solz, and in the Military Intelligence (Abwehr) section of the Army High Command. These provided niches within which resistance to the regime could be discussed and planned. Similarly, the fact that so many senior officers should have been sounded out about the possibility of a coup against the regime during 1938–44 without them betraying the instigators to the Gestapo, even when they themselves were not prepared to participate, suggests that the professional and social *esprit de corps* of the military continued to act as a barrier to Nazi control — at least at the highest levels. Here, the process of social dilution or levelling and of ideological penetration had not yet had time to take effect.

The best source for the social relations of the traditional noble élite during the war years is *The Berlin Diaries of Marie 'Missie' Vassiltchikov*. Marie Vassilitchikov was a young Russian aristocrat living and working in Berlin during the war. The picture that emerges from her diaries is of a group of nobles, many of whom were from the highest ranks of the

European aristocracy — the Hohenzollerns, the Wittelsbachs, the Metternichs, the Bismarcks, the Lichtensteins, the Schwarzenbergs, the Fürstenbergs and many others — who, although doing their patriotic duty as fighter-pilots, tank commanders, civil servants, office workers, or nurses, were more or less totally detached from the regime and regarded it with a mixture of contempt and disgust. Their international connections, both family and social, acted as a barrier to its extreme nationalism and their upbringing led them to despise the crude and parvenu behaviour of its officials. In short, their common background, shared set of values and their family and social links provided a kind of insulation from the regime, and the basis for a critical perspective, even for those — like Bismarck-Schönhausen or Fritz-Dietlof von der Schulenburg — who still held senior positions within it.

The insulation was not total. There were still a number of members of the nobility who supported the regime and, for example, 'Missie' Vassilitchikov's mother was denounced to the Gestapo by Count Carl-Friedrich von Pückler-Burghaus, the husband of a childhood friend with whom she was staying, for her criticisms of German policies in Russia. Pückler-Burghaus became a *Brigadeführer* in the SS and the German police chief in Prague. Nevertheless, social and family loyalties normally prevented such denunciations even when there might be a conflict of views.

Through its social activities this group of nobles formed a kind of alternative high society to the official one, which increasingly atrophied under the impact of the war. There were informal lunches and dinners at Horchers or the leading Berlin hotels — the Eden, the Adlon and the Kaiserhof. There were dinners and receptions at those embassies that were still functioning, such as those of Latin America and Spain. There were parties at their homes in the villas of Potsdam and Dahlem. When the stresses of life in wartime Berlin became too great, Marie Vassiltchikov could seek rest and recuperation at the castles and palaces of various friends where of course there were plentiful supplies of home-grown food. There were skiing holidays up until as late as February 1943. Moreover, the fact that some members of this social set still had influential positions within the regime enabled strings to be pulled on occasions.

The biggest society event during the war was the marriage of Princess Maria-Adelgunde of Hohenzollern to Prince Konstantin of Bavaria, which took place at Sigmaringen Castle on 31 August 1942. According to the description by Marie Vassiltchikov, it was an extraordinarily feudal occasion in which the local officials of the regime were allowed to pay court but were kept in their proper place:

> At 10 a.m. on the dot we started off, again in pairs. I myself arm-in-arm with Didi Tolstoy. Slowly and solemnly the procession, the guests first, the bridal party and the immediate family last, wound its way out of the castle, across the many courtyards, down the wide ramp, through the town and into the church. The whole neighbourhood seemed to line the streets to watch, as had a score of photographers and newsreel cameramen ... When we arrived back at the castle we found the main reception rooms crowded with people gathered to congratulate the newly-weds, each room being allotted to a given group according to their position, i.e. the local officials in one, the staff in another, the outside guests in a third, and we, the house guests, in a fourth. Luncheon, a veritable banquet, was served in the so-called Portuguese Room (named after its magnificent wall tapestries). The food was delicious, starting with crab cocktail and vol-au-vents filled with caviar, and the wines out of this world.

These upper-class activities provoked some popular resentment which was exploited by the Nazi Security Service (SD) in its reports. For example, on 12 March 1942, the SD reported that

> there are increasing complaints about the life-style of well-off families, above all of young women, which is particularly crassly apparent in the winter-sports districts. The young women in their ski outfits and with sun-burnt faces have a really provocative effect on the national comrades who are working. There are also frequent complaints from soldiers, who are travelling south and can hardly get a seat on the overcrowded trains, about the fact that the 'upper classes' are going skiing. Exhausted officers and soldiers have to put up with spending hours standing in the corridors watching the ladies sitting in the compartments playing a cosy game of bridge. People do not understand why the state cannot prevent this and ensure that these national comrades adopt a life-style which is more in line with that of the rest of the community (Berlin, Munich, Vienna, Stuttgart).

Goebbels, who increasingly took the lead in matters of morale was particularly sensitive to these popular criticisms. In March 1943, for example, he tried to close down Horchers, organising a night-time demonstration in which windows were broken. But he was confronted with the implacable opposition of Goering, who, unlike Goebbels, was a gourmand and a regular patron of Horchers. This indeed was the point.

Much of the Nazi leadership indulged in various forms of high living, despite regular reminders from Hitler and Bormann of the need for them to set a good example. But, by now, although the two groups — the Nazi leaders and the traditional German élites — visited the same restaurants and hotels, they indulged themselves separately. High society, in the sense in which it had operated even into the late 1930s, that is as a group whose basis was their social intercourse, had ceased to exist.

Nazism and High Society
Bella Fromm, *Blood and Banquets* (New York, 1942); Michael Kater, 'Hitler in a Social Context', *Central European History*, vol. 14 (1981); Jeremy Noakes, 'Nazism and Revolution', in N. O'Sullivan (ed.), *Revolutionary Theory and Political Reality*; ibid., 'German Conservatives and the Third Reich: An Ambivalent Relationship', in M. Blinkhorn (ed.), *Fascists and Conservatives* (London, 1990); *The Berlin Diaries of Marie 'Missie' Vassilitchikov, 1940–1945* (London, 1985); Herbert Ziegler, *Nazi Germany's New Aristocracy: The SS Leadership, 1925–1939* (Princeton, 1989); Hellmuth Auerbach, 'Hitlers politische Lehrjahre und die Münchener Gesellschaft 1919–1923' in *Vierteljahrshefte für Zeitgeschichte* 25 (1977); Martha Dodd, *My Years in Germany* (London 1939); Gerhard Grainer, *Magnus von Levetzow. Seeoffizier, Monarchist und Wegbereiter Hitlers. Lebensweg und Ausgewählte Dokumente* (Boppard 1982); G.H. Kleine, 'Adelsgenossenschaft und Nationalsozialismus' in *Vierteljahrshefte für Zeitgeschichte* 26 1978, pp. 100–141; *The Berlin Diaries of Marie 'Missie' Vassiltschikov, 1940–1945* (London 1985); Albrecht Tyrell, 'Der Wegbereiter. Hermann Göring als politischer Beauftragter Hitlers in Berlin 1930–1933' in M. Funke et. al. *Demokratie und Diktatur, Geist und Gestalt politischer Herrschaft in Deutschland. Festschrift für Karl Dietrich Bracher* (Düsseldorf 1987), pp. 178–197.

CHAPTER IV

UNDERSTANDING NAZI RACISM: PRECURSORS AND PERPETRATORS

Paul Weindling

A FTER THE SECOND WORLD WAR an American intelligence officer investigating the Kaiser Wilhelm Institute for Anthropology, Human Heredity and Eugenics in Berlin commented that one German scientist was a thousand times more guilty than 'an idiotic SS man'. Although Nazi Germany has been paradigmatic for the abuse of medicine and biology in human experiments and in justifying killing of the mentally ill and of Jews, 'Gypsies' and Slavs, until the 1980s there had been little study of the role of doctors, biologists and anthropologists in the formulation and implementation of Nazi racial policies. Given that during the Cold War there was concern to protect genetics and human genetics from Lysenkoism, eugenics was seen as a legitimate branch of medicine and public health, and sharply differentiated from non-scientific racial ideology. The concentration on a handful of criminal doctors and human vivisectors meant that normal science and medical systems were not scrutinised. The burden of guilt could be shifted on to racial ideologists. It was overlooked that eugenicists had commandeered public health and welfare services in order to make Germany an all-embracing medical utopia, in which health and the reproduction of future generations sound in body and mind were priorities.

Nazi racism has been interpreted primarily as a populist variant of a Germanic ideology of racial purity and cultural regeneration, harking back to archaic rural and aristocratic values of a pre-industrial society. Less historical attention has been given to other variants of race propagated by social groups associated with scientific, medical and welfare experts, and institutions with an interest in social modernisation. The distinctive composition and influence of professional and scientific élites under Nazism have until recently been overlooked. Most of the burden of guilt could be shifted on to party-political racial ideologists. The concentration on a handful of criminal doctors and human vivisectors meant that conventional science and medical systems under Nazism did not come under scrutiny until the publication of a recent wave of historical studies generated by concern over the power wielded by professional experts.

The notion of a one-nation community, or *Volksgemeinschaft*, was central to Nazi propaganda and racial policy: it was reinforced by the ideology of Germanic racial purity. The Nazi attempts to inculcate sentiments of social cohesion were underpinned by a sense of common ancestral roots and notions of communal health, blood and genetic inheritance. The population policy for large 'child-rich' German families had implications for the disciplining of women and in setting models for the family in domestic welfare measures; the required living space (*Lebensraum*) was a justification for territorial expansion. Given the dispersal of Germanic ethnic groups throughout central and Eastern Europe, racial ideologies legitimated the military expansion of Nazi Germany and the inexorable brutality and killings that followed.

The extermination of those deemed to be threats to the biological and cultural unity of the race was an expansive programme. Racial pathology was liberally applied not only against so-called 'aliens', notably Jews and other ethnic groups such as Gypsies and Slavs, but also against the so-called 'asocial' — the mentally and physically ill and disabled, homosexuals, vagrants and criminals. Population policy meant women were either dragooned into motherhood or subjected to eugenic abortion and sterilisation. Heavy drinking, tobacco consumption or simply being 'workshy' or 'feeble-minded' could all be construed as deviant racial traits. Indeed, there were cases of Nazi Party members being brought before sterilisation tribunals, and some eugenicists darkly hinted that Hitler was himself a degenerate psychopath. Thus it can be seen that race, while intended to be a unifying ideology, was ultimately divisive, as the circle of degenerates was so enlarged it could foment disunity among élite social groups.

While Nazi racial ideology was part of the vapid rhetoric of a one-class society, or *Volksgemeinschaft*, historians should not be seduced by such propaganda into believing that race was a monolithic, standardised, simple and self-evident concept. Whereas there is consensus that the political structure of Nazi Germany consisted of diverse and overlapping authorities, Nazi racial ideology is often conceived of in simplistic terms of Germanic racial purity. It is ironic that the intensive historical research on the competing political structures, regional diversities and conditions in various economic sectors has not resulted — at least until very recently — in any attempt to work with anything more than a formulation of Nazi racial ideology so simplified that it is more a caricature than a true likeness. The mismatch between polycratic political structures and a supposedly monolithic racial ideology is a glaring inconsistency; if the Nazi state was a 'racial state' then the developing ideological forces, which integrated and created possibilities for further development, require analysis. Moreover, seen from an international perspective, given that there was wide variation in the racial and eugenic components of diverse fascist movements and states (notably Italy, where racial concepts were low on anti-Semitism but high in pronatalism and maternal and child welfare) the possibilities of divergent racial ideologies under Nazism become evident.

That racial ideology and movements contained conflicting elements and interests prompts the question whether the Nazis appropriated a science of eugenics that would have led to the biological categorising of the population, to incarceration and sterilisation as in Britain and the United States of America, but could have stopped short of anti-Semitism and genocide? Or whether the removal of democratic controls on the scientific community allowed a coercive and lethal potential in eugenics and more broadly in biology and medical research to become manifest? These issues become more complex when it is realised that the Nazis maintained massive investment in biological research programmes, resulting in innovations in ethology, virology and human genetics, which need to be assessed as powerful extensions of the racial state. Given that Hitler and Himmler were prepared to mix opportunistically quite divergent strands of scientific eugenics and mystic notions of Germanic racial purity, the way in which conflicting types of racism interacted provides insight into the ability of Nazi leaders to manipulate and control antithetical social interests. Racists had different targets: some were primarily anti-Semites and others were ideologists of rural peasant utopias, like H.F.K. 'Rassen' Günther for whom industry was a pathologically degenerative factor, whereas supporters of industrial social welfare schemes could regard rural populations as slow-witted and prone to in-breeding.

The question is did Nazi racial policies accord with the aims of scientific experts who wished to establish a professionally administered dictatorship replacing civil laws by the laws of biology, or did the Nazis give the eugenics movement lethal new marching orders? To understand the position of eugenicists under the Nazis, it is helpful to take a long-term view of German eugenics since the 1880s. Eugenicists, keen to assert their autonomy and authority in 1933, reminded the Nazis of their long pedigree as a scientific movement. A longer-term perspective shows not only the variations among racial groupings that continued to metamorphose under Nazism, but also the processes of social transformation that gave rise to eugenics and kindred forms of racism. The origins of eugenics indicate how it provided an alternative to notions of class conflict, being of interest to revisionist socialists seeking alternatives to Marxism, feminists and campaigners for social welfare measures.

The 1880s and 1890s in Germany were decades of rapid industrialisation; with the largest cities showing the highest rates of population increase, fears arose of physical and psychological degeneration. Chronic degenerative diseases such as tuberculosis, alcoholism and sexually transmitted diseases (all rife among youth and students of the period) were regarded as 'racial poisons', threatening the health of future generations. In protest against urban degeneration there was a spate of utopian colonies. The natural values of air, sun and light were the basis of utopian communes which cultivated a reformed lifestyle, nudist open-air bathing and organic foodstuffs. Dissident young artists, students and doctors condemned industrial society and the repressive politics of Bismarck's anti-socialist laws. One group of students formed a society called 'Pacific' and collected money to send a delegate, a medical student called Alfred Ploetz, to study utopian settlements in the United States. After working at a colony in Iowa, Ploetz returned home to condemn egalitarianism; instead, he drew up a scheme for a racial colony based on sound health as a means of recovering primitive racial vigour that had been sapped by urban life. Biology was to be a source of social salvation and to ensure that future generations would be sound in body and mind. The utopian values of a reformed way of life were to be scientised. Here lay the roots of Pletz's new philosophy of 'racial hygiene' — a term he introduced in 1895.

There was a demand for scientific solutions to the social problems of urban squalor and disease, as well as a disenchantment with liberal individualism as destructive of human lives and of the sense of common national and social interests. As a scientifically based creed of social corporatism with selective welfare benefits to promote health and fitness of future generations, eugenics represented a biologically based variant of revisionist socialism. Even such orthodox socialists as August Bebel and

Karl Kautsky had a critical interest in eugenics, and a number of early eugenicists had been socialist activists, for example Ludwig Woltmann, who launched a journal for political anthropology in 1903. Ploetz considered that the more one could understand the biological causes of the reproduction of weak progeny, the less the exterminating process inherent in the struggle for survival would be necessary. He hoped that it would be possible to have a science of reproductive hygiene by controlling the selection of favourable reproductive cells. Ploetz argued for scientific solutions to social problems — rejecting education, sexual selection and Francis Galton's suggestion that marriage be restricted to the hereditarily healthy.

Advances in therapeutic medicine and the boost that sickness insurance gave to individual doctor-patient relations were considered to be keeping the weak and degenerate alive. Thus, another young doctor, Wilhelm Schallmayer, suggested that there should be screening of the entire population by means of a system of health passports, annual medical inspection and the official notification of all diseases; instead of working for the individual sick patient, the doctor was to be a state official. The obligation to the state would mean that medicine would act in the interest of future generations.

A transition occurred from utopian counter-cultures to attempts to reform society as a whole by bringing social legislation into line with biology and medical science. In 1905 Ploetz founded both a periodical for racial and social biology and the German Racial Hygiene Society, in which doctors and biologists predominated. While rejecting notions of race based on cultural myths and psychological stereotypes, Ploetz attempted to base race on biology — to shift from a static classificatory concept of race to a dynamic concept of a *Vitalrasse* based on Mendelian genetics and reproductive biology. The 'rediscovery' of the Mendelian laws in 1900 prompted analysis of both paternal and maternal lines of inheritance for a range of medical conditions like spastic debility, shortsightedness, cancers and tuberculosis, for physical traits or reproductive tendencies like the birth of twins (by Wilhelm Weinberg) and for psychiatric illness, as with Ernst Rüdin's statistics on the incidence of schizophrenia which were linked to his calls for compulsory sterilisation. Medical researchers pointed out that attention to individual cases of illness obscured information about the incidence and transmission of diseases. They argued for research on entire populations and for measures that would give priority to the health of future generations. Such thinking undermined liberal notions of the individual's right to health and of choice in reproduction. Eugenic science supported authoritarian and collectivist forms of society, maintaining its appeal over a wide political spectrum. Certain eugenicists (for example Schallmayer) drew up models offering eugenic controls on reproduction as a means of eliminating poverty and disease in future generations.

The presence of eugenicists who also happened to be Jewish or part-Jewish (like Weinberg) indicates an interest in non-racial socio-biology in which population groups and medical problems were analysed according to biological categories. While Ploetz sought to keep eugenics separate from organised anti-Semitism, privately he and a number of other members were anti-Semitic — there was a secret Nordic inner group in the Munich Racial Hygiene Society. There was thus a complex interaction with other variants of racial ideology. Ploetz was critical of the Gobineau Society and of such racial philosophers as the Gestalt-theorist Christian von Ehrenfels, who advocated polygamy, seeking to marginalise them while remaining on good terms with their leaders. Other areas of ambivalence were those that involved the feminists, particularly the Nietzschean radical Helene Stöcker, who dominated the League for the Protection of Motherhood and Social Reform.

At the beginning of the new century there were competing schemes of racial and social biology, hygiene and sexual reform. These focused on reproduction and demographic issues as the key to the solution of the social problems of crime, poverty and disease. Abortion, the effects of sexually transmitted diseases in causing congenital syphilis and sterility, and birth control were much debated. Biological ideas were applied to explain homosexuality — including Magnus Hirschfeld's idea of an intermediate third sex. Eugenicists promoted maternal health with improved infant welfare: the League for the Protection of Mothers and Social Reform shifted from folkish rural colonies to schemes for maternity allowances. The anthropologist Eugen Fischer returned from studying the Rehoboth mixed race tribe in German south-west Africa to call for a national institute for the study of human heredity to correlate data on genealogy and disease. By 1912 state medical officials were asking to what extent degeneration was a cause of the declining birth-rate. Hereditary biology was permeating not only medical science but was also under consideration by the central state administration.

During the First World War the state sought to promote improved health and welfare provision on the domestic front, and the war can be

seen as midwife to a eugenically based welfare state. One wing of the
Racial Hygiene Society became committed to welfare and support for a
population policy to raise the birth-rate. The other wing demanded
foreign conquests for *Lebensraum* (literally, 'living space') and was
politically on the ultra-Right with links to the *Vaterlandspartei*. Racial
hygienists were horrified at the mass slaughter of the fittest in society, but
were enthusiasts for the conquest of new territories for rural settlement.
Although ideas of the unified nation waging a biological struggle for survival and the expansion of *Lebensraum* became a folk memory on the
ultra-Right in the 1920s and were later to be appropriated by Nazism,
this should not blur the conflicts among the eugenicists.

The fact that welfare became a state responsibility under the Weimar
constitution opened the way to state-sponsored eugenic research
and medical practices. For a time the German Racial Hygiene Society
was taken over by leading medical officials, who regarded eugenics as
part of the post-war reconstruction policy to overcome famine and
wartime losses. Among the health administrations most active in
pursuing a welfare oriented eugenics were Prussia, with a welfare minister
from the Catholic Centre Party, and socialist controlled Saxony. New
health centres included marriage advice clinics providing a eugenic
premarital health examination, and there were hereditary databanks
correlating the records of health centres, schools, police, the churches and
hospitals. The aim was hereditary prognosis; by studying the patterns of
inheritance, it was hoped that effective medical and crime prevention
schemes could be implemented. State authorities supported schemes
for 'total registers of biological populations'. For example the Saxon
eugenicist Eugen Fetscher recorded mental and physiological disorders,
alcoholism, character and indebtedness, as well as a range of sexual
information. Eugenics entered academic curricula. Among the students
of the geneticist Walther Haecker at Halle were Heinrich Himmler
(studying agricultural science; later to be in control of the SS) and
Joachim Mrugowsky (who was to head the Hygiene Institute of the
Waffen-SS). Eugenic notions flourished throughout the political
spectrum and there was acrimonious debate about eugenics, sexual and
reproductive issues among feminists, socialists and welfare experts, as
well as among the ultra-Right. Birth-control, sterilisation and abortion
were political battlegrounds. Notions of *Lebensraum* were supported by
those seeking to disperse the high-density (and often socialist) urban
populations into rural settlements, and by diplomats, who supplied

eugenic literature and material assistance to ethnic German communities in Eastern Europe.

Schemes for biological politics culminated in the opening of the Kaiser Wilhelm Institute for Anthropology, Human Hereditry and Eugenics in Berlin in 1927 as a national eugenics institute. This organised a scheme for a nation-wide programme of anthropological surveys correlating physical with psychological traits. By the time of the economic crisis there was a favourable atmosphere for the scientific experts of the Kaiser Wilhelm Institute to launch schemes for a scientific dictatorship. Eugenic experts were to tackle the root-causes of poverty and associated diseases: eugenics was thus integral to biologically-conceived systems of state welfare. Positive eugenic incentives with premiums for child-rich families of sound eugenic quality were matched by calls for sterilisation as well as other eugenic controls on reproduction for those of constitutionally less value. Biological concepts of a human economy thus displaced the categories of liberal political economy just as the concept of eugenic and medical controls supplanted notions of individual rights. In the telling formulation of Karl-Heinz Roth, eugenics represented the 'Final Solution' of the social problem of poverty, disease and crime. While racism flourished on the ultra-Right, Weimar eugenics was primarily concerned with offering scientific solutions to social problems, so countering radical socialist demands for a redistribution of wealth and property.

Yet the view of eugenics as a programme of bourgeois social rationalisation and modernisation does not satisfactorily account for the cultural force of racial ideologies and anti-Semitism. In contrast to the sophisticated genetics of the Kaiser Wilhelm Institute, Hitler's racial biology was scientifically antiquated, and much more closely linked to currents of mystic Germanic and Nordic racial purity. He might have been given the textbook of human heredity and eugenics by Baur, Fischer and Lenz while imprisoned after the Munich Putsch, but certainly its eugenics left little impact on his notions of racial purity, except perhaps regarding the possibilities of sterilisation and the problem of syphilis. Burleigh and Wippermann judiciously remark that Hitler's racism had 'inner contradictions': we do not know exactly which men provided the sources of Hitler's racism and many crucial aspects of policy-formulation of racial measures still require clarification. Hitler's *Mein Kampf* of 1924 relied on blending heredity in order to show the evils of racial intermarriage as leading to the sterility of hybrids, but had no understanding of particulate genetic characters. This had repercussions for the Nuremberg Laws of 1935, which banned racially mixed marriages. Hitler and Himmler were scornful of the snail's-pace of medical research, and called for a new dynamic action-oriented style of science. Racial policies relied on public health administrations to seek out the medically, socially and racially undesirable, and to implement such measures as sterilisation and, ultimately, the killing of mental patients and other racial undesirables.

The rifts over eugenics were reflected in criticisms of the concept of a Germanic branch of an Aryan race. Anthropologists pointed to the mixed racial composition of Germany and some privately commented (to their cost) that Hitler was a dark Alpine racial type with psychopathic and hysterical traits. Apart from a major role in drafting the Law for the Prevention of Hereditarily-diseased Progeny of July 1933, eugenicists were unsuccessful in the pursuit of their strategy of an expert dictatorship. Examples of tensions between the Nazi concept of race and such socio-biological measures as the sterilisation laws included the protest by the Reich Doctors Führer, Gerhard Wagner, that Nazi Party members were being forcibly sterilised under the law drafted by the veteran Mendelian psychiatric researcher, Ernst Rüdin. In-fighting between groups of eugenic experts was in the interests of the Nazi state, as eugenic pluralism — equivalent to what political historians term the polycratic structure of Nazi Germany — resulted in the radicalisation of racial policies. Wagner exploited these divisions to place the killing of mental patients and crippled children on to the political agenda. For eugenicists to survive, links had to be forged with the racial priorities of groupings in the Nazi Party, state and the SS, and racial categories increasingly dominated the social programme of the eugenicists.

A few years ago Müller Hill, a geneticist, showed that such SS doctors as Josef Mengele acted in league with the leading human geneticists. We know that the Nazis supported innovative research in areas such as population genetics: for example the Soviet geneticist Timoféef-Ressovsky remained as a researcher in Berlin throughout the war and Konrad Lorenz certainly endorsed views that domestication of animals led to degeneration being applied to human society, arguing that patients with hereditary diseases should not be treated. One trouble with Müller Hill's work is that he does not differentiate various levels of engagement in the Nazi racial machinery. His work exemplifies the interpretative approach, which can be characterised by borrowing the Nazi prescription for a more economical and nutritious way of cooking meals in a single pot — as the *Eintopf* school — for every eugenicist is seen to be part of a homogeneous racial ideology. A eugenicist supporting compulsory sterilisation for schizophrenics would not necessarily have supported their killing in the 'T-4 euthanasia' programme (see p. 101ff). Müller Hill and Robert Proctor (the author of an overview on Nazi racial hygiene) throw all eugenicists and racists into the same historical melting-pot, regardless of their different views and political affiliations.

The case of Wilhelm Weitz, a clinician expert in human genetics during the Nazi period, is instructive. The funding and scale of his research increased because the Nazi public health authorities needed geneticists in sterilisation tribunals. In 1936 Weitz established a Department for Twin and Hereditary Research in the Hamburg University Hospital, collecting data on 8,000 pairs of twins. Weitz supported the ideology that the duty of the German doctor was to defend the hereditary health of the population. While believing that hardly a disease was free from the taint of heredity, he was also interested in the interaction of hereditary and environmental factors. He established a central registry of medical records — with over a million records by 1939 — in order to locate monozygote twins. Such a databank was open to use by social workers and the police. Weitz was keen to extend compulsory sterilisation to neurological conditions, and joined the Nazi Party in 1937 and the SS in 1938. But this exact geneticist was also accused by a Nazi official of a complete lack of understanding of Nazi ideology. Weitz resigned in 1943 from the SS, apparently because an assistant informed him about the Holocaust. This resignation illustrates how participation in the Nazi medical killing programmes was essentially voluntary. Weitz's shock at the Holocaust did not deter him from continuing to build up his hereditary databank.

The case of Weitz suggests that concentration on eugenics provides only limited insight into Nazi racial policies. Other types of racism and the ultimate aims of the Nazi racial utopia need to be considered. The Holocaust was not self-contained, nor was it the result of a single coherent programme under a unitary authority (although the SS came close to achieving this) was an end in itself, but a stage in a vast programme of population engineering to be achieved by moving populations throughout Eastern Europe and Germanic rural settlement programmes (see pp. 140ff). Anthropologists were deployed to screen populations and to distinguish racially 'valuable' from 'worthless' populations. There was also a need for infectious diseases to be controlled to make such settlement possible. Ideologies of Germanic racial superiority reinforced the technical skills of eugenicists.

In acknowledging that professional élites and experts extended the capacity of the Nazi state to pursue its racial ends, the problem of the sheer lack of uniformity arises. The vacillations of policymakers, and the competition of different interests to attain control over the machinery of anti-Semitism are echoed in other areas of social policy. A state that was irresolute in deciding the fate of half and quarter Jews, showed a similar broad spectrum of opinion with conflicting interests and definitions of race. For if 'National Socialism was applied biology' (as Hess once said), biologists and other medical experts were divided over a wide range of issues associated with heredity and race, to which must be added competing allegiances (for example SS membership) and sectional interests. The implications of a polycratic interpretation of racial ideology are far reaching. Historians have to understand that the place of diverse groups of racial experts in the Nazi machinery was subject to continuing change and conflict. Thus the psychiatrist Ernst Rüdin, who advised on the Sterilisation Laws of 1933 was marginalised by the time of the killing of psychiatric patients, and was under severe pressure from the SS to allow them to control the German Institute for Psychiatry. By this time the SS were concerned with the implementation of genocidal policies in the East. Although the agenda was set by Hitler's *Mein Kampf* and by *völkisch* ideologists of *Ein Volk ohne Raum* (a nation without space), its realisation depended on technical expertise.

Eugenics has been studied with reference to domestic social policies in Germany — but not *vis-à-vis* foreign policy and strategic aims. The integration of eugenics with Holocaust history remains problematic. Many aspects of the Holocaust cannot be explained by reference to leading eugenicists, for example the geneticists portrayed by Müller-Hill had, at most, a marginal role in the planning and (apart from Mengele) implementation of the Holocaust. Similarly, the disillusion of Richard Walther Darré and Hans F.K. Günther as agrarian ideologists with the power of industrial lobbies in the Nazi state suggests the insufficiency of *völkisch* racism to explain Nazi genocidal policies. The 'utopian programme' has been limited to Hitler's visionary statements concerning 'the destruction of the Jewish race in Europe'. Self-interest is seen as taking priority over ideological rationales. The control of the Final Solution by the SS was strengthened by personal lust for status and power, and by departments seeking to justify their existence and economic motives.

The importance of a broader, biologically-driven aim of exterminating the causes of disease can be seen in Nazi medical killing programmes. The positive side to public health was the promotion of physical fitness through sport and exercise. There was also much emphasis on vaccination as a crucial element of preventive medicine. Ironically their very success in eradicating diseases made Germans vulnerable, something well illustrated in the case of typhus. When they invaded Russia, the Germans had to face the problem that they were encountering infectious diseases (including typhus) that could not only be hazardous to the troops, but might be brought back to Germany where the population could be non-immune and therefore highly susceptible. These epidemics also posed risks for any settlement programme. Given that ethnic Germans were to be brought back from the East and that peasant stocks from the heartland of Germany were to be transplanted to the East, there was a double risk of epidemics. Finally, the destruction, deportations, ghettoisation and concentration camps also posed severe epidemiological threats. The SS commanding concentration and extermination camps were fearful for their own health. The epidemiological threats that dogged the racial engineering and the Holocaust prompted a racialisation of epidemiology.

The Nazis were incapable of recognising that their actions were the causes of epidemics. Instead, they attributed these to congenital filth and the racial degeneracy of Slavs and Jews. Anti-typhus measures have been seen as simply providing a convenient rationalisation and cover-up for the brutality of racially motivated killings. Medical terminology of 'disinfection' and 'special treatment' were used to disguise the Holocaust, and sanitary engineering provided techniques of mass murder, including the disguise of gas chambers as showers. The Nazi perversion of preventive medicine provides insight into the rationales, implementation and extent of the Holocaust as extending from apparently harmless research by biochemists examining the effects of gases on the cellular metabolism or entomologists involved in louse-control studies, to those who manufactured, serviced and operated the gas chambers.

The routines of delousing developed by German military medical officers in the First World War shaped the routines of the concentration and extermination camps. Refugees had come to expect delousing at railway junctions and on entry to transit camps. The body of the concentration-camp prisoner was under the dictatorial regime of hygienic delousing requirements of short hair, a change of clothing and a scientifically calculated starvation diet. While the SS wished to accelerate the deaths of concentration-camp prisoners from starvation, harsh work-regimes and overcrowding, the SS feared epidemic infections arising from such conditions to which they themselves were vulnerable. It is in this context that the Hygiene Institute of the *Waffen*-SS under Joachim Mrugowsky merits consideration. An examination of Mrugowsky's career reveals that this key (and hitherto overlooked) figure whose career linked public health and the Holocaust, was a character of considerable complexity.

The image of the medical experimenters like Mrugowsky (who was condemned to death in the Nuremberg Doctors' Trial) has been that of abusers of science. Mrugowsky fits into the pattern of a Nazi activist of the younger generation: while Mengele had doctorates in anthropology and medicine, Mrugowsky had doctorates in botany and medicine. Mrugowsky's studies of the ecology and sociology of plant communities were applied to the teaching of racial hygiene from 1934 and in research on the health of the mining community of Mansfeld (published in 1938). His biological approach to the social problems of a mining community with a reputation for revolutionary socialism shows the importance of internal social problems of Germany in generating concepts and methods later to be applied in the Holocaust. In 1930 Mrugowsky joined the Nazi Party and SA and from 1931 he was in the SS. In 1937 he joined the sanitary department of the SS, and he had special responsibility for the health of the armed SS as director of the Hygiene Institute of the *Waffen*-SS. Mrugowsky's qualifying lecture in Berlin was on ethnic groups and disease in the 'German South East' (the Sudetenland, Ostmark and Slovakia) and marked a transition from domestic sanitary measures to issues associated with the expansion of German *Lebensraum*.

The organisation and expanding responsibilities of Mrugowsky's Hygiene Institute of the *Waffen*-SS merit comment. It had three departments: one each for epidemic control (by means of bacteriology and serology), chemistry and hereditary (or constitutional) medicine. Thus, measures were appropriated from a eugenically oriented public health system, in order to maintain the SS at the peak of racial health. These methods had a highly destructive potential when applied in the military context of Nazi expansion in the East. Mrugowsky also supervised typhus research in Buchenwald, where human experiments were conducted while testing vaccines. He personally undertook 'experiments' concerning the efficacy of different types of bullet, which involved the shooting of Soviet prisoners. The Hygiene Institute of the *Waffen*-SS supplied Zyklon (a fumigant gas) to concentration and extermination camps and received gold from the teeth of murdered victims.

The genocidal role of preventive medicine is revealed in the sanitary codes for SS units; the men were warned that all civilians were potential typhus carriers and thus their extermination could be justified. Despite such crude prescriptions, epidemiological rationales used sophisticated statistical and geographical methods to explain the vulnerability of the more civilised German to the lethal parasites carried by Jews and Slavs. As Browning has shown, high rates of typhus provided the pretext for sealing off the Warsaw Ghetto. Mrugowsky viewed this in the context of a vast system of geographical epidemiology (or geomedicine). The Ostgrenze (eastern frontier) as a cultural divide between Germans and menacing racial Slavs could be correlated with high rates of infectious diseases, for example typhus, typhoid and dysentery in Russia and Lithuania. Mrugowsky considered that control of cities such as Warsaw, Lublin and Lvov, crossing-points for communications to Ukraine and Belorussia, was the key to the control of epidemic threats from the East. Eugenics thus took a key role in combating 'Asiatic threats' of epidemic infections which were linked to the inferior races of Jews, Slavs and Gypsies.

The conventional view that the 'technical' implementation of the Final Solution was carried out by a few officials, implies that the processes of the implementation are reduced to be a mere working-out of the logic of genocidal policies. While Hans Mommsen has recognised that 'technocratic and subordinate attitudes could be as important as blind racialism or the mere parroting of National Socialist anti-Jewish clichés', there remains an unexplained gulf between the technocrats and the racists, and the distinctive forms of racism that might have motivated the technocrats are never considered. By leaving the distinctive constituents of Nazi racial utopias unexamined important elements of motives and the forms that the Holocaust took are obscured.

An example of the Nazis' complex blend of ideology and technology is the cremation movement, which combined medical notions of a pure earth, Nordic beliefs in fire as eternal life and Germanic cultural traditions. The Nazified cremation movement was under the direction of public health officials and there were complex links with other branches of Nazified medicine. Mrugowsky's interest in the holistic roots of German medicine reveals the ideology of clearance and of a purging fire with the flames of destruction necessary for a momentous scientific discovery. Doctors can be seen as supplying the methods and ideological rationales for the Holocaust and thus for the realisation of the Nazi racial utopia.

Race and its medical extensions were neither administratively nor ideologically monolithic. Thus, the eugenicist Fritz Lenz criticised Mrugowsky for advocating the holism of Adolf Meyer, who at this time was under attack from SS human geneticists and anthropologists, so revealing the in-fighting among the SS ideologists linked to non-SS eugenicists (like Lenz). In June 1942 Lenz resisted Mrugowsky's promotion in Berlin university to professor, arguing that his services in combating typhus on the Eastern Front were insufficient for an academic honour. While the SS was moving into a controlling position in universities and in the German Research Council, there was still pluralism within its ranks. There were racial mystics associated with the SS *Ahnenerbe* (Ancestral Heritage) and genetic reductionists, advocates of herbal medicines or of industrially produced drugs and vaccines. It might be argued that the co-existence of diverse strands within the SS strengthened its influence as a directive and controlling organisation.

The interpretation of public health and eugenics as modernisers by such historians as Aly and Roth has resulted in an impressive array of new evidence that brings academics into the mainstream of the Nazi power structures. Their important analysis of statisticians and demographers in the service of the state and SS shows how the state relied on experts to define categories and to implement policies. Yet they also rigidly defend a linear interpretation of eugenics as unchanging between the population policies formulated during the First World War and those of the Federal Republic, policies basically generated and sustained by economic demands for a healthy and fertile workforce. Denying any cultural relativism, ideas are reduced to the underlying interests of capitalism. Indeed, race hardly figures in Aly and Heim's account of economic planning as the key to Holocaust. I would suggest that once the diversity of competing groups of racial experts continually forming and dissolving alliances with diverse groups in the Nazi power structure has been mapped, then the social interests underlying key decisions in racial and social policies can be determined. Greater use can be made of the social history of ideas, of academic institutions, of the professions and of health and welfare in order to bridge the gap between studies of the ruling élite and of public opinion.

Returning to the problem of what weight to give to the Nazi ideologies of blood and soil, *Lebensraum* and racial health and purity, some deficiencies of the historical approach that marginalises the importance of race for the underlying economic conditions and political organisation of Nazi Germany should now be evident. Racial ideology was far more complex than just a chilling distillation of utterances emanating from Hitler, implemented by Himmler and the SS and disseminated by the Nazi Party's Racial Political Office (Rassepolitisches Amt). While it has been acknowledged that there was an impressive propaganda machine, these ideas have been reduced to manipulative techniques of social control. Historians dealt with the functions and organisation of the state and party, the effects on policies and the people, and indeed the complex problem of popular perceptions and responses. For all the sophistication of the categories used, this rested on assumptions of a rather simplistic binary social structure: of a ruling élite and the people. There was a lack of attention to middle-class professional groups such as doctors, lawyers and teachers, who were simply reduced to the status of purveyors of a uniform Nazi ideology, rather than recognised as interacting with the Nazi ideology and power structures. Instead, critical analysis concentrated on the interaction of party political groupings, functionaries and leading Nazis within the state, military, Party and SS.

The stress on the crucial importance of the interactive process of decision-making in the Nazi state, led to the conclusions that racial ideology could reveal little about the planning and decision-making that led to the Holocaust. With the Holocaust reduced to 'a complex political process', mass extermination was one more act of wartime social policy with complex origins — just as (to choose a humane counter-example) the British National Health Service might be seen as arising from wartime expediencies, and complex and controversial decisions among politicians and decision-makers. Instead, I would suggest that the types of ideologies and methods of extermination deployed can be used to indicate the power of involved groups in the Nazi ruling élites. Moreover, racial values provided connections to other related areas of Nazi social policy. That there was indeed a Nazi plan for the unification of health services as part of the medical campaign to boost Germany's racial élite indicates how racial concepts shaped health and welfare, as well as the Holocaust. It is all too easy to see Nazi Germany as positively innovative in the modernisation of social institutions, in the provision of medical care and in the generation of science and technology, if the values of race are artificially limited to the bloody rhetoric of Nazi anti-Semitism.

KARL ASTEL

Karl Astel exemplifies the transition made by those involved in the Munich Racial Hygiene Society before 1933 to their implementation of racialised medicine in the service of the SS. As director of public health in the Nazi state of Thuringia and as administrator of the university, he racialised public health and biology. He was responsible for surveys of the fertility of the élite party members and the peasantry, and screened the population for such 'asocial' groups as homosexuals. Despite the homogeneity of Thuringia's racialised public health services, Astel was, for personal and ideological reasons, at loggerheads with numerous Nazi officials. He was a believer in direct action, thus he discouraged smoking by punching cigarettes out of the mouths of students. He committed suicide in 1945.

Understanding German Racism

Götz Aly and Susanne Heim, *Vordenker der Vernichtung* (Hamburg, 1991); Götz Aly and Karl Heinz Roth, *Die restlose Erfassung* (Berlin, 1984); Gisela Bock, *Zwangssterilisation im Nationalsozialismus. Studien zur Rassenpolitik und Frauenpolitik* (Opladen, 1986); Christopher R. Browning, 'Genozid und Gesundheitswesen. Deutsche Ärzte und polnische Juden, 1939–1941', in Christian Pross and Götz Aly (eds), *Der Wert des Menschen. Medizin in Deutschland, 1918–1945* (Berlin, 1989), pp. 316–28; Michael Burleigh and Wolfgang Wippermann, *The Racial State: Germany, 1933–1945* (Cambridge, 1991); Michael Burleigh, *Death and Deliverance: Euthanasia in Germany 1990–1945* (Cambridge, 1994); Michael Kater, *Doctors under Hitler* (Chapel Hill and London, 1989); Alfons Labisch and Florian Tennstedt, *Der Weg zum 'Gesetz über die Vereinheitlichung des Gesundheitswesens'* (Düsseldorf, 1985); Hans Mommsen, 'The Realization of the Unthinkable: "The Final Solution of the Jewish Question" in the Third Reich', in Hans Mommsen, *From Weimar to Auschwitz. Essays in German History* (Oxford, 1991), pp. 224–53; Benno Müller Hill, *Murderous Science: Elimination by Scientific Selection of Jews, Gypsies and Others: Germany, 1933–1945* (Oxford, 1988); Jeremy Noakes, 'Wohin gehören die "Judenmischlinge"? Die Entstehung der ersten Durchführungsverordnungen zu den Nürnberger Gesetzen', in U. Büttner (ed.), *Das Unrechtsregime* (Hamburg, 1986);

R. Proctor, *Racial Hygiene: Medicine under the Nazis* (Cambridge, Mass., and London, 1988); Paul Weindling, '"Mustergau Thüringen". Rassenhygiene zwischen Ideologie und Machtpolitik', in Norbert Frei (ed.), *Medizin und Gesundheitspolitik in der NS-Zeit* (Munich, 1991), pp. 81–98; ibid., *Health Race and German Politics Between National Unification and Nazism* (Cambridge, 1989).

CHAPTER V

THE GERMAN *VOLKSGEMEINSCHAFT* FROM THE PERSECUTION OF THE JEWS TO THE 'FINAL SOLUTION'

Avraham Barkai

RACIAL ANTI-SEMITISM, AS IS generally well known, was a central theme of National Socialist ideology and propaganda. Nevertheless, many historians continue to question whether the electoral successes of the Nazis before 1933 can be attributed to the purchase exerted by crude and virulent anti-Jewish propaganda. As early as the 1870s, there were political parties in Germany whose programmes and solutions to the nation's problems were pronouncedly anti-Semitic. Moreover, from the mid-nineteenth century, German academics and scientists attempted to give racial ideology, particularly that concerning the Jews, an air of scientific respectability, although they were assisted in this enterprise by French and British popular writers. Despite this, it is impossible to maintain that the German people were more hostile towards the Jews than, say, the peoples of Eastern Europe; violent pogroms occurred during the 1880s in Russia and Romania, but nowhere in Germany. The most public, turbulent and politically divisive manifestation of anti-Semitic resentment was the Dreyfus Affair in France between 1894 and 1906. By this time, the fortunes of German anti-Semitic parties had waned and German Jews comforted themselves with the thought of increasing security and progressive integration into German society as a whole.

The ascendancy of the National Socialist German Workers' Party, or NSDAP, after 1930 was primarily a consequence of mass unemployment and the political crisis of the late Weimar Republic. However, the Nazis' anti-Jewish demagogy also contributed much to the unstable climate, and culminated in the vicious street fighting and pugnacious meetings characteristic of the final phase of the Republic. These disturbances did not deter potential voters because traditional hostility towards Jews was deeply rooted in almost every section of the population. This also explains the willing acceptance of racial anti-Semitism by the population at large once this had been elevated by the Third Reich to a state ideology and substitute religion. Anti-Semitism was integrated into a comprehensive, internally consistent, *völkisch* ideology, characterised by a number of specific features that may be described as being peculiar to Germany.

The concept *völkisch* is even less amenable to precise translation than the word *Volk* from which it is derived. The term 'nation' is conventionally used to describe the contractual coming together of a community of people sharing a common origin, language or other common characteristics and interests in a unified community. A 'people' represents the multiplicity of individuals living in a society; by contrast, in the German tradition the word *Volk* has profounder, mystical significance. In German the word signifies an autonomous, living organism from which the individual members of the *Volk* derive the true meaning and essence of their existence. A metaphor frequently used to make these distinctions comprehensible is of a heap of stones, juxtaposed against a seamless, indissoluble rock. The origins of these ideas lay in German Romantic literature and philosophy of the early nineteenth century. They were frequently, but not necessarily, associated with fanatical nationalism and also with anti-Semitism. *Völkisch* and anti-Semitic ideology were not always synonymous. Although their complex evolution need not detain us here, both *völkisch* and anti-Semitic ideas and organisations were intimately linked in the period under consideration.

In 1919 Adolf Hitler joined the German Workers' Party, one of the many *völkisch* splinter-groups operating in the Munich area, as an undercover *Reichswehr* (or military) agent. Most of these sects were led by cranky middle-class ideologues and demagogues; the support of reactionary conservative elements of the upper bourgeoisie, who preferred to stay out of the limelight in the revolutionary climate of the years following the First World War, enabled these groups to produce and disseminate vast quantities of propaganda. Hitler managed to merge these *völkisch* societies and sects into the National Socialist German Workers' Party under his own leadership. He had grasped the fact that *völkisch* ideas would only achieve considerable purchase in a modern industrial society if they became part of the programme of a broad mass-based party. Therefore he saw his specific task in terms of 'winning the workers once more for the German national community'.

The notion of a 'national community' (*Volksgemeinschaft*) was the National Socialist counterpart of the classless society to which Marxist and revolutionary parties aspired. Every racially pure German employer and worker, peasant and intellectual was to occupy his or her rightful place in the national community. The success and welfare of the national community in the worldwide struggle for power would determine the destiny of every individual 'national comrade'. The 'national community' therefore occupied the highest rung in the National Socialist scale of values. All individual rights and received moral norms were subordinated to the interests of the national community, which encompassed every sphere of life and justified any action. During the Third Reich these interests were determined solely by the Führer, who alone could establish the national community's goals and the stages for their implementation.

This total concentration of power in the hands of a dictatorial regime was by no means predetermined at the outset. It was achieved in stages, albeit with remarkable speed. Although the political terror exercised by the Gestapo may always have hovered in the background, this was not the decisive factor. More significant was the degree of consensus the regime enjoyed among broad sections of the population as a result of its economic and foreign policy triumphs, which led to increasing identification with the Nazis' ideological and political goals.

In January 1933, most Germans felt resigned and disappointed about democratic parliamentary politics. They were therefore ready to give the self-confident-seeming Nazis a chance to deliver them from economic and political crisis. The surrender of basic freedoms and the brutal use of terror against political opponents and the Jews were regarded as unpleasant side-effects, which had to be accepted even if one did not necessarily care for them. This mood of cautious expectancy was soon superseded by the ecstatic enthusiasm of jubilant masses of people celebrating their Führer.

The reasons for this phenomenon lay in the many tangible achievements of the regime. Dirigiste control of the economy enabled the Nazis to overcome unemployment more rapidly than the government of any other country affected by the Depression. The Nazis also effectively exploited the helpless inactivity of the Western Powers in the face of rearmament and an aggressive foreign policy. All of these things were celebrated as the achievements of a national community united behind the Führer, which had finally left behind the old class antagonisms and divisions of the Weimar Republic. Propaganda encouraged the feeling of belonging to a united people encompassing every 'national comrade'. A new social élite gradually emerged in the shape of such party organisations as the paramilitary SA and SS, which offered the reckless and talented members of the lower classes unheard of opportunities for social advancement. All of these factors, as well as the sense of belonging inherent in any mass movement, created the illusion of an egalitarian society, which gave every German rather more than he or she had had before.

These sentiments were accompanied by tangible, as opposed to illusory, benefits. The German Labour Front, the largest mass organisation in the Third Reich, endeavoured to achieve improvements in working conditions and gave the working class a sense of enhanced status. Its leisure organisation, Strength through Joy, enabled many people to go on outings, ski trips or visits to sanatoria, which would have previously been beyond their reach. Ideological considerations led to preferential treatment for the farmers who had been badly hit by the Depression. They received higher prices for their produce, state subsidies and agronomic advice, all of which served to improve their standard of living. The regime's propaganda celebrated them as 'bearers of Germandom', and, dressed in colourful traditional costume, they were honoured by the Führer at mass harvest festivals. Even impoverished national comrades were catered for by a special Nazi organisation, the National Socialist People's Welfare (NSV). Annual collections for 'winter aid' were celebrated in the regime's propaganda as a demonstration of national solidarity. One Sunday a month rich and poor families tucked in to a simple 'one pot meal', donating the money saved to national comrades in distress. On these occasions prominent Party figures ostentatiously rattled collection tins on street corners as living proof of a national community that had transcended the barriers of social class.

In the years before the outbreak of war, the cost in terms of loss of personal freedom or existential security was only paid by a minority of political opponents, socially marginal elements such as homosexuals, 'Gypsies', the chronically ill and, in particular, Jews, who are the subjects of this chapter. Since in the Nazi view of things Jews were not national comrades and, following the promulgation of the 1935 Nuremberg Laws, were no longer citizens of the Reich, they were excluded from the benefits outlined above. Only a few Jewish firms briefly benefited from the general upturn in the economy. Jewish workers and salaried employees were excluded from obligatory membership of the German Labour Front. They were therefore dismissed *en masse* from large firms, including those still owned or operated by other Jews. Despite the achievement of 'full employment' by late 1936, Jewish workers remained unemployed. Most of those still in work with Jewish firms lost their jobs in the course of the progressive liquidation of 'non-Aryan' businesses. Jewish academics, civil servants, doctors, lawyers, teachers and other professionals had already mostly lost their livelihoods following special discriminatory legislation in April 1933. In 1935 Jews were excluded from the general provision of 'winter aid'. Those in need — almost a quarter of those Jews living in Germany required welfare — were assisted by the Jewish community in a separate Jewish Winter Aid.

The people who were on the receiving end of this Nazi campaign of hatred were a small, demographically and economically declining minority group. In 1933 about half a million Jews lived in the German Reich or, in other words, about 0.7 per cent of the total population. Like most other small minorities, historical circumstances — even in an age of general and rapid industrialisation — had given them a specific demographic and economic profile. A higher proportion of Jews dwelled in the major cities than was true of the population at large. Their birth-rate had declined considerably since the turn of the century and from 1925 the number of deaths exceeded that of births. This means that the Jewish population was ageing and declining before the onset of persecution under the Nazi regime. Almost half of all Jews employed were independent small businessmen. The commercial sector accounted for almost half the Jews in employment. The largest concentration was in trade, particularly in the clothing industry. Jews were also strongly represented among self-employed doctors and lawyers. Because of the crisis occasioned by the Depression in these competitive professions, the large number of Jews concentrated in these sectors suffered grave consequences during the Nazi period.

During the nineteenth century, the general process of secularisation had led to the displacement of religious by economic arguments as the chief rationalisation for anti-Semitic hatred; Jews were accused of having enriched themselves unfairly through trade and banking, in ways prejudicial to the German economy, which was increasingly described as having been 'Jewified'. Nazi propaganda employed the hate-figure of an 'international Jewish financial oligarchy', as a sort of counterpart to the socialists' dilation upon major and monopoly capitalists. A totally spurious distinction between 'parasitic Jewish capital' and 'creative Aryan industrial capital' enabled the Nazis to appear to be anti-capitalist at a time when many German capitalists were nonetheless giving them their support. In Nazi and conservative ideology, the enemy stereotype of 'the Jew' embodied all the negative characteristics of a modern industrial society, whose principal casualties were the old *Mittelstand* of small farmers, craftsmen and merchants. Nostalgia for a bucolic society and the idealised harmony of a traditional way of life, easily degenerated into aggression against Jews, who were blamed for the absence of these values in the present. Jews were simultaneously held responsible for the Bolshevik Revolution in Russia and similar manifestations in Germany. They were identified as the so-called 'November criminals' of 1918, who by 'stabbing the armed forces in the back' had (according to the Right) denied the latter victory, in order to assume the leadership of the German people in the subsequent 'Jewish Republic of Weimar'. In this manner, the Jewish *Volksfeind* (enemy of the nation) was deployed as a simple and effective opposite to the ideology and propaganda of the *Volksgemeinschaft* or 'national community'.

This does not mean that anti-Semitism played a purely instrumental role in National Socialist propaganda before and after the 'seizure of power'. Nowadays, no serious historian holds the view that anti-Semitism performed a merely functional role, designed to offset the real or imagined prospect of a revolutionary upheaval through deployment of the Jewish scapegoat. Naturally, broadly based anti-Semitic resentments among the population were effectively exploited by Nazi propaganda; beyond this, however, the struggle against the Jews constituted the constant, unalterable core component in Hitler's world view. In National Socialist ideology, to which Hitler's personal contribution was greater than anyone else's, anti-Semitism enjoyed pride of place alongside the utopian vision of *Lebensraum* conquered and settled by racially pure German 'Aryans'. The murderous 'Final Solution of the Jewish Question' and the war of conquest against the Soviet Union were constant, fixed and interrelated objectives of National Socialist policy. Certainly, the successive stages of policy implementation were far from unilinear and were affected by changing political circumstances and possibilities. However, Auschwitz was latent in the anti-Semitic obsessions of Hitler and his Party from the beginning, in the way in which the embryo is in the egg or fruit within a bud.

This alone explains why persecution of the Jews not only failed to slacken following what the Nazis referred to as their 'seizure of power', but rather became ever more vicious, escalating into increasingly radical measures against Jews residing in Germany. In this phase, anti-Semitism was no longer necessary as an instrument of political mobilisation. On the contrary: henceforth the basest instincts of suppressed aggression, personal envy and sheer greed could be directed against Jews. Because of this, the National Socialists' initial measures were directed against Jewish economic activities.

Acts of violence against Jews, and attempts to take over their businesses, began immediately after the 1933 'seizure of power'. As trusted 'old fighters' of the movement, SA and SS men believed that the time had come to implement the Party's slogans, and to enrich themselves at the expense of the Jewish enemy of the people. The government, which included such coalition partners from the German National People's Party as the Minister of Agriculture Alfred Hugenberg, could not tolerate these so-called 'individual actions'. Individual attacks on the economic activities of the Jews were channelled into the more orderly lines of systematically implemented policy. In this phase, the objective was to undermine the economic base of the victims' existence, to isolate them from society as a whole and to force them to leave their homeland through mass emigration.

These policies commenced on 1 April 1933 with the officially inspired enforced boycott of Jewish businesses. Within a few days, 'action committees' were formed in even the most remote villages, which, accompanied by noisy propaganda, undertook measures against Jewish shopkeepers, doctors and lawyers. Uniformed and sometimes armed Nazis were stationed outside Jewish shops and legal and medical practices in order to deter customers and clients. People who refused to be intimidated were insulted and photographed so that they might subsequently be denigrated as 'traitors to the *Volk*' in the Press or public display cases. Shop windows were daubed with viciously offensive slogans or covered with specially prepared posters and flysheets. Although the official boycott only lasted for one day, it gave the signal for the beginning of officially sanctioned and remorselessly pursued exclusion of the Jews from the economy. From now on, the same scenes were sporadically repeated on the streets, particularly in the provinces but also in primarily Jewish residential quarters of the bigger cities.

Jewish lawyers and professors were forcibly expelled from the courts

A·I·Z

ERSCHEINT WÖCHENTLICH EINMAL • PREIS 20 PFG., Kč. 1,60
30 GR., 30 SCHWEIZER RP. • V. b. b. • NEUER DEUTSCHER
VERLAG, BERLIN W8 • JAHRGANG XI • NR. 42 • 16. 10. 1932

DER SINN DES
HITLERGRUSSES:

Motto:
**MILLIONEN
STEHEN
HINTER MIR!**

Kleiner Mann bittet um große Gaben

1 John Heartfield's 1932 illustration of the standard Marxist 'line' on Fascism explains 'the meaning of the Hitler salute' with the ambiguous slogan 'Millions stand behind me!' The millions of votes cast for the Nazis suggest that the party was more than the creation or 'tool' of a small class of industrialists and bankers.

2 Hitler attending the opening of a section of the Autobahn network. Nazi popularity in the early 1930s was in part a result of their success in putting the unemployed back to work through a range of economic policies including improvements to the infrastructure.

3 The German Labour Front was designed to integrate the working classes into the 'national community'. Its strategies included improvements to the workplace itself, and attempts to make a middle and upper class 'High' culture accessible to the workers. The photograph shows a symphony orchestra playing in a tram depot.

4 During the war, German agriculture and industry became increasingly reliant upon foreign forced labour, primarily to avoid conscripting German women for labour service. Treatment of foreign forced labour reflected racial criteria, with 'eastern workers' from Russia or the Ukraine experiencing the worst conditions. This photograph shows a group of Soviet prisoners of war huddled around a stove in a camp attached to the Volkswagen factory.

5 A children's home run by the Volkswagen factory at Rühen. It was stipulated that all female forced labourers had to give up their children two weeks after birth. They were raised in the most basic conditions, and from the autumn of 1944, all newly born children taken to the home at Rühen, died.

6 The patrician Jewish painter Max Liebermann passing a man canvassing for Hitler during the 1932 presidential elections in which the other candidates were Hindenburg and the Communist, Thälmann.

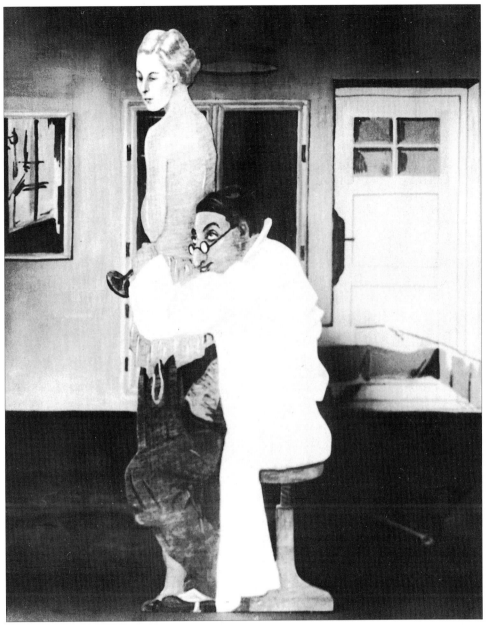

7 A cheap slur used to drive Jews from the medical profession was to claim that they were misusing their positions of trust to sexually abuse female 'Aryan' patients, a claim given visual form in this 1935 illustration of the new Reich Doctors' Decree.

Mann und Frau sind körperlich und seelisch verschieden

8 *After the Dresden Hygiene Exhibition of 1911, gigantic anatomical figures were used for mass public health education. During the 1920s, the 'visible man' and 'visible woman' were devised using an innovative new technique of anatomical preparation. Under the Nazis, the tone of educational displays became more authoritarian and directive, including propaganda on race, euthanasia and eugenics. The photograph (above) shows a man and woman from the 'Gesundes Leben – frohes Schaffen' exhibition on the Kaiserdam,. Berlin in 1938.*

9 (left) *The Nazi racial scientist, Karl Astel.*

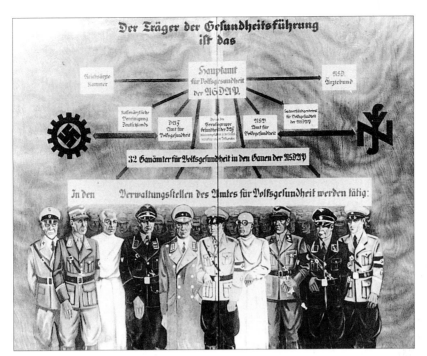

10 Doctors played a key role in the implementation of Nazi racial policies. No longer concerned with the health of the individual, they constituted a new class of 'experts' patrolling the hereditary health of the entire nation.

11 The enforcement of Nazi racial policies depended upon the willingness of the public to denouce people to the authorities. This photograph, taken by a member of the Nazi Party, proves that a fellow member was socialising with Jewish people. The cross identifies the house where these 'crimes' took place; the arrow indicates the Jews.

12 Jewish people assembled with their meagre belongings in Wiesbaden prior to their deportation to extermination centres in the East, 1941.

13 Handicapped child killed during the so-called 'children's euthanasia' programme. In 1939 Hitler authorised the medical murder of mentally and physically handicapped infants.

14 A registration form used to identify victims of the adult 'euthanasia' programme (left). This form concerns an elderly patient suffering from arteriosclerotic dementia. Among the non-medical 'symptoms' described here is that the man is 'inactive, and looks very bad'.

15 Buses from the 'Community Patients' Transport Service' were used to transport selected groups of patients to one of six asylums used as extermination centres.

16 Gypsies were persecuted because they were deemed to be both racially 'alien' and 'antisocial'. This picture shows a traditional Gypsy wedding.

17 The National Socialist persecution of Gypsies built upon earlier traditions of hostility towards this minority. They were persecuted for being 'racial aliens' and because of their allegedly biological predisposition towards criminal patterns of behaviour.

18 This painting (1942-43) by Emil Scheibe allegedly shows Hitler visiting the Front. In fact, despite his habitual identification with the ordinary soldier during the First World War, an experience with which he regularly used to browbeat his generals, Hitler rarely, if ever, visited any Front, and was utterly indifferent to the sufferings of ordinary soldiers.

19 A German armoured column advances through a Russian village in June 1941. The Germans sought a swift victory, but the Allies' economic power, fierce Russian resistance and the hostile climate proved to be insurmountable.

20 The Nazi soldier was required to sacrifice all for the Fatherland, but was also likely to succumb to the strain.

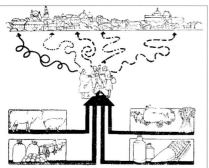

21 The main guard house (above) leading onto Auschwitz II-Birkenau and a railway siding used from 1944 to transport Jews to their deaths. In addition to Chelmno, Belzec, Sobibor and Treblinka, Auschwitz was the main camp used to murder the Jewish population of Europe.

In der früher unregulierten Marktordnung stand der Jude als Vermittler der landwirtschaftlichen Erzeugnisse.

22 Before and after graphics (left and right) illustrating
the supposed economic benefits resulting from the
rationalisation- meaning removal- of Jewish middlemen
from the rural economies of eastern Europe. Such
arguments may have been a means of rationalising
racially-motivated hatreds.

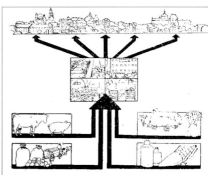

Jetzt sorgt eine geregelte Marktordnung für die
Erfassung und Verteilung der Produktionsgüter

23 *Homosexuals were persecuted by the Nazis because they did not contribute children to the 'national community' and because they undermined conventional notions of masculinity. Ironically, Nazism itself was partly based on the idea of intense male camaraderie, with women relegated to subordinate functions.*

24 Peasant women in folk costume at the annual Bückeberg harvest festival in 1935 welcoming their Führer. Photographs like this were used to demonstrate the allegedly hysterical enthusiasm of women for Hitler, as if he was an early version of a modern popstar. There is, however, no substantive evidence of this phenomenon.

Der Deutsche

SALZ
HERING

DIE GESUNDE VOLKSNAHRUNG

25 During the 1930s, housewives were encouraged to 'buy German', in this case in order to feed their families with German salt herrings, rather than imported foodstuffs. The role they were expected to play in developing a self-sufficient national economy may have contributed to a reevaluation of the housewife and mother in line with Nazi ideological imperatives.

and lecture theatres even before a law promulgated on 7 April 1933 ordered the dismissal of Jewish civil servants, academics and teachers from the public service, schools and universities. Doctors were excluded from hospitals and health insurance schemes. Initially, Jewish war veterans and relatives of war dead were allowed to pursue their trades and professions, following the intervention of President Hindenburg. But even they were affected by the progressive boycott and soon their clients consisted almost entirely of other Jews. Craftsmen and other business-men were also increasingly dependent upon the isolated Jewish sector of the economy. Local authorities ceased to grant them official contracts. Trade associations and co-operative credit associations took it upon themselves to issue 'Aryan paragraphs', whose effect was to render Jewish businesses uncompetitive, before the introduction of correspon-ding legislation.

The direct effect of these measures was the gradually escalating liquida-tion of Jewish economic activity. Some 100,000 individual businesses were owned by Jews in late 1932; this number included a few large mer-chant banks and a smaller number of major department stores or industrial concerns. Most, however, were middling, small or one-man enterprises. By mid-1935 almost a quarter, and by mid-1938 over two-thirds, of these enterprises had already ceased to exist. Their owners had either gone into liquidation or been obliged to sell at knock-down prices to 'Aryan' buyers. In most cases the Jewish sellers were ruthlessly pressurised by 'Aryan' purchasers. Since each 'Aryanisation' sale had to be confirmed by Nazi Party agencies, with preference being given to 'old fighters' wishing to make a killing, the years before 1938 represented an 'open season' for minor Nazis on the make. However, even major industrialists were not slow to join in when the chance arose to 'Aryanise' Jewish businesses. Threats from the Gestapo, followed if necessary by arrest and consign-ment to a concentration camp, were used without restraint to render Jewish businessmen more amenable to selling.

The indirect influences of the boycott and Aryanisation programme were far more portentous. The propaganda that accompanied them gave the vulgar jibes of the boycott and the greed manifested by Germans in the course of Aryanisation the nimbus of ideological legitimacy. The special status of the Jews was gradually anchored in popular conscious-ness. In their case, the received norms of civilised behaviour and com-mercial probity were no longer valid. The Nazi Press published bemused and laudatory reports about 'holiday-making schoolchildren' who mobbed and traduced elderly Jewish shopkeepers and also their non-Jewish customers on the streets. The pressure exerted upon commercial values by the most extreme Aryanisers was also effectively sanctioned by Nazi ideology. Since all property was regarded as part of the 'nation's wealth', Jews were not entitled to any part of it. Moreover, since in the eyes of anti-Semites, the Jews had come into possession of their wealth through the fraudulent exploitation of German 'national comrades', removing their property was a service to the nation rather than a criminal offence.

Economic marginalisation was only one aspect of a comprehensive policy designed to isolate the Jews within German society and as human beings. Even the education of young children was included in this process. The publishing house which produced the paper *Der Stürmer* on behalf of the rabidly anti-Semitic Gauleiter of Franconia, Julius Streicher, produced illustrated childrens' books which warned the very young against the Jewish enemy of the people. Racist sentiments were also encouraged in the schools and among the Hitler Youth who played an active part in the hooliganism which accompanied the boycotts. *Der Stürmer*, which was exclusively dedicated to the most primitive and quasi-pornographic type of anti-Semitic propaganda, was displayed everywhere in special showcases. Jews were depicted in caricatured form, with beards and sidelocks and clothed in a medieval style of dress which was still only used by the Jews of Eastern Europe. Represented with unattractive features and gestures, they were accused of seducing German women and girls, as bloodthirsty ritual murderers or as crafty participants in a world conspiracy. Real Jews living in Germany, who of course looked quite otherwise, were identified as being merely a more cunningly disguised version of the same species.

Identification of one's Jewish neighbours, with whom one frequently enjoyed amicable relations, with the travesty represented by the Nazis' 'traitor to the *Volk*' was only possible because of a tradition of Christian anti-Semitism. The Nazis did not need to invent any of the odious anti-Semitic stereotypes that they employed. They were able to find most of them in ecclesiastical teaching, in the folklore of antiquity or the Middle Ages, or in the secular anti-Semitic literature which circulated in nineteenth-century France, Germany or Russia. At Christmas 1933 the Munich cardinal Michael von Faulhaber delivered a number of sermons which are often interpreted as evidence of resistance to the Nazis irreligious policies. It is striking what he had to say about the Jews:

Following the death of Christ, Israel was debarred from the task of revela-
tion. They had denied the Lord's Anointed, depraved, they expelled him
from the City and nailed him to the Cross. The veil of the Temple of Zion
was rent asunder and therewith the union between the Lord and his people.
The Daughter of Zion [the Jewish people] was cast aside and henceforth the
eternal Ahasver wandered ceaselessly across the earth.

It is significant that one of the most murderously anti-Semitic films pro-
duced and shown during the Third Reich was entitled *The Eternal Jew*.
Even though traditional anti-Semitism was no more widely diffused in
Germany than in other countries, it had sufficiently deep roots to provide
a receptive breeding ground for systematic indoctrination in which the
Volksgemeinschaft-Volksfeind polarity was a central element.

However, this objective was not achieved overnight. The Nazis needed
a number of years to clear aside the received moral inhibitions of the average German citizen. In the early years, the violent scenes that frequently
accompanied the boycotts often encountered popular disapproval. A man
called Richard Schneider, who described himself as a veteran Party member, wrote in disgusted terms to the Ministry of the Interior in December
1934 regarding the boycott in Frankfurt am Main:

> Half-grown boys of 16 to 17 years of age barred the entrances . . . Elderly,
> but rather distinguished-looking gentlemen, including men who had made
> the greatest sacrifices fighting for four years for their Fatherland, had to ask
> leave to enter from these rascals and scallywags, having to answer the
> question: 'Are you a German?' And this was done with police protection,
> by a vulgar pack of people whose inclusion in the national community
> should be absolutely rejected.

Nothing in the records tells us about the Minister's reply or the fate of
the man who signed off with the words: 'Ugh to the Party! Ugh to the
new Germany!'

In summer 1995 an increase in the boycott was accompanied by violence.
The Minister of Economics Hjalmar Schacht protested to his colleagues
in the government about the illegal behaviour of the Party, which was
endangering economic recovery, relations with foreign countries and
thereby Germany's rearmament programme. This time there was much
less evidence of negative popular response. When Hitler promulgated the
notorious Nuremberg Laws on 15 September 1935, the population
accepted these measures without demur. Evidently, it was no longer
regarded as objectionable that a group of people should lose elementary

civil rights and be socially marginalised up to and including the forfeiture of the most intimate human relations. Following the so-called Law for the Protection of the German Blood marriages between Jews and Gentiles were prohibited and extra-marital sexual relations thenceforth constituted the punishable offence of 'miscegenation'. In order to 'protect' German girls, Jews were no longer allowed to employ Aryan domestic servants. In one small town local Nazi leaders took this stipulation so seriously that, accompanied by the drunken cries of those who took part, they dragged housemaids out of Jewish households on the very same night the law was promulgated.

The next and most notorious station in the continuing exclusion and depersonalisation of the Jews was the pogrom of 9 and 10 November 1938. The pretext was the assassination of a German diplomat in Paris by the seventeen-year-old Hershel Grynszpan, in revenge for the forced expulsion of his entire family. During the night of 28 October about 18,000 Jews of Polish nationality had been taken from their beds by the police and hounded across the Polish border. There is no record of disapproving reactions on the part of the German population *vis-à-vis* this first deportation of 'Eastern Jews', who in any case enjoyed little sympathy among the wider population. Nazi propaganda used the murder in Paris to whip up support for a campaign of hatred orchestrated by the Minister of Propaganda Josef Goebbels. During the night of 9 November, every synagogue in Germany went up in flames on Goebbels's instructions. The 7,500 businesses still in Jewish ownership, as well as many Jewish homes, were ransacked and their occupants violently mishandled. The following day about 25,000 Jews were sent to the concentration camps. About 100 Jews died in the pogrom and hundreds more were badly injured; how many died subsequently in concentration camps is not known.

This time, broad sections of the population were shocked by the brutality of the pogrom and a small minority bravely gave vent to their opposition. A considerably larger minority took an active part in these attacks, plundering Jewish businesses and rejoicing with open expressions of *Schadenfreude*. Most Germans silently shook their heads and averted their gaze. Criticism was mostly directed against the destruction of material goods, which might have benefited the 'German national economy', or concerned incidents that disturbed public law and order. The majority of Germans had so internalised the exclusion of the Jewish 'enemy of the people' by this time, that the physical abuse of Jewish neighbours and sacriligious incendiarism against their places of worship were regarded as unavoidable.

The November pogrom marked the opening of the final, tragic stage in the existence of German Jewry. The Jewish businesses that had been wrecked could not be re-opened. All firms still in Jewish hands were liquidated or compulsorily 'Aryanised' through transfer to state-appointed trustees. Half of the property still owned by Jews went to the Nazi state. Hermann Goering imposed a collective 'payment of atonement' of a billion Reichsmarks for the murder in Paris. Jews, who were now fleeing en masse, had to pay a large part of their capital in the form of a 'tax on flight from the Reich'. The state, as well as individual Party members and national comrades, prised out further considerable sums through a whole series of 'gifts' and supplementary deductions. Those Jews who remained in Germany were able to subsist for a few years more on the remains of the property of Jewish communities, organisations and private persons. From the end of 1941 even the costs of their own deportation to the extermination camps were withdrawn from these funds by the Gestapo.

About two-thirds of the Jewish population in Germany in 1933 had emigrated or died before mass deportations to extermination camps began in October 1941. By this date about 165,000 Jews still lived within the pre-1938 borders of the Reich, i.e. before the annexation of Austria and parts of Czechoslovakia. The majority were elderly, with more women than men, and lived a desolate existence totally isolated from the non-Jewish population in special 'Jewish houses' or forced labour camps. A few thousand of them survived the war, thanks to the courageous assistance of a few Germans who sustained their underground existence. Many more were delivered into the hands of the Gestapo by neighbours and acquaintances. The rounding up and deportation took place in full public view, without protest from either the population or the Churches.

Between 1933 and 1941 the National Socialists succeeded, through education and propaganda, in totally isolating the Jews in Germany. A striking exhibition of Jewish everyday life in this period is entitled 'From neighbours into Jews'. Real Jewish people were converted into a collective and depersonalised mythical enemy stereotype. It was only a small step from that figure to the total dehumanisation that made possible the murder of six million European Jews. How that was achieved can be seen from the film *The Eternal Jew*, which was shown everywhere in Germany and occupied Europe from 1940 onwards. It compared the

Jews with vermin who, emanating from 'breeding grounds' in the ghettos of Poland, streamed across the entire world in different garb in order to spread sickness and pestilence, and finally to achieve power. Deliverance from this threat was identified in the film with the words Hitler delivered in a speech to the Reichstag on 30 January 1939 when he prophesied:

> If the international Jewish financiers in and outside Europe should succeed in plunging the nations once more into a world war, then the result will not be the Bolshevising of the earth, and thus a victory of Jewry, but the annihilation of the Jewish race in Europe.

In thousands of books and articles historians seek to explain how a civilised people in the heart of Europe could cause or, at least, passively watch the state murder millions of people — men, women and children — in a bureaucratically superbly organised operation, solely on account of their membership of a 'race'. So far none of them has found a satisfactory explanation. Many conclude that the Holocaust was a unique, totally inexplicable phenomenon, beyond the understanding of historical research. This overlooks the fact that the perpetrators were not extra-terrestrial monsters, but rather tens of thousands of perfectly ordinary people. After carrying out their abominable activities, they spent evenings with their children, played cards at their regular tables in bars and canteens or delighted themselves through the music of Mozart or Beethoven. Because of this it is simply not possible to give up the attempt to understand and explain what happened. The account given here does not claim to supply a complete or final answer to these frightening questions. It simply seeks to show how seven or eight years of fanatical ideological indoctrination and concrete visual instruction in racial matters could befog the consciences of millions of Germans and corrode their moral inhibitions. Without these prior developments the Holocaust would not have been possible. From this perspective, the persecution of the German Jews seems the necessary, although not sufficient precondition, for the murder of European Jews.

Point 4 of the National Socialist German Workers' Party Programme dated 24 February 1920
Only national comrades can be citizens of the State. Only persons of German blood can be national comrades, regardless of religious affiliation. No Jew can therefore be a national comrade.

Reich Citizenship Law of 15 September 1935
A citizen of the Reich is that subject only who is of German or kindred blood and who, through his conduct, shows that he is both desirous and fit to serve the German people and Reich faithfully.

Express letter from the Reich Minister of Finance dated 4 November 1941
Jews who are not employed in concerns of major national economic importance are to be pushed out to a town in the eastern territories in the coming months. The assets of those Jews who are to be deported are to be confiscated in the interests of the German Reich . . . The deportation of the Jews will be carried out by the Gestapo. The Gestapo will take care of the securing of Jewish assets.

SS Economic and Administrative Main Office instruction to the commanders of the concentration camps dated 6 August 1942
The Head of the SS Economic and Administrative Main Office has decreed that all human hair collected in the concentration camps is to be utilised. Human hair is to be recycled into industrial felt and spun into thread. Therefore it is hereby decreed that the hair of female prisoners collected after disinfection is to be preserved.

The German *Volksgemeinschaft*

Avraham Barkai, *From Boycott to Annihilation: The Economic Struggle of German Jews 1933–1943* (Hanover and London, 1989); Michael Burleigh and Wolfgang Wippermann, *The Racial State: Germany, 1933–1945* (Cambridge, 1991); Hermann Graml, *Antisemitism in the Third Reich* (Oxford, 1992); Raul Hilberg, *The Destruction of European Jews* (New York and London, 1985); Ian Kershaw, *The 'Hitler Myth': Image and Reality in the Third Reich* (Oxford, 1987); Robert Gellately, *The Gestapo and German Society: Enforcing Racial Policy* (Oxford, 1990).

CHAPTER VI

SAVING MONEY, SPENDING LIVES: PSYCHIATRY, SOCIETY AND THE 'EUTHANASIA' PROGRAMME

Michael Burleigh

IN GERMANY PSYCHIATRY EMERGED FROM the First World War with its already poor image as a futile and scientifically dubious branch of medicine tarnished even further. Some 70,000 patients had died during wartime from a combination of hunger, disease and neglect. Exhausted or 'neurotic' soldiers had been systematically abused by crude shock therapies. Revolutionaries arrested after the abortive Munich Soviet were regularly diagnosed as 'psychopaths' by forensic psychiatrists. Post-war austerity engendered a decline in the physical fabric of the asylums, while economy cuts affected everything from books, drugs and heating to light-bulbs and soap.

In Wilhelmine Germany criticism of psychiatry had often come from the Right, for example from the anti-Semitic court chaplain Adolf Stöcker, and was primarily directed against psychiatry's medicalised denial of individual liberty. In Weimar Germany a temporarily powerful psychiatric reform movement, including groups demanding patients' rights, went on the attack, demanding enhanced patients' rights, checks on committal procedures and an effective inspectorate. On the Right many questioned the efficacy and value of the entire psychiatric project, for there was frequently no tangible 'cure' for mental illness. And in 1920 the lawyer Karl Binding and the psychiatrist Alfred Hoche, dared to raise the delicate question of whether a nation faced with a dire emergency could actually afford to sustain what they dubbed 'life unworthy of life'. In a controversial tract, which was essentially a search for a post-Christian utilitarian ethics, Binding and Hoche deliberately conflated the issues of suicide and voluntary 'euthanasia' with the non-consensual killing of the mentally ill; stressed the historical relativity of such notions as the 'sanctity of human life'; highlighted the objective futility of such emotions as 'pity' — 'where there is no suffering there can also be no pity' — and emphasised the emotional and economic burden allegedly represented by 'entirely unproductive persons'. The altruistic heroism of British Polar explorers, such as Captain Robert Scott, was invoked to justify jettisoning 'dead ballast' from the 'Ship of Fools'. The tract was symptomatic of how received liberal or humanitarian values were breaking down, with concern for narrow or wider collectivities, such as the good of a class, the economy, race or nation usurping respect for the rights and value of the individual.

Faced with such variegated assaults upon their activities, German psychiatrists began to think more kindly of a handful of farsighted reformers in their own midst who had hitherto been cold-shouldered. Two rather remarkable men, Gustav Kolb and Hermann Simon, had long advocated breaching the walls between asylums and the wider society, and between sickness and the world of work. Their liberal recommendations found a ready response from Weimar governments obsessed with cutting costs. Patients were discharged into the arms of a new range of urban outpatient clinics or perambulatory community psychiatrists in rural areas or, indeed, into paid family fostering, where a family was paid a fee to house a former patient. The economic advantages of this were clear: whereas the annual overheads of an outpatient clinic in Munich were RM2,000 a year, it cost RM1,277 to keep one patient for a year in Munich's Eglfing-Haar asylum. However, patients in asylums were not free from the attentions of the reformers either. Depressed by the effects of long-term institutionalisation in environments with next to no therapy, the psychiatrist Hermann Simon decided to use occupational therapy to engender self-satisfaction and hence repress the depressed or excitable moods that resulted from enforced idleness. Soon, asylums were humming with patient activity, with the complexity of the work performed, and hence the degree of freedom and responsibility enjoyed, being the objective indicator of recovery. In many asylums, up to 80 per cent of patients did some form of work, which made the asylums largely self-sufficient or capable of generating modest surpluses. Judging by the flood of articles devoted to community care and occupational therapy published in the professional journals in the 1920s, psychiatry began to be a more optimistic profession.

Inevitably, there was a disadvantage to these developments. First, as psychiatrists began to follow their discharged patients out into the wider world, they inevitably encountered hitherto unknown ranges of 'abnormality'; what had passed before them in the asylums was literally the tip of an iceberg. Being of an increasingly hereditarian cast of mind, they began to construct genealogies of the patients' families. Instead of addressing themselves to questions concerning the socio-economic environment, which in any case they were powerless to effect, they opted for the control function of registering widespread deviance in primitive databanks. The sheer scale of illness they discovered engendered a certain pessimism, and hence their susceptibility to radical eugenicist solutions. Experience had taught them that people they deemed degenerate or feckless could not be counselled into voluntary birth control, so many psychiatrists began to think in terms of compulsory sterilisation. This would enable the person to return to the productive process without risk of reproductive damage ensuing to the collective biological substance of the race or nation. Furthermore, the widespread introduction of occupational therapy in asylums increasingly meant that patients were measured in terms of their economic productivity. Unfortunately, not all patients were capable of rolling cigars, weaving baskets, running errands or answering the telephone. Each asylum therefore had a quantity of 'incurables', languishing 'unproductively' in back wards, where conditions were often parlous. The adoption of occupational therapy implicitly meant separating the able-bodied and willing from the therapy-resistant chaff. Long before the National Socialist government appeared on the scene, some psychiatrists advocated (or considered) killing this permanent reminder of the limits of their own therapeutic capacities and permanent burden upon the nation's scant resources. Paradoxical as it may sound, psychiatric reform had actually established most of the conceptual framework for the sterilisation and later elimination of psychiatric patients. The year 1933 did not mark a decisive break; most of the policies of the Nazi period were more or less latently evident in the Janus-faced health and welfare apparatus of the Weimar Republic.

Nonetheless, the advent of a National Socialist government had dire consequences for the asylum population. Asylums became freak-shows, with thousands of members of Nazi formations being given tours to illustrate the inherent uselessness of the patients. Between 1933 and 1939 21,000 people trooped through Eglfing-Haar, including 6,000 members of the SS, some of whom came out recommending setting up machine guns at the entrance to mow down the inmates. Party newspapers and journals such as the *Völkischer Beobachter* or *Schwarze Korps* dilated upon the Goyaesque scenes in the asylums and advocated killing the mentally ill, often coupling this with heroic instances of 'mercy killing' carried out by individuals.

With the regional health authorities increasingly in the hands of men who explicitly advocated killing mental patients, it is hardly surprising that conditions in the asylums soon deteriorated sharply. Specialist facilities were closed and patients were removed from the private or religious sectors and crammed into cheaper state institutions to save money and increase control. An asylum such as Eichberg in the Rheingau had 793 patients in 1934 and 1,236 by 1940. The ratio of doctors to patients deteriorated from 1:162 to 1:300 between 1935 and 1938. In some institutions it was as high as 1:500, which made basic care — hygiene, watering and feeding — let alone any treatment, totally impossible. The meagre sums expended upon patients' food were cut, for example, at Haina in Hessen from RM 0.69 per day in 1932 to RM 0.54 in 1935; this was against a background of general economic recovery. Enthusiastic lower-class National Socialist administrators replaced disinterested boards of upper-class philanthropists in the running of institutions such as the Idstein reformatory (also in Hessen), gradually marginalising medical control in these institutions. With doctors no longer necessarily in charge, economic efficiency became the primary goal. Many of the psychiatrists — who tended to be recruited from the dross of the medical profession anyway — were SS members inherently antagonistic towards their patients. Below them, a host of thoroughly unsuitable people, armed with Party cards and SA membership, flooded into nursing in order to escape the dole queues in many cases. Nursing had always been an occupation for those who had failed in other fields or for women who had yet to find a husband. Independent inspectors, some of whom deplored the fact that patients were sleeping on straw on the floor or going about virtually naked, and who objected to the brutal language used by senior health administrators, were simply barred from further visits.

Apart from the continuing deterioration of general conditions, psychiatric patients were directly affected by the 1933 Law for the Prevention of Hereditarily Diseased Progeny, which sanctioned compulsory sterilisation for a range of putatively hereditary illnesses. This Law was promoted through various forms of propaganda, including film, whose intention was to degrade and stigmatise mental patients. Psychiatrists were responsible for initiating the procedures leading to a patient's sterilisation and, indeed, often sat on the 220 local Hereditary Health Courts that made the final decisions. At this time, the hereditary character of the illnesses concerned was more a declaration of faith than a matter of scientific certitude. Leaving aside the fact that one genuinely hereditary illness — haemophilia — was actually omitted, the prefix 'hereditary' was dropped from schizophrenia in order to sterilise those where the cause was exogenous, while reformed drunks or people with low alcohol tolerance who did not actually drink much, were sterilised as 'chronic alcoholics', on the grounds that alcoholism reflected some underlying 'asocial or psychopathic disorder', neither of which separate conditions was specified in this legislation. Nor did the courts confine themselves to the people who actually came before them. In Bavaria, for example, after he had ordered the sterilisation of a young woman, the Kaufbeuren psychiatrist Hermann Pfannmüller, who was also a judge in the court at Kempten, spent a week isolating twenty-one additional 'degenerates' in her family, recommending the sterilisation of ten of them as being 'highly urgent since the danger of reproduction appeared immanent'. In a thoroughly pernicious development, schoolteachers were encouraged to set their pupils the task of constructing their own family trees, with a view to helping identify any defective members, while mayors reported single mothers primarily to curtail the costs involved in looking after their illegitimate children.

Apart from the permanent psychological damage sterilisation caused those affected, it was not uncommon for people to die on the operating table or to commit suicide shortly afterwards. The regime's remorseless propaganda campaign to sell these policies inevitably entailed generating mass resentment against the 'burden' represented by the asylum population. Propaganda films also regularly disputed the human 'personality' of the mentally ill and severely handicapped, deliberately and indiscriminately conflated criminals and the insane, and advocated a reversion to Social Darwinian elimination of the weak and the abandonment of a counter-selective welfare apparatus.

From the mid-1930s, what had once more become a very desolate psychiatric landscape was temporarily brightened by the arrival of a new range of somatic therapies. The Viennese psychiatrist Manfred Sakel pioneered insulin coma therapy for schizophrenia, which essentially involved starving the central nervous system of the glucose circulating in the blood, for it cannot metabolise substitutes for even short periods. Glucose solutions were used to arrest the drop in blood-sugar levels before they became critical. This was in turn augmented by Ladislaus von Meduna's cardiazol convulsive therapy, based upon the alleged biological antagonism of epilepsy and schizophrenia, and which employed the cerebral stimulant cardiazol to induce epileptic fits. Finally, in the late 1930s the Italians Bini and Cerletti developed electro-convulsive techniques, which had the advantage over other therapies of not involving injections and which rendered the subject instantaneously unconscious. However, none of these therapies was free from serious risks to the health of the patients treated in this fashion.

The major psychiatric journals quickly filled with enthusiastic accounts of these therapies. They often included detailed 'before and after' case-histories and the testimonies of people who felt miraculously relieved of isolating and oppressive illnesses. For example, a young woman treated for persecution mania with insulin and cardiazol wrote to relatives:

> Now I can write to you as once more as the Hilde of old! Imagine Mummy, Saturday evening in bed, it just dawned following a conversation with the others. Naturally I am eating again, for not eating was just part of the persecution mania. You cannot imagine the feeling of being freed from every fear. One is born again, so to speak. Now I look forward to Sunday and to seeing you dear Mummy. It should have clicked together before, then you would have noticed something, but nonetheless, we should thank our lucky stars. How are you then? I am so very happy.

A new optimism was abroad, for with these therapies, psychiatrists could argue that they actually cured people.

Paradoxically, these limited psychiatric successes with acute patients only heightened psychiatric embarrassment about that proportion of patients for whom they could do nothing. Acute cases could be treated with occupational therapy or one of these new somatic therapies. Any danger they might represent to the collective hereditary health of race and nation could be neutralised through compulsory sterilisation before, or as a condition of their release into the community. But this still left the problem of, the incurable or refractory, upon whom these therapies made no impact whatsoever, and whose care still cost money. In November 1939 director Hermann Pfannmüller of Eglfing-Haar responding to a report from local auditors, commented on this last group of patients, 'The problem of whether to maintain this patient material under the most primitive conditions or to eradicate it has now become a subject for serious discussion once more.' Selective therapeutic intensity had once again pushed a certain patient constituency to the margins, but this time, in a political climate where the masters of the state had no moral inhibitions about murder, and wished to clear the economic decks for the war they were bent on waging.

Before turning to the 'euthanasia' programme, one final element needs to be introduced into this discussion, namely the extent to which these policies were consensual. Matters are a little more complicated than the conventional polarised triad of victims, bystanders and perpetrators, because mental illness and severe disability are issues where attitudes are not clear cut and prejudice and social stigmas operate. Most discussions of the National Socialists' justification of their policies quite reasonably alight upon the intellectual influence of Binding and Hoche's utilitarian tract for the times, without noticing that very often they actually refer to an author who was, in fact, the tract's main critic. In 1925 Ewald Meltzer, the director of the Katharinenhof asylum for backward juveniles at Grosshennersdorf in Saxony, published an extremely powerful critique of Binding and Hoche, which stressed both the joy handicapped people took in life and the positive sentiments caring for them engendered in others, and which condemned the inflationary and materialist character of the arguments used by the two professors.

Unfortunately, Meltzer decided to carry out a poll of the views on 'euthanasia' held by the parents of his young charges. His assurance that the results of the poll would be non-consequential did not stop one or two people removing their relatives from his asylum. Much to Meltzer's surprise, some 73 per cent of the 162 respondents said that they would approve 'the painless curtailment of the life of [their] child if experts had established that it is suffering from incurable idiocy'. Many of the 'yes' respondents said that they wished to be relieved of the burden represented by an 'idiotic' child; some of them expressed the wish that this be done secretly and that they should be told that the child had died of some illness, in a manner which resembled later National Socialist practice. Only twenty of the forty-three 'no' respondents in fact rejected all four propositions put to them by Meltzer — for example some countenanced killing in the event of their own deaths leaving the child orphaned — it thus being a minority who, either from ethical and religious convictions or powerful bonds to their child, would not sanction their deaths under any circumstances. Surveying National Socialist propaganda on these subjects, it is not entirely surprising that Meltzer was as much cited as Binding and Hoche. Silent collusive assent was as much involved as outrage and protest.

Indeed, the origins of the 'euthanasia' programme were very much bound up with requests for 'mercy killing'. The reason Hitler decided to assign the task to the Chancellery of the Führer was not simply because this small prerogative agency could act secretly outside the regular channels of government, but because the Chancellery handled incoming petitions, which included requests for 'euthanasia'. These came from, for example, a woman dying of cancer, a man blinded and severely injured after falling into a cement mixer, and the parents of a handicapped infant called Knauer, languishing in a Leipzig clinic, blind and without a leg and part of an arm. Hitler despatched Karl Brandt, the accident surgeon attached to his retinue, to Leipzig to authorise the death of this child. He then empowered both Brandt and the head of the Chancellery of the Führer, Philipp Bouhler, to make further authorisations in similar cases in future. A Reich Committee for the Scientific Registration of Serious Hereditary and Congenital Illnesses was formed, consisting of three leading paediatricians, whose task was to make decisions on euthanasia killings on the basis of information they received following the introduction of compulsory registration of such conditions. A number of special paediatric clinics was established, which promised the parents the latest forms of treatment, with the revealing rider that there were real risks involved. Parents who had exhausted every medical avenue and who were worn down by having to cope with several children had few reservations about handing their child over to these clinics, in some cases in the knowledge that he or she would be killed there. An army of welfare snoopers equipped with coercive powers could easily bring pressure to bear on the recalcitrant by, for example, conscripting single mothers for labour service.

The children concerned were killed by a combination of starvation and powerful sedatives. The nurses involved may have found the work disturbing, but they also thought it right to 'release unfortunate creatures from their suffering', and appreciated the regular bonus payments. The doctors were volunteers. That it was possible to refuse such work is demonstrated by, for example, the case of Dr Friedrich Hölzel, who used the opportunity of a vacation ruined by rain, to write to Pfannmüller declining the post of running Eglfing-Haar's paediatric killing centre.

Although he approved of these policies, it was another matter to carry them out in person, a distinction that 'reminded [him] of the difference which exists between a judge and executioner'. He thought he was too weak and too concerned with helping his patients to be able to 'carry this out as a systematic policy after cold-blooded deliberation'. Pfannmüller never pressed him any further on the matter. In total, as many as 6,000 children were killed in this programme, with the age range being surreptitiously extended to include adolescents.

Hitler's wartime authorisation of an adult 'euthanasia' programme was conceived as an economy measure, a means of creating emergency bed space for military casualties, and, although this has not been much explored, hostels for ethnic German repatriates from Russia and eastern Europe. In the eastern areas of the Reich, SS units under Kurt Eimann and Herbert Lange were subcontracted to shoot psychiatric patients to create army and SS barrack space in a parallel operation. The Chancellery of the Führer created an elaborate covert bureaucracy based at Tiergartenstrasse 4 (hence the code name Aktion T-4), whose task was to organise the registration, selection, transfer and murder of an anticipated, and previously calculated target of 70,000 victims. This apparatus was run by a group of economists, agronomists, former businessmen and commercial lawyers — many of whom were old friends — with an expanded panel of academics and psychiatrists whose job was to handle the medical side of mass murder. Many of the professors were of modest social origin, men for whom education was hence a form of social mobility, with their fragile egos being bolstered by titles and semi-official positions in Hereditary Health Courts or by working for the SS on a freelance basis. For instance T-4's first medical chief, Werner Heyde of Würzburg, had worked part-time in concentration camps since the mid-1930s, and was a provincial, latently homosexual, university professor of modest social circumstances, literally tantalised by the indirect power radiating from the Chancellery of the Führer.

Together this odd assortment of highly educated, morally vacant humanity set about registering and selecting victims; finding asylums quietly to kill them in; establishing an effective means of so doing; and, last but not least, a staff of people willing and able to commit mass murder. Both Herbert Linden, the desk officer responsible for asylums in the Ministry of Interior, and regional health bureaucrats such as Walter 'Bubi' Schultze in Munich or Ludwig Sprauer in Stuttgart proved very co-operative, because they had already been advocating these policies for several years. They either identified suitable asylums, organising transfers of ownership, or recommended doctors, orderlies and nursing staff whose track-record and level of ideological commitment singled them out as suitable; Heyde provided the names of his past students. The SS, which was at one remove from these policies, provided a pool of insensate hard men from the concentration camps who could deal with the horrible physicality of murder. Teams consisting of these people were sent to six asylums in order to convert them into extermination centres: the former hard labour prison at Brandenburg; Bernburg, near Halle; Grafeneck, high in the Swabian Alb; Hadamar, near Limburg; Schloss Hartheim, near Linz, and Sonnenstein, outside Dresden. The doctors who monopolised killing were gradually inducted into their grim work, beginning by watching and moving on to turning a gas-valve themselves, a simple enough task, but one apparently requiring a medical degree. Most of these doctors were quite young, socially insecure and hugely impressed by big names and grand places, i.e. the usual accompaniments of petty-bourgeois academic ambition. Their narrow professional training added no element of moral inhibition. The nurses and orderlies were the products of a professional and societal culture of obedience, and often had proven records of ideological commitment, believing in the rightness of these policies. It was a culture of compliance.

Registration forms were completed for every patient and then despatched via T-4 to various assessors. Many asylum directors made the fatal mistake of deliberately underestimating a patient's capacity to work in order not to lose valuable workers, a depressing reminder in itself of how the asylums had been turned into units of production. Low productivity, and the length of institutionalisation, usually signed a patient's death warrant. The T-4 assessors received batches of 200–300 forms at a time, and were paid on a piecework basis, which probably accounts for the diagnostic virtuosity of such Stakanovites of the psychiatric profession as Josef Schreck, who alone completed 15,000 forms in a month. On the basis of these forms, batches of patients were then removed by the Community Patients' Transport Service either directly to the gas chambers or to holding asylums, designed both to mislead relatives and to stagger the burden on the crematoria.

These killings inevitably meant contacts between T-4 and a host of private, state and religious asylums. Ecclesiastical resistance to these policies was slow in coming, not least because many directors of religious asylum networks, such as the director of the Protestant Inner Mission Hans

Harmsen, had supported negative eugenic strategies in the 1920s and 1930s, and because the Church hierarchies preferred high-level private talks to open confrontation with an anti-clerical government. Indeed, the chief Roman Catholic negotiator with T-4 headquarters (in itself a striking development), Bishop Heinrich Wienken, seems to have made a series of unfortunate compromises, impressed, no doubt, by the elaborate theological arguments T-4 had elicited beforehand to justify 'euthanasia'. Half of the 70,000 victims of T-4 came from asylums and homes which were part of ecclesiastical charitable networks. Protests from individual churchmen came too late to be effective and were simply sidestepped. Difficulties with individuals within the judiciary or state prosecution service were ironed out by inducting their superiors into an operation that had no formal legal sanction whatsoever.

Some asylums tried to subvert the operation by delaying completion of the registration process once they realised that this had a malign hidden agenda. This practice was countered by roving teams of T-4 assessors, some of whom would go off sight-seeing leaving their students to process entire cohorts of patients. A few asylums tried pre-emptive discharge, or indeed hid a few vulnerable patients. But discharge depended upon the willingness of families to have the patient at home; in many cases the response was that there was no room in the inn. Refusing to have his brother home from the Mariaberg asylum, a man wrote that Otto 'would never be forgotten' and promised a 'little something' in the post for Christmas. Otto did not last until Christmas — he was gassed at Grafeneck on 13 December. Most asylum staff co-operated, rationalising what they did by the weak excuse that they had haggled over the life of this or that patient, for T-4 naturally included room for a little plea-bargaining to anticipate the element of bad conscience. It was always possible to point to this or that saved individual, quietly overlooking the disappearance of bus-loads of others. Capacity to work, the dominant therapeutic criterion, now became the basis of selection. In many cases, psychiatrists had no difficulty effecting the transition.

In total, T-4 killed over 70,000 people. A final report translated the monthly kill-rate into graphs, while precisely calculating how much money or foodstuffs would be saved by 70,273 'disinfections', extrapolated down to 1951. These graphs, discovered by the Americans in a safe at Hartheim, showed actual savings on, for example, marmalade — assuming each person consumed 700 grams a year — of 5,902,920 kilograms with its money equivalent of RM7,083,504.

Following the cessation of the mass gassing of patients in August 1941, because the initial target had been slightly exceeded and protests were mounting, the T-4 medical assessors were turned loose on the inmates of concentration camps, where they perfunctorily rediagnosed people the SS had already deemed 'sick' and hence dispensable. Many of the 20,000 or so victims of 'Aktion 14f13' — the code designating the death of a sick camp inmate — were killed simply because of their criminal records, or because they were Jewish. In the winter of 1941, a T-4 team under Viktor Brack was despatched to Minsk where it is very probable they quietly disposed of seriously injured German soldiers *en route* from field hospitals to rear areas. That autumn, a busy Brack had also met Himmler, for whom he had once been a driver and for whom his doctor father had once helped Frau Himmler with a difficult pregnancy, who allegedly said that 'Hitler had some time ago given him the order for the extermination of the Jews. He said that preparations had already been made, and I think that he used the expression that for reasons of camouflage one would have to work as quickly as possible.' The T-4 men were to be one of the separate groups involved in the various competitive, experimental pushes set in motion finally to 'solve' the European 'Jewish Question'. As experts in mass gassing, they were given the largest part of the operation, apart from Rudolf Hoess's death factory at Auschwitz.

Some ninety-four temporarily redundant T-4 personnel were 'loaned' by Philipp Bouhler to the Higher SS and Police Leader in Lublin, the ex-bricklayer Odilo Globocnik. With the SS 'euthanasia' expert Herbert Lange already disposing of the Jewish population of the Warthegau at Kulmhof, this T-4 team formed the hard core whose task was the massive operation of murdering the entire Jewish population of the Generalgouvernement, the part of Poland not simply absorbed into greater Germany. Thus, a motley array of former cooks, lorry-drivers, labourers and ex-policemen, such as Kurt Franz, Lorenz Hackenholt, Josef Oberhauser, Franz Stangl, Christian Wirth, together with T-4 doctors such as Irmfried Eberl, moved up several social notches to pre-side over the murder of nearly two million people in what came to be called 'Aktion Reinhard', i.e. the extermination camps of Belzec, Sobibor and Treblinka, which wiped out the poor Jewish masses of Poland and the Jewish bourgeoisie of Western Europe. These men were hardened killers, inured to death and destruction, although few of them were con-victed psychopaths like Hoess at Auschwitz. They did not become extremely violent; most of them started off like that, indefinitely deferring and evading recognition of their own awfulness through black humour and talk of production targets. Indeed, the final statistical reckoning, drawn up by Globocnik in December 1943 precisely enumerated the vast sums garnered in the process, as well as nearly two thousand waggonloads of bedding, towels and clothing, and such things as sunglasses, opera-glasses, powder-puffs and silver cigarette cases.

Following the silent eradication of these three killing centres, many of the T-4 men involved were despatched southwards to the Dalmatian Coast to operate an extermination and torture centre in the Risiera — or rice warehouse — at Trieste. There they killed bottlenecked transports of Jews *en route* to Auschwitz, as well as Italians and Yugoslavs vaguely suspected of partisan activities.

Meanwhile, in the asylums of Germany, 'euthanasia' killings went on, using slow starvation on specially conceived diets, designed to minimise the cost of lethal drugs necessary to complete the process. At meetings in the regional health ministries, psychiatrists exchanged 'menus' consisting of nothing more than root vegetables in fluid, whose express object was to kill patients. There were no actual food shortages, since most asylums produced large surpluses on the backs of patient labour, which the administrators then sold at profit to Nazi organisations. There is also the matter of doctors such as Friedrich Mennecke and his wife Eva gorging themselves to excess while his patients expired through hunger. Death was visited upon anyone deemed unproductive or whose behaviour or manner irritated the staff, with patients sometimes being co-opted into killing their fellow inmates. Many of the victims were foreign forced labourers, for killing them on the spot was deemed cheaper than repatriation. In cases where nurses were drawn from religious orders, hardened T-4 killers such as Pauline Kneissler were brought in, with the recorded mortality rate spiralling high, only to fall when, in her case, she went on holiday for a week or two. In other institutions, the nursing staff participated in killings because their training had told them to do what they were told, because institutional culture desensitised what little sensitivity they possessed and because they were often bitter, frustrated, disillusioned, tired, underpaid and undervalued.

Obviously, policies like the ones described above, which were impossible to keep secret, did nothing for the image of either asylums or psychiatry. More importantly, they were like sawing off the branch upon which one was sitting, for depopulated asylums were usually alienated for non-medical purposes. In order to counteract these unwanted tendencies, psychiatrists working for T-4, such as Paul Nitsche or Carl Schneider, put forward various proposals for the 'modernisation' of psychiatry by using the funds saved through these killings to provide up-to-date therapies for acute cases. The more or less explicit subsidiary agenda was to build up university-based research activities by integrating them with the neurological 'material' made available to the professors through the 'euthanasia' programme. These plans were thus about reasserting professional psychiatric control over policies that were economically driven, whose effect was to put young recruits off entirely and whose logic threatened the existence of this entire branch of medicine. They were thus a form of *ex post facto* rationalisation, a means of evading the fact that these men had in fact created conditions in the asylums which a few enlightened doctors there described as a 'reversion to the psychiatry of the Middle Ages', with untended and skeletal patients lying naked in their own excrement and urine on straw sacks, and people locked alone in dark vermin-infested bunkers. Doctors strode the wards not as 'modernising' idealists but as self-styled 'soldiers' for whom the patients, particularly if they were people who spoke not a word of German, had literally become 'the enemy'.

Saving Money, Spending Lives
Michael Burleigh, *Death and Deliverance: 'Euthanasia' in Germany c. 1900–1945* (Cambridge, 1994); Jeremy Noakes and Geoffrey Pridham (eds), *Nazism, 1919–1945: A Documentary Reader* (Exeter, 1989), vol. 3; Paul Weindling, *Health, Race and German Politics Between National Unification and Nazism, 1870–1945* (Cambridge 1989).

CHAPTER VII

CHRISTINE LEHMANN AND MAZURKA ROSE: TWO 'GYPSIES' IN THE GRIP OF GERMAN BUREAUCRACY, 1933–60

Wolfgang Wippermann

O N 17 JANUARY 1942 TWENTY-TWO YEAR OLD Christine Lehmann was summonsed by the criminal police in the Ruhr town of Duisburg. She was ordered immediately to abandon the 'marriage-like relationship' she was having with the van driver Karl H. Refusal would result in 'assignment to a concentration camp', for Christine Lehmann was 'a member of the Gypsy clan Lehmann', and 'membership of a clan' constituted 'an impediment to marriage'. There was also no question of Christine Lehmann and Karl H. continuing to live together out of wedlock, for this would prejudice 'the maintenance of the purity of Aryan blood'.

In order to understand what lay behind the inhumanly pedestrian language used in this and further communications with Christine Lehmann, it is necessary to say a little about the legal position of so-called 'Gypsies', or Sinti and Roma as they prefer to call themselves in the Third Reich. The Roma, or Romany, differed from Sinti — many of whose forefathers had been in Germany since the fifteenth century — with respect to their customs and pronunciation of the Romanes (or Romany) language. However, few outsiders beyond a handful of so-called experts on 'Gypsies' were aware of these differences. The authorities certainly did not differentiate between Sinti and Roma. As far as they were concerned, both ethnic groups were simply 'Gypsies', who were subject to special laws, and who could be summarily deported if they could not prove German citizenship.

Strictly speaking, Sinti and Roma were already second-class citizens before Hitler's accession to power. By virtue of the Bavarian Law for the Combating of Gypsies, Travellers and the Workshy of 16 July 1926, Sinti and Roma could be sent to a workhouse for up to two years if they were unable to provide proof of regular employment. Following the National Socialists' abrogation of all residual civil rights between 1933 and 1934, Sinti and Roma were in even less of a position to protect themselves against discrimination than before. Low-ranking officials and some local authorities used this new situation further to inhibit their right to earn a living or their freedom of movement. From 1934 onwards various towns endeavoured to confine Sinti and Roma in so-called 'Gypsy camps', which were hardly fit for human habitation. Initially there was no legal sanction for this, since Sinti and Roma were not specifically mentioned in National Socialist racial legislation. This was true of, for example, the Law for the Restoration of the Professional Civil Service of 7 April 1933, which licensed the dismissal of Jewish civil servants; the law of 14 July 1933 sanctioning the compulsory sterilisation of the allegedly hereditarily ill; and finally, of the Nuremberg Laws of 15 September 1935 which effectively took away the citizenship of German Jews and forbade them to marry or have sexual relations with 'citizens of German or related blood'. Sinti and Roma were not even mentioned in the so-called Marriage Health Law of 18 October 1935 to which the Duisburg criminal police were referring in their summons to Christine Lehmann. These deficiencies were remedied in the successive decrees that accompanied the implementation of these laws. For example the 'first decree concerning the implementation of the Law for the Protection of German blood and honour' stipulated that marriages could not be contracted if, in general, 'the progeny would constitute a threat to the purity of German blood'. A decree issued by the Minister of the Interior on 26 November 1935 concluded that this would be so in the case of 'marriages between persons of German blood with Gypsies, Negroes and their bastards'.

In the absence of formal legislation concerning Gypsies, the Duisburg criminal police availed themselves of this decree in the case of Christine Lehmann. How, one might ask, had she and Karl H. managed to stay together until 1942? As early as 8 December 1938 Heinrich Himmler had ordered the 'final solution of the Gypsy Question in accordance with the nature of their race' and in May 1940 some 2,500 German Sinti and Roma had been deported from westerly regions of the Reich to the Generalgouvernement in occupied Poland. Among the latter were the parents and six siblings of Christine Lehmann, who may herself have been spared because at that time 'Gypsies married to persons of German blood were to be excluded from deportation'. Such caution was no longer in evidence by 1942. The Duisburg criminal police now regarded the 'marriage-like relationship' of Christine Lehmann and Karl H. as being 'asocial'. They put the town health authorities, with their army of professional snoopers, on the case. A few months later, a zealous female welfare official reported that she had 'encountered' Christine Lehmann 'with her husband'. Christine Lehmann had cooked for him and 'the home looked as though two persons with children slept (!) there'. Christine also delivered express letters for Karl H.

In other words, Christine Lehmann was exactly what the authorities normally wanted Gypsies to be, in the sense that she was manifestly socially conformist. She looked after her family as a wife, mother and provider of income. Paradoxically, it was precisely these prosaic activities that led to her being categorised as 'asocial' on racial-ideological grounds. She was summonsed once more on 30 January 1943 by the Duisburg criminal police, who by this time had compiled a comprehensive 'hereditary and life history questionnaire' about both her and her entire family. In the box asking: 'Which members of the clan have led a markedly irregular, unsteady, drifting way of life, or have frequently changed their habitation and place of work? Which are workshy or vagrants? Which seem to be criminals?' the Duisburg criminal police wrote: 'The Lehmann clan belongs to the Gypsy people and, until they settled, continually moved around, deriving their living from the sale of haberdashery. With the exception of the person under consideration here, the entire clan was resettled in the East on 16 May 1940.' This was a *de facto* death sentence for Christine Lehmann. However, at first she appeared to be fortunate. Unlike the majority of German Sinti and Roma she was not deported to the 'Gypsy camp' at Auschwitz in early 1943. The records are imprecise as to why this oversight occurred. Perhaps the reason was that at this time she had not yet been subjected to 'racial investigation', which was one of the necessary preconditions for the 'regularised' deportation of a Sintiza (a Sinti woman) to Auschwitz.

This deficiency was remedied in June 1943, according to a communication dated 10 June from the Essen criminal police to their colleagues in neighbouring Duisburg. They used Christine Lehmann's 'Gypsy' name and added the letters 'ZM' after it to signify (*Zigeunermischling*) or 'Gypsy halfcaste'. This took care of all the preliminaries needed to send someone to Auschwitz. However, this still appeared impossible. The criminal police in Essen went on to remark that 'assignment of Gypsy persons to the concentration camp at Auschwitz is not possible at present on sanitary grounds'. Of course, the criminal police did not simply release Christine Lehmann. She was detained in 'police preventive custody by virtue of the general provisions for the 'preventive fight against crime'. Her 'asocial' and 'community-endangering behaviour', as the pleonastic jargon had it, or in other words her illicit sexual relationship with a German, was sufficient pretext for her continued detention. The gentlemen from the police also drew attention to 'her constant efforts to flee so as to avoid the projected confinement'.

Without evidently realising it, the criminal police in Duisburg had made an error. People taken into 'police preventive custody' were normally detained in nearby concentration camps rather than sent to the extermination camps in the East. A higher department of the Essen criminal police spotted the error, drawing attention in a letter dated 10 June 1943, regarding the 'detention order' issued against Christine Lehmann — for this was paper dealing with more paper — to the fact that 'in her case one is dealing with a Gypsy person whose transfer to the Gypsy camp of the concentration camp at Auschwitz is in accordance with the decree of the Reich Main Security Office of 29 January 1943'. This recommended improvement was relayed to the Reich Criminal Police Office in Berlin. They, in turn, decreed that Christine Lehmann should not be sent to a concentration camp in Germany, where her chances of survival would have been marginally better, but rather to the extermination camp at Auschwitz-Birkenau, where her chances would be practically nil. Almost as an afterthought, the Reich Criminal Police added that since Christine Lehmann's children were 'Gypsy half-castes', they should accompany their mother too. They meant four-year-old Egon and twenty-month-old Robert.

Executing these orders proved difficult for the criminal police in Duisburg. The parents of Karl H. — who by this time was serving at the Front — refused to surrender the two children. The criminal police in Duisburg decided, *faute de mieux*, to deport Christine Lehmann unaccompanied by her small children. Somewhat frustrated they reported on 3 February 1944 that Christine Lehmann was on her own in the concentration camp at Auschwitz. In the meantime, baby Robert had been taken in by a sister of Karl H. who lived in Luxemburg. This presented the police with a taxing problem; their colleagues in the Duisburg welfare department refused to oblige by making available a nurse to pick up the child, because Allied bombing had made travel more than usually arduous.

Eventually, the criminal police in Duisburg nerved themselves to send an officer to bring the child back. The 'costs . . . up to the handing over of the prisoner to the concentration camp' were 'defrayed by the responsible criminal police office under heading 14, item 33'. On 12 March 1944 the police could finally regard the job as having been properly done. They reported that five-year-old Egon and Robert, who was almost two, had 'been transferred to Auschwitz by individual transport'. It is doubtful whether the family enjoyed even the briefest of reunions. Christine Lehmann died on 28 March 1944, 'as a result of enteritis and physical weakness in the sick-bay of the camp at Auschwitz'. The criminal police officer responsible for the case made a final laconic entry in his records: 'There are no known relatives here. In so far as there was a relationship between Lehmann and the van driver H. — who is in the army at present — the latter's mother has been informed of the demise. The legal heirs are Lehmann's two children Egon and Robert who are in the camp at Auschwitz.' Egon, Robert and Christine Lehmann were among the 500,000 people whom the National Socialists murdered because they were Sinti and Roma.

Mazurka Rose was spared this fate. However, although he survived persecution by the National Socialists, he was not recognised as a victim by the Federal German authorities after 1945, and indeed experienced continued discrimination in the post-war period. He shared this fate with many other Sinti and Roma who had survived Nazi persecution.

Mazurka Rose was born on 20 July 1911 in Bärwalde near the East Prussian city of Königsberg. He came from a Roma family which had migrated to Germany from Hungary in the nineteenth century. In common with other Sinti, Roma or, for that matter, Polish or Jewish nineteenth-century immigrants, the Rose family had acquired German citizenship.

In 1937 Mazurka Rose, his wife, mother and some of his brothers and sisters were confined in the 'Gypsy camp' set up at Marzahn in Berlin, where they occupied 'waggon 75'. This camp was established in the summer of 1936 on the joint initiative of the municipal welfare authorities, the police and the Racial Political Office of the National Socialist Party. The ostensible motive was the desire of the National Socialist government to remove 'blots' on the image of the city currently hosting the summer Olympic Games. The blots included sites occupied by Sinti and Roma scattered across the city. On 16 July 1936 the police herded together about six hundred Sinti and Roma in a so-called 'Gypsy camp' on an insalubrious site in the north-eastern suburb of Marzahn, which was thenceforth put under permanent guard and ringed with fencing. The inmates of the camp received inadequate accommodation, elementary sanitary facilities, poor food and minimal medical attention. In early 1939 the authorities noted 'numerous cases of scarlet fever, diphtheria and tuberculosis', and were concerned about 'the danger that the population of Marzahn might contract these diseases'. They therefore recommended the 'physical reconstruction' of the camp, and the introduction of a strict regime along the lines of a concentration camp. Such an arrangement would also have the merit of regular legal status. In 1941 the camp's one-class school was closed. At the same time it was decreed that 'in so far as they are still capable of work, aged and infirm Gypsies should carry out . . . clearing work,' while able-bodied Gypsies should be employed in construction work or in factories. Mazurka Rose was sent to work at Soff, the cap manufacturers. However, shortly afterwards he was denounced to the Gestapo and sent to the work training camp at Berlin-Wuhlheide.

This forced labour camp was established in early 1940, following an agreement between the Gestapo and the national railway construction department in Berlin. There were similar forced labour camps in other towns or attached to large concerns. They were retrospectively legitimised by a decree issued by Himmler on 28 May 1941, who simultaneously ordered every Gestapo regional office to set up camps of this sort. Conditions in the camp at Wuhlheide seem to have been particularly squalid. The barracks were overcrowded and food and medical provision were totally inadequate. A large number of inmates fell ill. Prisoners were beaten up by their guards, thrown into drainage ditches and cesspits, or subjected to sadistic tortures such as being crushed between two portable cement-mixing trays. Many of the inmates did not survive. The local registry office at Berlin-Karlhorst gave false information on death certificates, using such stereotypical formulae as 'died from pneumonia', 'heart failure' or 'circulatory disorder' to account for deaths due to maltreatment.

After a few weeks, Mazurka Rose was released and allowed to return to the camp at Marzahn. He was rearrested on 5 October 1942 by the criminal police in Berlin. The latter handed Rose over to the Gestapo, who consigned him to Sachsenhausen concentration camp on 16 December

1942. This was done on the authority of Himmler's circular of 14 December 1937 categorising Sinti and Roma as 'asocial' and sanctioning their detention in police 'preventive custody'. In Sachsenhausen, Mazurka Rose was categorised as 'Aso [asocial] Gypsy'. On 17 July 1944 he was transferred to Dachau, where he was categorised under the rubric 'AZR' (Reich Forced Labour) in reference to the large-scale raids against the 'asocial' conducted under the operational heading 'Action Workshy Reich' in June 1938.

In 1945 Mazurka Rose was liberated by the Americans from Blaichach, a satellite camp of Dachau. Although he had survived, his wife, children and mother had been murdered in the extermination camp at Auschwitz following their deportation from Berlin on 5 May 1943. After the war, Mazurka Rose resumed his job as a carpet and rug dealer and remarried. On 21 December 1950 he applied to the Bavarian regional compensation office for compensation for the physical and material damage he had incurred in various concentration camps between 1942 and 8 May 1945. In other words, he failed to claim compensation for his detention in the 'Gypsy camp' at Marzahn or the 'work training camp' at Wuhlheide, which he would certainly be entitled to do today with considerable chance of success. This reticence turned out to be mistaken, for on 10 August 1953 the Bavarian regional compensation office rejected his application on the grounds that 'he had not been imprisoned because of his race, but because he was not engaged in regular employment'. Mazurka Rose decided to contest this decision in the courts. However, on 18 August 1954 the third compensation chamber of the Munich regional court rejected his appeal. The court argued that in contrast to his relatives, Mazurka Rose had been sent to a concentration camp 'too soon', that is before Himmler's decree of 16 December 1942 despatching all German Sinti and Roma to Auschwitz. Mazurka Rose had actually been sent to Sachsenhausen on the day this decree was issued. Unfortunately, on 7 January 1956 the Federal Supreme Court decided to endorse the view that Sinti and Roma had only been subject to racial persecution following the decree sending them to Auschwitz. All previous measures, notably the deportations of April 1940, whose legal status was the question at issue in this hearing, were evidently not inspired by racial-ideological motives. This had particular relevance for those Sinti and Roma who had been categorised as 'asocial' by the decree issued by Himmler on 14 December 1937 and had thence been sent to concentration camps. In other words, the Federal Supreme Court had decided that it was completely legitimate to confine Sinti and Roma and the 'asocial' in general in concentration camps.

The decision of the Munich regional court reflected this thinking, managing to emulate the language and outlook of the Nazis in the reasons given for their judgement. The court declared that Mazurka Rose had been sent to Sachsenhausen and Dachau as an 'Aso Gypsy' because 'he was workshy, refusing to work', and had 'carried out sabotage at the workplace'. In the concentration camps he had worn the 'black triangle which designated the workshy'. The court came to the following conclusion: 'All of these circumstances suggest that the plaintiff was not categorised as being workshy on account of his membership of the Gypsy people; rather, how [the authorities] regarded one individual proved crucial, and this cannot be taken to justify the claim of persecution upon racial grounds.' Setting aside the unfortunate choice of words in the second part of this sentence, with its implication that it might be possible to justify racial persecution, it is necessary to emphasise that the National Socialists did indeed deduce 'asociality' simply from 'membership of the Gypsy people'. Even a passing acquaintance with the publications of a Nazi expert on Gypsies, such as Dr Robert Ritter, would have been enough to set the court to rights on this question.

The court's judgement had certain untoward consequences for Mazurka Rose. The only 'expert' witness called was a criminal police inspector called Geyer. This was the same Georg Geyer who, along with other colleagues, had been responsible for the deportation of Bavaria's Gypsies before 1945, but who nonetheless was still operating in the Travellers Department of the Bavarian Regional Criminal Police. On 19 August 1954, one day after the completion of the oral hearing of Mazurka Rose's case, Geyer put in a special request to the residents' registration office in Essen and both the trade inspectors and criminal police in Hamburg. Because the Munich criminal police had Mazurka Rose in their records as a 'traveller', and because he had been unable to produce a birth certificate at the time of his second marriage, and finally, because he had described himself to the court as 'a member of the so-called Romany people', Geyer had decided that Rose's 'nationality remains unclear'. Henceforth, the Munich criminal police office had decided to regard Rose as being 'stateless . . . until such time as unimpeachable proof exists concerning his nationality'. Geyer asked the authorities he contacted 'carefully to re-examine the information which led to Rose being issued with identity papers, including both his passport and itinerant trading licence'.

This threatened Rose's entire professional existence. Without German identity papers he would find it very difficult to obtain an itinerant trading licence which he needed in order to continue to purchase and sell rugs and carpets.

On 30 August 1954 Geyer asked the criminal police in Hamburg to check whether Rose's brothers Karl Rose, Alfred Weiss and Josef Rose had legitimately acquired German citizenship. Geyer justified this request by remarking that the Rose family were 'Roma Gypsies, whose forefathers had illegally entered Germany from Hungary in about 1870'. In a further communication, dated 14 October 1954, the Bavarian criminal police openly admitted where they had got the intelligence that the forefathers of Rose and his family had illegally come to Germany in about 1870. They had discovered 'watertight evidence' in the Bavarian regional criminal police headquarters gleaned from 'investigations of individuals'. What they omitted to mention was that these records were those of the Reich Central Office for the Combating of the Gypsy Nuisance, the Nazis' central agency involved in persecuting Sinti and Roma, and also the findings of the 'racial hygienic research institute in the Reich Office of Health', the agency run by the notorious Robert Ritter. The department for nationality questions within the office for legal affairs of the city of Hamburg also referred on 18 August 1955 to the research materials of Ritter's agency which, during the Nazi period, 'had refereed every Gypsy'. This material led the department for nationality questions to conclude on 27 April 1956 that there were no grounds for claiming that Mazurka Rose had 'ever possessed or acquired German citizenship' and that therefore he was to be regarded as being 'stateless'. It is almost incomprehensible that the scientifically dubious findings of Ritter's agency, which before 1945 had played a critical role in the persecution of Sinti and Roma, should have been used by the Federal authorities after the war not only to deny claims to compensation, but even to challenge the victims' right to German citizenship.

The 'research' on the Roma in question was carried out first by Ritter's colleague Dr Karl Moravek, and then by Ritter's girlfriend and quondam postgraduate pupil Eva Justin. She wrote an article about her research in the journal *Neues Volk* published by the National Socialists' Racial Political Office in 1944. She began by remarking that 'in the sixties and seventies of the last century several clans of a semi-nomadic Gypsy tribe from the Hungarian-Slovakian border region traversed the open frontier with Germany'. Once there, they had 'paid large sums of money to native

Sinti Gypsies, German travellers and even indigeneous Germans in order to acquire documents and identity papers' and thus 'had illicitly come into possession of German citizenship'. This same claim was repeated almost word for word by the post-war officials of the Bavarian regional criminal police. Naturally, Eva Justin had no hard evidence for her assertion that all Roma had illegally assumed German citizenship. Today it is possible neither to prove nor disprove this assertion, any more than it is to establish the exact origins of all those Germans — and a glance at a telephone book would reveal the scale of the problem — who have Polish, Russian, Czech, Slovak, Huguenot or Hungarian names, whose deportation on the grounds of illegal entry is presumably on no one's agenda.

In any case it is indisputable that many Roma, including the Rose family, were in possession of German citizenship, and that not even the notoriously racist Nazis had endeavoured to contest this. Mazurka Rose's mother Lisa and some of his sisters were only formally declared 'enemies of the state and nation' or 'enemies of the Reich' after their deportation. The object of this strategy, which was also used in the case of German Jews deported to the East, was to facilitate confiscation of the goods they left behind under the provisions of the Law for the Confiscation of the Property of Enemies of the State and Nation of 14 July 1933. In the case of Mazurka Rose's mother, some RM30 was confiscated 'for the benefit of the Reich'. As seen above, Mazurka Rose himself was sent to a concentration camp following Himmler's decree of 14 December 1937, something that could only be done in the case of German citizens. Put briefly, in the eyes of the Nazis the Roses were indisputably German citizens.

In this respect therefore, the Bavarian regional criminal police were far more radical and hostile to Gypsies than the Nazis had been, and were content merely to rely upon the research 'findings' of Ritter's racial hygienic research bureau to legitimise their actions. It is time to return once again to Eva Justin's article about the Roma Gypsies. In order to prove her claim that the Roma had illegally acquired German citizenship, Eva Justin referred to a number of anthropological and sociological characteristics of the Roma that allegedly distinguished them in a negative light from indigenous Sinti. She was not referring to alleged or real differences in language or their system of taboos, but rather to differences in appearance and behaviour. While the 'undemanding' Sinti 'eked out a miserable living through music-making and seasonal work, but mainly through begging, fortune telling and minor acts of deception, and almost without exception had more or less lengthy criminal records consisting of short spells in prison', the Roma were by contrast 'casually but elegantly dressed textile dealers', the 'most intelligent of whom' were wealthy people who 'even in the first years of the war had driven past our institute in heavy foreign lorries'.

However, in ways reminiscent of Christine Lehmann's unimpeachable lifestyle, it was precisely this evidence of socio-economic success that both Eva Justin and her disciples in the Bavarian criminal police used negatively against the Roma. According to criminal police officer Eller, 'all Roma Gypsies . . . were extremely cunning and for the most part well-off dealers . . . who once used to be horse dealers, but who for the last twenty years or so have mostly worked as textile traders'. The same claim can be found in Eva Justin's article, which moreover claimed that 'up to 1942 most of the 2,000 odd Roma Gypsies in Germany managed to make a living from large-scale black-market trading in textiles and other consumer goods in short supply'. Predictably, there was no evidence for this claim. Justin merely referred to the painstaking and tenacious endeavours of Berlin-based experts in Gypsy matters under one Leo Karsten, who had succeeded 'in bringing about 200 of the 400 adult Roma in Berlin before the courts as parasites on the nation'. Among those 'parasites' brought before the courts by the Berlin 'Gypsy' police was Mazurka Rose.

Justin considered it 'of racial-biological interest' that 'the worst Roma blackmarketeering families . . . evinced fewer physical characteristics typical of Gypsies'. Indeed, a few of them were beyond racial 'diagnostic classification' altogether. It was difficult to ascertain whether they were Gypsies or South-East Europeans. This was an involuntary admission of just how difficult it was to achieve precision in this branch of 'scientific' research, none of which stopped Justin from further flights of academic fancy. She went on to claim that in the case of a few Roma, 'their overwhelmingly Near Eastern or oriental physical characteristics, their gestures and smoothly cunning trading practice left a pronouncedly Jewish impression'.

It is more than shocking that racial differences between Sinti and Roma 'discovered' by Nazi 'experts' should have been perpetuated by Federal German authorities after 1945, and that the latter frequently had recourse to the findings of the former. This is evident in a letter written by a senior police official in Hamburg on 3 November 1960 which referred to materials left on file by the 'former expert on Gypsies L. Karsten'. This was the same Karsten who had decided that Mazurka Rose and a further 200 Roma Gypsies were 'parasites on the nation', and who had sent Rose's mother and sisters and another 252 Berlin Gypsies to Auschwitz. Relying upon his expertise in this matter was tantamount to asking Adolf Eichmann for expert testimony in compensation cases brought by Jews. But this was precisely what the Hamburg criminal police were doing as they wrote in this letter of the 'valuable materials' from the Racial Hygienic Research Bureau which 'according to the testimony of former staff members of the archive on Gypsy clans had survived the collapse of 1945' and now lay 'in the form of microfilm with the Bavarian regional criminal police'.

Mazurka Rose never regained his German citizenship. He died prematurely on 14 July 1962 at the age of fifty-one, quite possibly because of damage to his health sustained during his spells in various camps. An official physician whom Rose had asked for a report on his state of health, had categorised his condition as 'hereditary'. Mazurka Rose's son Georg Rose, who was born in 1949, was still 'stateless' in 1992; his attempts to gain German citizenship had been totally unsuccessful. The judgements against his father were confirmed, notwithstanding the fact that they were unjust and unconstitutional. Article sixteen of the German Constitution says: 'German citizenship may not be withdrawn. Loss of citizenship can only ensue following the promulgation of a law and against the will of the person affected in so far as the person affected is not thereby rendered stateless.' Article sixteen is a basic law. Like other basic laws, such as freedom of the Press, of assembly and the inviolability of one's own home, 'its essentials ... can never be challenged' (Article 19.2 Basic Law).

Two 'Gypsies' in the Grip of German Bureaucracy
Ute Brucker-Boroujerdi and Wolfgang Wippermann, 'Die Rassen-hygienische und Erbbiologische Forschungsstelle im Reichsgesund-heitsamt', *Bundesgesundheitsblatt*, vol. 32 (Bonn, 1989); Michael Burleigh and Wolfgang Wippermann, *The Racial State: Germany, 1933–1945* (Cambridge, 1991); David Crowe and John Kolsti, *The Gypsies of Eastern Europe* (New York, 1991); Donald Kenrick and Grattan Puxon, *The Destiny of Europe's Gypsies* (London, 1982); Wolfgang Wippermann, 'Nationalsozialistische Zwangslager in Berlin, 1936–1945', in Wolfgang Ribbe (ed.), *Berlin-Forschungen*, vol. 2 (Berlin,

1987); Michael Zimmermann, *Verfolgt, Vertrieben, Vernichtet. Die Nationalsozialistische Vernichtungspolitik gegen Sinti und Roma* (Essen, 1989).

CHAPTER VIII

SAVAGE WAR

Omer Bartov

BETWEEN 1941 AND 1945 THE THIRD REICH conducted the most savage military campaign in modern history. The invasion of the Soviet Union, code-named Operation Barbarossa, cost the lives of between 20 and 30 million Soviet citizens, well over half of whom were civilians, and devastated vast areas of western Russia from Leningrad in the north to Stalingrad in the south. Over three million Red Army prisoners of war, or 60 per cent of the number of Soviet soldiers captured, died in German captivity. Although the Soviet Union emerged from the war as a military superpower, it took decades to recover from the human tragedy and economic disaster of the German occupation.

The German war in Russia raises a number of important questions, relevant both to the history of the Third Reich as a whole and to the history of modern warfare. First, why Barbarossa was conducted in such a savage manner and what ends this policy was expected to serve; second, to what degree the soldiers fighting at the Front participated in the murderous actions of the regime and what effect the character of the fighting had on their morale, motivation and perception of reality; third, whether the war in the east was indeed a unique and unprecedented phenomenon in modern history by comparison to other instances of brutal warfare.

War played a central role in Nazi ideology. It was no coincidence that Hitler called his book *Mein Kampf*, that is, 'my battle'. According to the Nazi world-view, life consisted of a constant struggle for survival in which the best would win, or rather, in which the very fact of victory and survival would show the inherent physical and spiritual superiority of the winner, on the one hand, and the inferiority and moral depravity of the vanquished, on the other. Traditional norms of behaviour, ethical conventions and legal restrictions had nothing to do with this eternal battle; all that mattered was survival through victory and total annihilation of the enemy. Conversely, battle did have a profoundly ennobling effect, for in it the best qualities of the individual were called forth and the nation was purged of all slackness and degeneration. Thus war was not merely an inevitable condition, but also a necessary and welcome one. War forged a community of battle, a *Kampfgemeinschaft*, which in turn would produce the community of the people, the *Volksgemeinschaft*, that Nazi ideal of a racially pure, militarised, fanatically determined society, where affinities of blood and endless conquest would compensate for class inequality and lack of political freedom.

The ideal war, according to Hitler, was one of conquest, extermination and subjugation; the ideal area in which to conduct such a war was in the east, where the German people would win for itself the living space, or *Lebensraum*, necessary for its moral and racial purity, as well as for its ultimate emergence as the master race (*Herrenvolk*) of Europe and Asia, if not indeed the whole world. However, due to political and military constraints, this ideal could not be immediately realised. Before turning to the east, the Third Reich first had to make certain that its western flank was secure. Germany had experienced a two-front war between 1914 and 1918, and Hitler was determined to prevent a recurrence of such a hopeless strategic situation. Also, while the Western Powers were quite willing to let Germany fight it out with Bolshevik Russia, Stalin was unwilling to take the main brunt of Nazi military might and concluded a pact with Hitler which enabled the Third Reich first to smash Poland and divide its territory with the USSR, and then to turn against France.

The fighting in the west was inherently different from what was soon to be seen in the east. This had to do both with ideological determinants and with political calculation. Nazi racial theory placed the Jews at the very bottom of the racial ladder; they were to be simply done away with, whether by exclusion and expulsion (as was done in the early years of the regime) or by extermination, which began to be practised on a mass scale simultaneously with the attack on the Soviet Union. Only slightly higher were the Slavs, who were considered subhumans (*Untermenschen*), to be either murdered, worked and starved to death, or used as slave labour for the German colonisers of their lands. As for the French, and even more so the English, Nazi racial 'experts' remained rather vague, whether because of what they perceived as racial affinities with the German 'Aryans', or because of the 'higher' culture of Western Europe. Thus, while France was seen as a 'degenerate' civilisation, it was not marked for subjugation, but rather for a secondary role in the Nazi scheme of a German-dominated Europe. Politically, Hitler was always keen on reaching some settlement with the British, both because of his ambiguous view of the 'Anglo-Saxon race', and because of his fear of a two-front war.

Consequently, the German army fighting in the west was given strict orders to conduct itself according to the rules of war. This was easier also because the average German soldier had far fewer prejudices about the French and the English than about the Russians, and because Western Europe seemed to him more similar to his homeland than the Russia he was soon to invade.

Once France was defeated, and following Hitler's realisation that he would be able neither to persuade the British to reach an agreement with Germany nor to destroy British military strength whether from the air or by a landing from the sea, the German army was given orders to prepare for an invasion of the Soviet Union. Now at last Hitler could have the war of destruction (*Vernichtungskrieg*) and ideologies (*Weltanschauungskrieg*) he had always wanted to fight. In this he was far from alone, for his generals were in full agreement with the need to conduct a wholly different kind of war against what they called 'Judeo-Bolshevism' and the 'Asiatic hordes' of the east.

The Barbarossa Decree was composed of the operational orders for the attack on the Soviet Union, as well as of what have come to be called the 'criminal orders', a set of instructions regarding the manner in which the army was to conduct itself during the campaign. These included the infamous 'commissar order', calling for the immediate execution of all Red Army political officers captured by front-line units; the curtailment of military jurisdiction, which stipulated that soldiers could not be tried for offences committed against enemy soldiers and civilians as long as they did not thereby impinge on combat discipline; regulations regarding the behaviour of soldiers in the occupied territories, which called for ruthless punitive action against guerrillas and anyone assisting them, as well as against members of the Communist Party and Jews; and orders for the army closely to collaborate with and furnish military and logistical assistance to the death squads (*Einsatzgruppen*) of the SS, whose task was the mass murder of Jews and all other Soviet citizens belonging to 'biological' and political categories deemed unworthy of life by the authorities of the Third Reich.

To these orders the army added a series of logistical instructions, based on the assumption that in order to conduct a rapid campaign deep into Russia the units should not be hampered by a cumbersome supply apparatus, whose maintenance was expected to confront numerous difficulties because of the Soviet Union's primitive transportation infrastructure and a serious shortage of vehicles in the *Wehrmacht*. The conclusion was that, as far as possible, the army should sustain itself from the resources of the (often wretchedly poor) occupied population, with scant regard for the obvious repercussions this policy would have on the civilians' chances of survival. Moreover, the cold utilitarian calculation of operational efficiency was allied with the determination of the Nazi leadership not to allow any undue hardship among the German population in the rear as a result of the war, thereby preventing the outbreak of protests and demoralisation of the kind that had swept Germany during the latter phases of the First World War. Consequently, the army and the civil administrative authorities that followed it into the Soviet Union were ordered to exploit the agricultural, industrial and demographic resources of the occupied territories to the benefit of Germany. It was estimated that this would cause the death by deprivation of tens of millions of Russians, but this was greeted with satisfaction in view of the perceived need to 'depopulate' the eastern *Lebensraum* so as to make it ripe for German colonisation.

Closely tied to the military aspects of the operation was the decision to use this opportunity to 'eliminate' European Jewry once and for all, a policy officially sanctioned (though actually already in an advanced stage of execution) at the Wannsee Conference of January 1942, during which the work of the various agencies involved in the Final Solution was brought under the overall control of the SS six months after the attack on Russia was launched. The so-called 'Final Solution of the Jewish Question' by mass, industrial murder of the Jewish population of Europe, could hardly have taken the form which characterised it between 1941 and 1945 had the *Wehrmacht* not created the necessary military, logistical, demographic and psychological precondition for its implementation by its invasion of the Soviet Union and the vicious war it conducted there.

Thus it is clear that Barbarossa was conceived as an ideological war of extermination and enslavement; its goal was to wipe out the Soviet state, to enslave the Russian people after debilitating it by famine and all other forms of deprivation, systematically to murder all 'biological' and political enemies of Nazism, such as the Jews, the Gypsies, members of the Communist Party, intellectuals and so forth, and finally to turn western Russia into a German paradise of Aryan colonisers served by hordes of Slav helots.

For many years after the Second World War it was commonly assumed that although the Nazi regime was obviously criminal and had made use of murderous organisations such as the SS to carry out its policies of extermination, the army was not involved in such actions and in many ways resisted them, or at least kept itself in a position of critical isolation from the more unsavoury aspects of Nazi rule. It is therefore necessary to emphasise that this is a wholly erroneous view, based mainly on apologetic post-war literature by German veterans and its indiscriminate acceptance by Western military historians who remained quite ignorant of the realities of the Eastern Front and tried to apply their experience in the west to the totally different conditions that reigned in Russia between 1941 and 1945.

The fact of the matter is that, once Barbarossa was launched on 22 June 1941, the German combat troops on the ground showed little reluctance, indeed often demonstrated much enthusiasm, in carrying out the 'criminal orders' issued by the regime and the high command of the army. Nor did the field commanders do much to restrain the troops; quite the contrary, in many cases formation commanders exhorted their soldiers to act with even greater ferocity and determination against the 'racial' and political enemies of the Reich.

The commander of the Sixth Army, Walthar von Reichenau, appealed to his troops on 10 October 1941:

> Regarding the conduct of the troops towards the Bolshevik system many unclear ideas still remain.
>
> The essential goal of the campaign against the Jewish-Bolshevik system is the complete destruction of its power instruments and the eradication of the Asiatic influence on the European cultural sphere. Thereby the troops too have *tasks*, which go beyond the conventional unilateral soldierly tradition [*Soldatentum*]. In the East the soldier is not only a fighter according to the rules of warfare, but also a carrier of an inexorable racial conception [*völkischen Idee*] and the avenger of all the bestialities which have been committed against the Germans and related races.
>
> Therefore the soldier must have *complete* understanding for the necessity of the harsh, but just atonement of Jewish subhumanity. This has the further goal of nipping in the bud rebellions in the rear of the *Wehrmacht* which, as experience shows, are always plotted by the Jews.

On 20 November 1941 General Erich von Manstein, commander of the Eleventh Army, issued the following order:

> Since 22 June the German *Volk* is in the midst of a battle for life and death against the Bolshevik system. This battle is conducted against the Soviet army not only in a conventional manner according of the rules of European warfare . . .
>
> Judaism constitutes the mediator between the enemy in the rear and the still fighting remnants of the Red Army and the Red leadership. It has a stronger hold than in Europe on all key positions of the political leadership and administration, it occupies commerce and trade and further forms cells for all the disturbances and possible rebellions.
>
> The Jewish-Bolshevik system must be eradicated once and for all. Never again may it interfere in our European living space.
>
> The German soldier is therefore not only charged with the task of destroying the power instrument of this system. He marches forth also as a carrier of a racial conception and as an avenger of all the atrocities which have been committed against him and the German people.
>
> The soldier must show understanding for the harsh atonement of Judaism, the spiritual carrier of the Bolshevik terror . . .

On 25 November 1941, the commander of the Seventeenth Army, Colonel-General Hermann Hoth, issued this order:

> It has become increasingly clear to us this summer, that here in the East spiritually unbridgeable conceptions are fighting each other: German sense of honour and race, and a soldierly tradition of many centuries, against an Asiatic mode of thinking and primitive instincts, whipped up by a small number of mostly Jewish intellectuals: fear of the knout, disregard of moral values, levelling down, throwing away of one's worthless life.
>
> More than ever we are filled with the thought of a new era, in which the strength of the German people's racial superiority and achievements entrust it with the leadership of Europe. We clearly recognise our mission to save European culture from the advancing Asiatic barbarism. We now know that we have to fight against an incensed and tough opponent. This battle can only end with the destruction of one or the other; a compromise is out of the question.

The enormous death-toll among the Russian prisoners of war and civilian population was thus a direct result not merely of the heavy fighting but to a large extent of the implementation of Nazi policies in the occupied regions of the Soviet Union. Hitler had stated unambiguously before the campaign that German troops should not recognise their Soviet enemies as 'comrades in arms'; there were to be, in his words, *keine Kameraden*. Consequently, in the first few months of fighting, the *Wehrmacht* shot out of hand some 600,000 political commissars, and by the end of the first winter in Russia some two million prisoners were already dead. Unlike the Western campaign, the *Wehrmacht* had made no provisions for the very high number of prisoners it expected to capture thanks to its tactics of encirclement. Instead, captured Red Army troops were marched hundreds of miles to the rear or carried in open freight trains in midwinter, and those who survived were then herded into empty fields surrounded by barbed wire and armed guards and allowed to starve to death. The troops became so used to this treatment of Soviet soldiers as *Untermenschen* that even when the orders were changed due to the decision to conscript prisoners for forced labour in the Reich, they refused to relent and kept shooting them out of hand against the express orders of their direct superiors.

As the logistical situation of the *Wehrmacht* deteriorated during autumn and winter 1941, the troops were ordered to resort to extensive requisitions which stripped the population of its last reserves of food and caused widespread famine and death. Intensified guerrilla activity against the *Wehrmacht*, caused not least by desperation occasioned by the horrifying conditions in occupied Russia, brought brutal retaliatory measures which included not merely the hanging of anyone suspected of partisan activity, but also the destruction of thousands of villages and the murder of their inhabitants as part of a policy of collective punishment. Following the Red Army's counter-offensive of December 1941, and thereafter whenever the *Wehrmacht* was forced to retreat, German combat units resorted to a policy of 'scorched earth' which devastated vast regions of abandoned territory and led to the death by deprivation of whoever was not killed right away by the withdrawing troops or sent back to the Reich as slave labour.

Wehrmacht commanders were initially anxious lest such policies should cause demoralisation among their troops. In fact, the result was quite the opposite, for the fighting morale and motivation of the troops seem to have been fortified by the increasingly savage nature of the fighting.

This can be explained by reference to the perception of reality among the troops fighting in the east, which in turn owed much to their ideological training before and during their service in the army. The combat troops of the *Wehrmacht* were young men who had spent their formative years under the Third Reich and were exposed to large doses of indoctrination in Nazified schools and especially in the Hitler Youth and the Reich Labour Service. Thus, by the time these young men were conscripted many of them had already accepted the Nazi view of the war as a racial and ideological struggle for survival against a horde of demonic enemies. This was strongly reflected in their letters home, just as much as in their actual conduct at the front.

In mid-July 1941 Private Fred Fallnbigl wrote from the front:

> Now I know what war really means. But I also know that we had been forced into the war against the Soviet Union. For God have mercy on us, had we waited, or had these beasts come to us. For them even the most horrible death is still too good. I am glad that I can be here to put an end to this genocidal system.

A soldier's letter from Russia in late August 1941:

> Precisely now one recognises perfectly what would have happened to our wives and children had these Russian hordes . . . succeeded in penetrating into our Fatherland. I have had the opportunity here to . . . observe these uncultivated, multi-raced men. Thank God they have been thwarted from plundering and pillaging our homeland.

On 1 September 1941 Lance-Corporal O. Rentzsch wrote:

> It is good to know that this confrontation has already come. If otherwise those hordes had invaded our land, that would have . . . made for great bloodshed. No, now we want to shoulder ourselves all endeavours, in order to eradicate this universal plague.

A non-commissioned officer's letter in July 1942:

> The great task given us in the struggle against Bolshevism, lies in the destruction of eternal Jewry. Once one sees what the Jew has done in Russia, one can well understand why the Führer began the struggle against Jewry. What sorrows would have come to our homeland, had this beast of a man had the upper hand?

Moreover, it was precisely because they were allowed to vent their anger and frustration at the enemy in the course of a costly and increasingly hopeless war, that the soldiers accepted without opposition the extremely harsh, indeed brutal combat discipline enforced by their commanders, which resulted in no less than 20,000 executions of soldiers charged with offences such as desertion, cowardice and self-inflicted wounds. Both the absence of any serious mutinies in the *Wehrmacht* throughout the war and the outstanding determination with which the German army kept fighting until almost the very end, testify to the fact that the troops were both terrified of their own commanders' wrath and, even more so, of the enemy, whom they viewed as a faceless, Satanic entity out to destroy everything they believed in and cherished.

Social historians of the Third Reich have pointed out that the Nazi ideal of creating a *Volksgemeinschaft* where class tensions and inequality would be replaced by national and racial unity under a benign Führer was, in fact, never achieved. Instead, German workers retained a strong class-consciousness and kept up the struggle to improve their material condition and, by implication, to gain political recognition. Evidence has been found of resistance to the regime among the working class, manifested in strikes and intentional lower productivity, as well as in political organisation, quite apart from active resistance to the dictatorship (which was ruthlessly curbed in the first years of the regime). However, what such historians have neglected to address, is the extent to which the tensions between the working class and the regime were expressed once the younger workers were conscripted to the *Wehrmacht*. Although this issue has not been thoroughly researched, it does seem that, contrary to expectations, from the moment such workers became soldiers they no longer presented the regime or their military superiors with any problems of discipline and motivation. We have no evidence of mutinies of soldiers stemming from class-consciousness and lingering opposition to a regime that had obviously not fulfilled its perceived promises of at least partial equality. On the other hand, some recent work on attitudes among workers in the Ruhr industrial region, based on interviews conducted in the 1980s, seems to indicate that many workers were in fact quite pleased with the economic achievements of the Nazis, which meant that unemployment was drastically reduced (thanks to a vast programme of rearmament) and consequently led to a significant improvement in the standard of living. Moreover, it now seems that Nazi ideology was also much more successful in penetrating the strongholds of the working class than had been previously thought, particularly among the young. Men interviewed forty years later stated that they had joined the Hitler Youth with a great deal of enthusiasm, and did not view it as contradicting their identity as workers.

Gustav Köppke, son of Communist workers in the Ruhr industrial region, was interviewed in 1981. On watching the *Kristallnacht* pogrom in 1938 at the age of nine, he said:

> It was terribly impressive, when the SA marched . . . I was on the side of the strong guys; the Jews, they were the others.

On being a member of the Hitler Youth:

> Our workers' suburb and the Hitler Youth were in no way contradictory . . . this idea of the Hitler Youth versus the people, you shouldn't see it as if we young lads had to decide for something or against something; there was nothing else . . . and whoever wanted to become something belonged to it . . . The Hitler Youth uniform was something positive in our childhood.

On experiencing the defeat of Germany as a volunteer to the SS Hitler Youth Division:

> I was raised then, in the National Socialist time and had seen the world just as they had shown it to us . . . And suddenly nothing made sense any more.

Gisberg Pohl, another son of a working-class family interviewed in 1981, had this to say on participating in the suppression of the Warsaw rising as a member of an SS Division:

> Being a young man one easily made too much of it. We had after all gone to Russia, we wanted there [to destroy] subhumanity — That is, I was, strongly convinced of my task, that I was right. And once it goes that far, then you don't think about it much, then only one thing remains, then you know very well, either him or me.

These findings, taken together with the general high motivation of German troops, seem to indicate that even if the *Volksgemeinschaft* remained largely a myth (though a highly potent one nevertheless), its military counterpart, the *Kampfgemeinschaft*, or the community of battle, served not only as a powerful ideal but was very much seen by many soldiers as a true reflection of reality. Hence, by observing the conduct of soldiers at the front we can now gain a new perspective on the social history of the Third Reich as a whole. Furthermore, considering that once the war was over the survivors returned to their previous occupations, one must ask to what extent their experience as Hitler's main instrument of conquest and subjugation moulded their self-perception in the post-war era. This is a particularly pertinent question, because the *Wehrmacht* was in every sense of the word the army of the people, namely a vast conscript army composed of members of all social strata. It was these young men who, following the capitulation, built German post-war society, and it was they who gave it the character it has retained ever since, for better or for worse. The collective memory of the war is thus a crucial element in the new/old German national identity, and still plays a major role today as the newly reunited Germany regains its political stature and increases its already considerable economic might.

This brings us to the question of comparability and uniqueness, key factors in what has come to be known as the process of 'coming to terms with the past' (or as the Germans call it, *Vergangenheitsbewältigung*, roughly translated as 'overcoming the past'). This somewhat ambiguous term stands for the complex confrontation between personal and collective national memory (and its repression), on the one hand, and the memory (or amnesia) of individuals and groups belonging to other national entities, along with historical documentary evidence, on the other; it also refers to the use and abuse of the past by individuals and groups with the view of legitimising either past actions or current opinions and aspirations. While the past is constantly interacting with the present (both forming it and being informed by it in return), some past events and periods are of greater impact and significance than others. There is little doubt that the Nazi regime still plays a major role in the political consciousness and individual psychology of many Germans today. This was witnessed in the 1980s in a number of public debates in the Federal Republic and, particularly, in the German historians' controversy, or the *Historikerstreit*, which began in 1986, and in spite of (or perhaps very much due to) the upheaval of reunification, has remained in the background of much recent scholarship and public debate, thereby reflecting the growing political relevance of the Nazi past to a Germany searching for a new definition of national identity.

The *Historikerstreit*, as the subtitle of one German publication on the issue had it, concerned 'the controversy over the uniqueness of the National Socialist extermination of the Jews'. However, in an even wider sense, the debate was over the uniqueness of everything and anything that took place under the Third Reich, indeed over the meaning of uniqueness in history. From the purely scholarly point of view, the argument against uniqueness raised a valid point; namely, that if uniqueness implies incomparability, then it introduces an ahistorical terminology, that is, it decontextualises the event by wrenching it out of the course of history and thereby rendering it inexplicable, even mythical. In other words, the historian cannot accept that any event in the past is wholly unique, since that would mean that this event would defy any rational historical analysis and understanding. More specifically, however, the argument regarding the uniqueness of the Holocaust does not necessarily mean that it is incomparable. Comparison does not aim to show that two things or events are the same, but rather to shed light on two or more objects or phenomena by demonstrating both their similarities and their differences. Yet the 'revisionists', that is, the German scholars who called for a revision of the history of the Third Reich by means of 'contextualising' it through comparison and 'demystifying' it through 'detached' analysis, had a different aim in mind when they objected to the presentation of Nazism as unique. As their opponents claimed, the 'revisionists', or at least their more extreme representatives, were interested in 'relativising' the history of Nazism, that is, in demonstrating that although the Nazi regime was indeed evil and criminal, there were many others like it, and therefore the Germans had no reason to feel more guilty about their past than any other people, and could calmly go about re-establishing a proud national identity based on a history of great political and cultural achievements.

While these arguments met with fierce opposition in Germany and abroad in so far as they concerned the murder of the Jews, they were received with far more sympathy when applied to the German army's conduct of the war. When the 'revisionist' Ernst Nolte claimed that the only difference between the Holocaust and the Soviet gulags was the use of gas for killing, and that in any case the gulags were the begetters of Auschwitz because Hitler behaved as he did out of fear of the Bolsheviks, both the ethical import of and the documentary evidence for his assertion were forcefully challenged by many of his colleagues. But when Andreas Hillgruber, another highly respected 'revisionist', argued for the need of the historian to identify with the German soldiers' 'heroic' defence of the

Reich from the 'orgy of revenge' with which the Red Army threatened the German civilian population, he touched on a sensitive point for the Germans. The murder of the Jews could be ascribed to a relatively small circle of criminals, that is, could be isolated from the main bulk of the German population (and, as some would have it, from the main current of German history). Not so in the case of the *Wehrmacht*, based as it was on mass conscription and therefore highly representative of German society as a whole. Moreover, the powerful sense of abhorrence of war in post-war Germany, following the destruction visited upon it during the closing phases of the Second World War, has made many Germans view war, any war, as hell. Paradoxically, this view has in turn legitimised the actions of German soldiers in the war as being in no way essentially different from those of all other soldiers. Thus, one finds a combination of anti-war sentiment, apologetics and a sentimental admiration for the men who 'saved' Germany, indeed the whole of Europe, from the 'Bolshevik-Asiatic hordes', along with a powerful rejection of the notion that the *Wehrmacht* had served as Hitler's main instrument in implementing his policies of conquest and genocide.

The view of the *Wehrmacht* as an army like any other is shared by many non-German scholars, especially in the West, and reflects a wider trend in public opinion. This was given expression in former President Reagan's assertion that the soldiers of the *Wehrmacht* buried in the military cemetery of Bitburg were also victims of the Nazi regime. It is therefore of some importance to point out in what respects the German army's conduct in the war was essentially different from that of any other army in modern history.

War is a highly brutal affair, and there is little doubt that individual soldiers can and do become brutalised in the course of fighting. On the individual level there is no difference between, for instance, the killing of civilians by a *Wehrmacht* soldier in Russia, an American soldier in Vietnam or a Soviet soldier in Prussia. Once we shift a little from the individual level, however, we begin to see the differences. German soldiers fighting in Russia were allowed, indeed were ordered, to commit mass killings of people who were clearly not of any direct military threat to them. This was not the case of American GIs in Vietnam, nor of Red Army troops in occupied Germany, even if many such instances did occur. And because this was not the policy, but rather an unauthorised action, the scale of the killing was smaller. The Red Army in Germany had no policy of decimating the German population and turning

Germany into a wasteland fit for Russian colonisation. Had this been the case, we would not have seen the recent reunification of Germany, for there would have been nothing to reunite with. The German army in Russia, on the other hand, followed a clear policy of subjugation and extermination. Had Germany won the war, Russia would have disappeared as a political entity and millions more Russians would have been murdered, with the rest being enslaved by their German colonisers. Nor did the US Army have a policy of genocide in Vietnam, even if it did cause the deaths of hundreds of thousands of innocent civilians. If the Soviet Union installed brutal dictatorships in the East European countries it conquered, these were nevertheless not genocidal regimes, just as an American victory in Vietnam would not have meant the destruction of the Vietnamese people (whose existence under the victorious Communists has not been particularly cheerful either). The strategic bombing of Germany, another example often used by Germans, had no intention of wiping out the German people, even if it was of dubious military value and morally questionable. Moreover, one cannot forget that both the English and the Americans, as well as the Russians, were fighting against Nazi aggression: it was the Third Reich which had striven to conquer Europe, not the British, Americans or even the Soviets.

The *Wehrmacht* did not behave in the same manner everywhere. As has been seen, it was on the Eastern Front that the German army conducted a uniquely savage war. This was possible because of the agreement between the regime and its soldiers on the need to wipe out the Soviet Union, its political system and much of its population. Shared racist sentiments acted as a powerful motivation in the conduct of war in the east. Doubtless, many other armies have known the effect of racism; the US army, both in the Pacific War and in Vietnam, as well as the Japanese army have acted brutally, not least because of a racially-oriented perception of the enemy. Yet racism was not the official policy of the US government, nor was the education of American youths as deeply grounded in racism as that of the German youths of the 1930s. When Japan was occupied by the US army it was not enslaved, even if many American GIs had clearly evolved strongly racist views of the Japanese. The Japanese, on the other hand, did carry out highly brutal policies of occupation motivated by a mixture of imperialist policies and a sense of racial superiority propagated by the regime; it is true that the Japanese army's conduct in China, for instance, comes close to that of the *Wehrmacht* in Russia, just as their treatment of prisoners of war was abominable. Yet even here one must make the qualification that the Japanese did not adopt a policy of genocide. Hence, for instance, the rate of survival of prisoners of war in Japanese hands was twice as high as that of Soviet soldiers in German hands.

It is, indeed, on the issue of genocide that the German army must surely come out worse than any other modern army. This is both because the army itself actively pursued a policy of mass killing of Russians and because it was an essential instrument in the realisation of the Final Solution. The attempt to differentiate between the *Wehrmacht* and the SS, between the fighting at the front and the death camps in the rear presents a wholly false picture of the historical reality. As a number of highly detailed and thorough works have shown, the army was involved in the implementation of the Final Solution at every conceivable level, beginning with the conquest of the areas that contained the highest concentrations of Jewish population, through rendering logistical and manpower support to the *Einsatzgruppen* and the death-camp administrations, to the bitter determination in which it resisted the final and inevitable defeat of the Third Reich at a time when the rate of the industrial killing of millions of human beings reached its peak. The *Wehrmacht* was thus a crucial factor in the most horrendous crime perpetrated by any nation in modern history.

Savage War

O. Bartov, *Hitler's Army: Soldiers, Nazis and War in the Third Reich* (Oxford, 1991); A. Dallin, *German Rule in Russia, 1941–45*, 2nd ed. (London, 1981); W. Deist (ed.), *The German Military in the Age of Total War* (Oxford, 1985); R.J. Evans, *In Hitler's Shadow* (New York, 1989); G. Hirschfeld (ed.), *The Policies of Genocide: Jews and Soviet Prisoners of War in Nazi Germany* (London, 1986); E. Klee et al. (eds), *Those Were the Days: The Holocaust as Seen by its Perpetrators and Bystanders* (London, 1991); C.S. Maier, *The Unmasterable Past* (Cambridge, Mass., 1988); K.-J. Müller, *The Army, Politics and Society in Germany, 1933–45* (New York, 1987); R.J. O'Neill, *The German Army and the Nazi Party, 1933–39* (London, 1966); T. Schulte, *The German Army and Nazi Policies in Occupied Russia* (Oxford, 1989).

CHAPTER IX

THE PLANNING INTELLIGENTSIA AND THE 'FINAL SOLUTION'

Götz Aly

THERE IS A BROAD CONSENSUS among scholars that no rationally conceived motives informed the Nazis's murder of European Jews. The political philosopher Hannah Arendt, for example, emphasised that what made this crime unique was not the number of victims, but rather the absence of any concern for the economic utility of the victims on the part of the perpetrators. When it comes to motives, historians prefer to stress 'irrational racial hatred', 'destruction for destruction's sake', a 'black hole of historical understanding', or the self-propelling radicalising capacities inherent in modern bureaucratic structures.

For many years historians have sought in vain for an order from Hitler to destroy the Jews of Europe. However, from a careful examination of the documents that are assumed to have ordered the murder of German psychiatric patients or the deliberate starvation of 'many millions' of Soviet citizens, it is clear that they 'commission' or 'authorise', which means that recommendations or concrete plans were submitted to Hitler, Himmler or Goering for a decision: to be approved or rejected, redrafted or put on hold. Goering also expressed wishes about how these measures should best be disguised. Regarding the murders perpetrated by SS taskforces in the former Soviet Union, Hitler simply remarked: 'as far as the world at large is concerned our motives must be in accordance with tactical considerations . . . we will carry out all necessary measures — shootings, resettlements etc. — regardless of this.' This raises questions about the authorship of these 'necessary measures', and above all questions regarding aims and motives.

My starting point is that the Nazi regime relied to an exceptional degree upon academically-trained advisers and that it made use of their skills. Their ideas were transmitted upwards to the highest echelons by civil servants, especially by the secretaries of state attached to the various ministries, many of whom belonged to the General Council of the Four Year Plan agency, in which capacity they ranked higher than their own ministers. The Four Year Plan was designed to boost production in strategically vital areas of the economy and it reached the apogee of its power between 1938 and 1942, during which time programmes for the socio-political and economic reorganisation of Europe were developed and converted into both policy and military strategy.

The concept of an 'economy of the Final Solution' was developed by German experts — above all economists, agronomists, demographers, experts in labour deployment, geographers, historians, planners and statisticians. They made up the planning committees of such agencies as the Reich Office for Area Planning, the Reich Commissariat for the Strengthening of Ethnic Germandom and the Four Year Plan authority. They conceived and discussed solutions to the various 'demographic questions', and calculated the possible 'release of pressure' that would be the result of excluding Jews from the economy. They recommended converting the Ukraine into Europe's breadbasket — taking into their calculations the deliberate starvation of 'many millions' of Soviet citizens. They calculated the losses occasioned by the economies of the ghettos and thus delivered arguments for the mass murder of their inhabitants.

The approach adopted in this study is not that of the conspiracy theory, but to name those who were responsible, and to expose the role of a careerist, academically-trained, intelligentsia in the extermination of millions of people. There were probably a few thousand members of this 'scientific community', who, notwithstanding the usual animosities and petty institutional and personal jealousies, contributed to the formation of the prevailing opinion. It has sometimes been said that these people were not 'real' scholars, but rather half or totally crazy third-rate figures, but arguments such as this fail to explain the involvement of people more usually described as being major intellects, for example the historians Werner Conze and Theodor Schieder, who went on to dominate their profession in the post-war period. The expertise of this 'community' was not a form of *ex post facto* rationalisation of policies upon whose formulation they had exerted no real influence, but rather the basis upon which decisions were made by ministers and state secretaries. The reports produced by the Reich Committee for Economic Affairs concerning the 'conversion' of trade in Vienna or later in the Generalgouvernement in Poland provided the basis for decisions subsequently taken which sought to combine the 'dejudaisation' with the 'rationalisation' of their economies. The Reich Commissar for the Strengthening of Ethnic Germandom had detailed information regarding the optimum distribution of commercial and manufacturing firms in the areas from which Jews and 'Aryan' Poles were dispossessed in the interests of incoming ethnic German repatriates. In other words, both expulsions and compulsory 'germanisation' were carried out according to calculated economic, as opposed to racial-biological criteria. On the basis of these initial practical steps, in whose conception they had played a material part, the economists, demographers and planners could develop yet more elaborate plans. Thus, the Aryanisation of Vienna served as a model for all similar policies, and the expulsion of undesirable ethnic groups to the Generalgouvernement resurfaced later in discussions regarding the economic reconstruction of this territory, in the form of solutions to a self-imposed dilemma. Population pressure urgently demanded 'disburdenment'.

The reason why the links between long-term economic planning and the extermination of people have scarcely been investigated may largely be attributed to the initial connections forged between the uniqueness of the Holocaust and the alleged or assumed absence of any rational, utilitarian calculation. It is also the result of a gross underestimation of the power wielded by professional experts in a regime whose ideological statements were imprecise, vague and open-ended. This can be illustrated by looking at the various 'contributions' to the Nazi 'euthanasia' pro-gramme. On 3 April 1940 Viktor Brack, a senior official in the Chancellery of the Führer, speaking at a meeting of senior mayors, out-lined recent developments in German psychiatric hospitals. (In what follows, the agencies, individuals or interests responsible for various elements within the 'euthanasia' programme have been included in brackets):

> In many of the asylums in the Reich there are innumerable incurable patients of all descriptions [the doctors and psychiatrists], who are of no use to humanity [Hitler, the doctors]. They only serve to take away resources from other healthy people [military logistics experts, Hitler], and often require intensive nursing [doctors]. The rest of humanity has to be protected from these people [Hitler]. If today one has to make decisions regarding the maintenance of healthy people, then it is all the more essen-tial first to remove these creatures, if only to ensure better care of curable cases in the asylums and hospitals [doctors]. One needs the vacant bedspace

for all sorts of important military purposes [army medical corps experts]: sickbays, hospitals, auxiliary hospitals [army medical corps experts]. For the remainder, the action will greatly disburden the local authorities, since each individual case will no longer occasion any future costs for care or maintenance [war finance experts, local authorities].

To this list should be added the bureaucratic ambitions of the officials in the Chancellery of the Führer itself. A close examination of this relatively well-documented decision-making process should disabuse anyone of the idea that 'the bureaucratic machinery functioned automatically', as Hans Mommsen repeatedly states with reference to the murder of European Jews, where there is much less surviving evidence of the decision-making process. Three successive stages can be distinguished in deciding whether there was an 'economy of the Final Solution'.

1. Pogroms and Rationalisation

On 12 November 1938, two days after the pogroms of Reich Crystal Night, an important part of the Nazi leadership gathered for a discussion on the Jewish Question. The chair was taken by Hermann Goering, the Plenipotentiary for the Four Year Plan. Among those invited were Goebbels, Reinhard Heydrich and an array of economic experts: the Ministers of Finance and the Economy, a representative of the insurance sector and about one hundred experts, policy advisers and senior civil servants. Goering, the leading light in the economic affairs of the Greater German Reich, introduced himself with the modest disclaimer that he was 'not well versed enough in economic affairs', but then informed the participants that 'since the problem is mainly an economic one, it will have to be tackled from an economic perspective'. The measures necessary to Aryanise the economy would have to be taken 'one after another', with the Jews being excluded from the economy and 'put into the poorhouse'.

It was not a matter of enriching the petty-bourgeois grassroots supporters of the National Socialist German Workers Party (NSDAP), or, indeed, of Aryan competitors expropriating Jewish banks or department stores, but rather that there were too many one-man stores, artisan workshops and small factories in Germany in general. Within a few weeks of the conference state agencies closed two-thirds of all Jewish-owned one-man concerns and small businesses, selling off their stock to Aryan traders and adding the profits to national funds. This was part of what Goering called 'an action to convert non-essential units of production into essential ones', which was also scheduled to take place in the near future. So-called Aryanisation was therefore primarily a matter of economic rationalisation and concentration, what is now known as 'restructuring'.

The decisions taken at this conference were informed by the experiences derived from the annexation of Austria, experiences that were relayed to the participants by the Minister for the Economy and Labour in Austria, Hans Fischbock, who made the trip to the conference from his office in Vienna. According to calculations by the Reich Committee for Economic Affairs, 90 per cent of Jewish concerns in Vienna had been shut down entirely, with only 10 per cent being put up for sale. Fischbock boasted that the closures were based upon studies of each sector of the economy and had been determined in accordance with local needs. This *modus operandi* was adopted a few days later in Berlin and then by the German occupying authorities in Czechoslovakia, Poland and The Netherlands.

Any concerns about adverse socio-political consequences stemming from the Viennese model were allayed by Heydrich who, referring to co-operation between the Ministry of Economics, foreign humanitarian agencies and Adolf Eichmann's SS office for Jewish Affairs, pointed to the 50,000 Jews who had been removed from the economy since the Anschluss by being forced to emigrate. Only some 19,000 Jews had been removed from the Old (pre-expansion) Reich in the same timespan. The Special Plenipotentiary for Jewish Emigration was the President of the Reichsbank Hjalmar Schacht. Only one person present evinced any scepticism, the conservative nationalist Minister of Finance Schwerin von Krosigk who remarked: 'the crucial point is that we don't end up with the whole proletariat. Dealing with them will always be an appalling burden.' The conference ended with the slogan 'out with what can be got out', by which they meant the Jews. At the same time it was immediately obvious that because of shortages of foreign exchange this would only be partially successful, and that those Jews who remained — the old, sick and unemployed — would 'be a burden on the state'. If before Reich Crystal Night in November 1938 there had been rivalries and clashes of competence between the various agencies occupied with the Jewish Question, this changed dramatically after 12 November 1938. Goering declared: 'Once and for all I prohibit any separate action. The Reich has taken the matter in hand.' Thenceforth, anti-Semitic measures were co-ordinated by the Four Year Plan apparatus; special responsibility devolved upon Erich

Neumann, the State Secretary for Exchange Questions and 'special tasks of a general economic nature'. The business of deportations and later extermination was transferred to the Reich Main Security Office of the SS.

2. Developmental Policy and Demographic Questions

The second phase in the economically motivated radicalisation of policy towards the Jews began after September 1939 with the conquest and deliberate territorial fragmentation of Poland. In the eyes of German economic planners, Poland was underdeveloped and its economy both badly organised and starved of capital. Above all, however, too many people derived their livelihood from the land. The economy was characterised by subsistence agriculture: the rural population satisfied most of its own demands for foodstuffs and consumer goods, and in the villages barter rather than money was the normal means of exchange, in other words it was 'a system insufficient for rationalisation', basically impervious to the logic of capitalist penetration and exploitation. In the minds of German, and indeed other international economists, Poland's main problem lay in rural overpopulation. A third of the population would be deemed surplus to requirements should modern means of cultivation be adopted. The 'surplus population' was a 'burden on the national economy', or what Theodor Oberländer called, 'a symptom of socio-economic sickness'. Overpopulation had nothing to do with the density of population, but was rather a question of perceived deviation from an allegedly normal or 'optima' population.

The theory of optimum population had been developed at the turn of the century by a number of economists with the aid of Paul Mombert's theory of diminishing returns, or what is known as the Mombert Formula. Mombert (1876—1938) was Professor of Political Economy at Giessen until his compulsory retirement as a 'non-Aryan' in 1933. His formula consists of a simple equation which relates population numbers to economic resources. According to this formula, $F = P \times L$, food-supply (F) equals population numbers (P) times living standard (L). This reductionist abstraction enables the 'explanation' of every misrelationship between resources and living standards to be made in terms of population figures, regardless of such factors as unemployment, lack of capital or raw materials, absence of markets or low productivity and so forth. Every type of economic crisis, including those occasioned by war, could be redefined in terms of the 'population question'.

According to this theory, population becomes an economic variable like any other, which can therefore also be manipulated like any other. Mombert himself seems to have expressly ruled out this possibility, but this was overlooked by his disciples. To German economists, with their sights set upon a vast, dependent, integrated European economy under German hegemony, the size and composition of a population became the factor which, given wartime conditions and the relative scarcity of raw materials, they could adjust most easily. Population policy in the form of 'resettlement' became a way of overcoming capital and foreign currency shortages, of regulating wartime finances and of releasing foodstuffs and raw materials, while at the same time achieving the longer-term goal of a more rational economic structure and enhanced exploitation of labour.

By 1932 Mombert had already calculated the burden upon the national economy of the surplus population created by the Depression. The cost to the state of maintaining the unproductive was of the order of four billion Reichmarks, money which could otherwise have been employed productively by expanding the economic base in the form of domestic investment or export capital. At the time Mombert was thinking in terms of financing colonial projects in Africa, however his model also suggested ways in which capital could be more rapidly accumulated via a 'cessation of population growth'. According to the academics who serviced the occupying authorities in Poland — and who again and again referred to the 'irrefutable Mombert formula' — this was precisely the answer they needed to the underlying problems they discerned in the Polish economy. A reduction of the population would simultaneously break the vicious circle of overpopulation and lead to capital accumulation necessary for the modernisation of the economy. If this did not succeed, then occupied Poland would become a 'burden' upon the entire German-dominated *Grossraum*. The extermination of millions of people would halt population growth in eastern Europe for a few critical years, 'thus' releasing capital resources, which could be used to promote industrialisation and the mechanisation of agriculture, or in other words developments that were in Germany's economic interest. The German academic planners generated quantities of plans and developmental models, which at a stroke rendered entire peoples surplus to requirements and therefore subject to resettlement or deportation as forced labour. 'Negative demographic policy' was the lever of a new type of German developmental economics.

According to German calculations, every second rural Pole was 'nothing more than a dead weight', and overpopulation 'effectively a barrier to capital formation'. Theodor Oberländer, subsequently a minister in Konrad Adenauer's post-war cabinet, reckoned that in many areas of Poland the population was as much as 75 per cent superfluous. Expressed in absolute terms, this meant that some 4.5 to 5.83 million Poles were surplus to requirements. Thinking bigger, the economists calculated that in south-eastern Europe, whose overpopulation would also have to be regulated, there were between twelve and fifteen million workers on the land who would have to be 'set in motion'. If one included their families, then there were about fifty million people who would have to be pushed out of their domestic subsistence lifestyle if the German industrial economy was to benefit. Having occupied large parts of the Soviet Union, the German economic and agrarian experts revised their figures upwards by another thirty million, in other words by precisely the increase of population in Russia that had occurred between 1905 and 1939.

This theory of overpopulation described relatively backward economies. Underactivity and unemployment were the norm, or as economists would say, labour capacity was being only partially used. Disharmony between people and capital resulted in considerable rural and urban poverty; outside intervention designed to rationalise this state of affairs, would necessarily result in the population being divided into those who would have to work more intensively and those who would not be working at all. The state would decide who was deemed to be productive or non-productive. This was precisely the point at which Nazi racial criteria fused with the scientific criteria of population economy.

3. The War against the Soviet Union

The third phase in this demographically conceived programme of mass murder began with the planning for the war against the Soviet Union. The initial aim was to achieve a '180 degree turn' in the direction of the economy of the Ukraine, which should no longer feed Soviet workers, but rather secure the foodstuffs and hence immunity to blockade of Central Europe. The plan of attack incorporated the deliberate starvation of 'many millions' of people in order to secure food for the inhabitants of Western and Central Europe. According to printed guidelines:

> Many tens of millions of people will become superfluous to requirements
> in these areas [i.e. the forests and industrial towns of the north] and will die
> or have to move to Siberia. Attempts to prevent the population there from

starving by moving food surpluses from the black earth zone, can only be done at the cost of supplying Europe. This would undermine Germany's capacity to prevail during the war, and would undermine Germany and Europe's capacity to resist blockade.

Underlying these bleak calculations was the knowledge that Germany was only able to provide some 87 per cent of her food requirements, that the only occupied country able to deliver food supplies without starving its own citizens was Denmark and that the rest actually needed to import foodstuffs from Germany. Because of the way in which agriculture tended to become more and more extensive during wartime, involving the cultivation of unsuitable land, the food situation was bound to deteriorate from harvest to harvest. This problem, the only one that might have adversely affected the mood of the German population, was to be resolved by organising the deaths of about thirty million Russians. The plans, which were unparalleled in their clarity, never mentioned the word 'race', but constantly referred to the logic of economic circumstances. 'Negative demographic policy' was the imperative of the hour, with hunger acting as a form of geo-strategic tourniquet. These plans, which were developed some months before the 'Final Solution of the Jewish Question' once again emanated from Goering's Four Year Plan agency. The two million Soviet prisoners of war who died of starvation in German camps before the end of 1941, did not die because of any problems in food supply, but were victims of deliberate murder. In November 1941 Goering remarked that 'this year twenty to thirty million people will starve in Russia. Perhaps that's a good thing, since certain people will have to be decimated'.

These plans connected with the supply of food were accompanied by others — notably the Generalplan Ost — which were concerned with strategies of power and settlement policy. During the preparations for the war against the Soviet Union, the horizons suddenly appeared limitless to German planners. The Institut für Deutsche Ostarbeit in occupied Cracow considered *inter alia* 'the resettlement of the Poles', while a Berlin professor of anthropology who carried out studies of Soviet prisoners of war recommended 'the liquidation of Russiandom'.

The invasion of Russia opened up new ways of solving every social problem, not just in the occupied areas, but also in the Reich itself. As the chief of the Generalplan Ost project noted: 'the victory of our arms and the expansion of our frontiers has destroyed all of the old limitations.' The massive tasks which had 'arisen' for the German nation were not just a matter of 'germanisation' and the reconstruction of conquered territories. Rather, a 'profound reordering of nation and available space' in the old Reich would ensue as a result of the new order created on the new frontiers. It would begin with the reorganisation of the economy and with the cleansing of overfull occupations. Production, markets and prices would be streamlined in accordance with purchasing power. Finally, the whole structure of settlement would have to be reorganised. The Generalplan Ost, which covered the whole area between Leningrad and the Crimea, presupposed the 'evacuation' of thirty-one million people. In the eyes of the authors of these documents, the Solution of the Jewish Question (for some five million Jews lived in the areas covered by the plan), was merely part of their 'great task'.

In the German Reich, in occupied Poland and, finally, in the entire area subject to German hegemony it was overwhelmingly people designated as being unproductive — the chronically sick, the so-called asocial, and then the Jews — in other words, groups who were already discriminated against and who were hence easy to isolate, who were to be removed from the economic process and denied any form of social security. This meant that in addition to Jews and Gypsies, vast parts of the Slav population were to be victims of extermination. The extermination of the Jews carried out under cover of war was the part of this agenda most fully realised. These plans were founded upon demographic and economic criteria as well as theories of racial hierarchy. Their initial premise was that the population of Europe had to be reduced for medium- and short-term economic and strategic reasons. The dynamics of extermination and the actual course of decision-making can only be understood if the demographic and economic goals which underpinned them are borne in mind.

In destroying the Jews one of the most tangible manifestations of poverty in Eastern Europe would be destroyed, in other words the poorest parts of the cities and towns. Genocide was a means of solving the social question. Because most of the Jews lived in towns, their deportation would set the surplus rural population moving in the direction of the towns, giving them the possibility of social advancement into trade and handicrafts. At the same time, these overcrowded sectors in the towns themselves could be modernised and rationalised, without creating a discontented, declassé, national petty-bourgeoisie which would have been a threat to the German occupiers.

Both in Eastern Europe and, above all, in Germany itself, the expropriation of Jewish property provided an unbureaucratic form of self-help, which provided household goods, housing, new jobs and so forth. In the case of large-scale capital, expropriation enabled German banks and industry to consolidate their holdings. All that remained were unemployed and propertyless people or, in other words, an artificially achieved population surplus. Liquidified assets set free as a result of the deportation of Jews and non-Jewish Poles were taken over by the Main Trustees for the East set up for the purpose and then distributed in the form of development credits in order to strengthen undercapitalised sectors and regions.

Similar calculations informed the cogitations of virtually every German economist, agronomist, demographer and statistician. One example from many is the Berlin economic adviser Alfred Maelicke. Writing in the journal *The German Economy* in 1942, Maelicke remarked:

> Only the total dejudaisation of economic life will facilitate the solution of what is still the main problem in many countries, such as south-eastern Europe and elsewhere, namely overpopulation and other social questions. The elimination of the Jewish trader mentality and profit-mindedness and the exclusion of the Jews will create space and security (full employment) for many hitherto rootless and impoverished workers and peasants, artisans and others ... By observing the fundamentals and practices of dejudaisation as applied in Germany one could effect profound changes in demographic relations, and even wider structural changes, without violently upsetting the nature of any given economy. There will be no need to dismiss workers and no difficulties of supply. One does not even need to worry about a contraction of turnover.

Maelicke had described a racially informed 'cleansing of the population problem' — the structural preconditions for the long-term re-ordering and exploitation of the *Grosswirtschaftsraum* (greater economic space) that once was Europe.

This explains the apparent contradiction between an economic or military interest in exploitation and the mass-extermination of potential sources of labour. In the eyes of German economists, overpopulation confirmed the alleged economic backwardness of economic structures and retarded the implementation of 'optimum labour productivity' within the *Grosswirtschaftsraum*. In other words, the economic experts presupposed that part of the overpopulation would have to be 'eradicated' if the labour potential of the *Grossraum* was to be effectively

THE PLANNING INTELLIGENTSIA AND THE 'FINAL SOLUTION' 151

exploited by being rendered 'mobile'. The Germans were not prepared to think in terms of capital investment designed to broaden overall resources. The low level of mechanisation to which the Jews were reduced in the ghettos and labour camps following their exclusion from the wider economy was further evidence of 'an effective brake upon capital', because resources were being tied up which, with the better organisation of labour and a more favourable combination of capital and labour, could otherwise have been used to produce greater profits. Himmler and Speer were in full agreement on this issue. The low wages paid to Jews working for German and Polish firms prevented rational-isation because in the short term, a Jewish labour force was a cheaper alternative than new machinery; the advantages that cheap labour obviously had for individual concerns were not mirrored by advantages for the economy as a whole. According to these criteria, it was economic-ally more rational to kill the Jews than to put them to work.

The fact that even Jewish munitions workers were only temporarily reprieved from the gas chambers suggests that these concepts were racially determined. Even the last Jewish craftsman was replaced by an 'Aryan' one. However it is incorrect to talk (as some historians do) of the 'primacy of racially-motivated exterminatory plans above any economic factors'. Rather, especially in the second half of the war, the imperatives of munitions production collided with other economic imperatives, namely the no less acute crisis of food supply, which demanded a reduc-tion of the population numbers and long-term economic restructuring by means of mass murder. Selection in accordance with racial criteria did not contradict economic calculation, rather it was an integral part of it.

Just as contemporary anthropologists, doctors and biologists regarded the marginalisation and extermination of allegedly 'less valuable' ele-ments as a scientific way of improving mankind or 'healing the body of the nation', so economists, agronomists and planners thought their work would result in the 'healing of the structure of society' in underdeveloped regions of Europe. The mere 'co-eaters' would be separated from 'economically really active people'. In so far as the Jews, active in such sectors as trade and handicrafts, which the Germans regarded as over-crowded and superfluous, were not already doomed, socio-political and economic restructuring pushed them yet further into a position where they lost their property and all means of earning a livelihood. In this way racial and economic selection criteria were harmonised, with a consensus replacing alleged conflicts of interest between rational planners and racial fanatics. This consensus and the social sanitising concepts which underlay it gave the systematic and centrally planned murder of millions of people its own gruesome dynamic. Evidence of a technocratically rational agenda does not make these crimes 'comprehensible' let alone 'understandable', in the sense of having empathetic understanding for something. But looked at in this way, the crimes Germans committed in these years assume a rather different character, and require us to undertake the search for causes and continuities afresh and perhaps with yet greater seriousness.

Finally, there is the question of uniqueness. We began by considering Hannah Arendt's statement that no rational motives informed the Final Solution, a view with which most historians concur. In her important work on the origins of totalitarianism, Arendt made the following pertinent observation:

> The imperative 'Thou shalt not kill' fails in the face of a demographic policy which proceeds to exterminate systematically or industrially those races and individuals deemed unfit and less valuable, not once in a unique action, but on a basis obviously intended to be permanent. The death penalty becomes absurd when one is not dealing with murderers who know what murder is, but rather with demographers who organise the murder of millions in such a way that all those who participate subjectively consider themselves free of guilt.

What did the demographic policies of both of the major dictatorships of this century have in common? The Stalinist population policy of the 1930s — the eradication of the kulaks (peasant farmers) — corresponded in many respects to the policies pursued by the Nazis between 1939 and 1944. Discrimination against minorities, the mobilisation of the rural population, forcible colonisation, slave labour, cultural and linguistic homogenisation, and progressive forms of extermination. Both dictatorships pursued strategies of more or less violent modernisation, based upon the degradation of people into 'human contingents', to be administered, dispossessed, resettled, privileged or marginalised at will. At the heart of such policies was the belief that in this way socio-economic structures could be revolutionised more rapidly, indeed almost overnight. Of course this belief was not unique to either Nazi or Soviet thinking. There are echoes of it in the progressive thought of the century as a whole, in the form of the 'agrarian or industrial question', or the 'refugee or overpopulation question'. The most striking example of this can be seen in the 1946 report of the United Nations on the economic reconstruction of Europe: 'In eastern Europe the large-scale elimination of the Jewish population has left the distribution system in a state of virtual disorder. On the other hand the pre-war phenomenon of agricultural overpopulation still prevails.' Only once, in Germany, did such ideas result in Auschwitz. The deed and the crime is unique. However, Auschwitz is part of European as well as German history. Only when one has fully understood this context is it possible to talk meaningfully of the 'limits of understanding'. The Holocaust was not a 'reversion to barbarism', nor a 'break with civilisation', still less an 'Asiatic deed'. But it was also far from being a 'historical black hole', somehow beyond language, poetry and historical understanding, but rather a possibility inherent in European civilisation itself.

The Planning Intelligentsia and the 'Final Solution'

Götz Aly and Susanne Heim, *Vordenker der Vernichtung* (Hamburg, 1991); ibid., 'The Economics of the Final Solution', *Simon Wiesenthal Center Annual*, vol. 5 (1988), pp. 3–48; Zygmunt Baumann, *Modernity and the Holocaust* (Ithaca, 1989); Michael Burleigh, *Germany Turns Eastwards: A Study of 'Ostforschung' in the Third Reich* (Cambridge, 1990).

CHAPTER X

FROM THE 'PEOPLE'S CONSCIOUSNESS OF RIGHT AND WRONG' TO 'THE HEALTHY INSTINCTS OF THE NATION': THE PERSECUTION OF HOMOSEXUALS IN NAZI GERMANY

Hans-Georg Stümke

FOLLOWING THE FOUNDATION of the German Reich in 1871, male homosexuality was declared illegal and punishable as an 'unnatural sexual act'. By contrast, female homosexuality remained non-criminal. Paragraph 175 of the Criminal Code regulated the precise details of the offence, and massive pressure from the state of Prussia ensured that this legislation was incorporated into the new unified national criminal code. This effectively marked the end of the comparatively liberal epoch that had prevailed for about fifty years in some of the other constituent states. A relatively enlightened understanding of the law meant that these states regarded sexuality as a private affair, which did not require punitive intervention by the authorities. The leading power in Germany proved unable to emulate their example.

In order to defend itself against enlightened critics of its policy on this issue, the Prussian state made uncharacteristic play with references to 'the people'. An official commentator noted that 'The people's consciousness of right and wrong condemns these activities not merely as vice but also as a crime.' Therefore the state had a duty to defend this conception of the law by punishing homosexuality. Admittedly, only 'activities resembling sexual intercourse', that is to say where penetration similar to that practised by heterosexuals had occurred, seem to have offended 'the people's consciousness of right and wrong'. Since most homosexual relations seem to have been consensual, it was forensically difficult to establish the offence. Accordingly, the number of convictions was relatively modest. Between 1871 and 1924 some three to seven hundred people were convicted each year; between 1925 and 1933 between eight and eleven hundred.

However, from the turn of the century there was a clear tendency to punish homosexuality more severely. In 1909 a draft law recommended not only sentences of five years' hard labour in certain cases, but also the criminalisation of female homosexuality. Continuities in the state's interest in persecution were implicit in the comment 'The stipulations of Paragraph 175 do not merely correspond with the healthy outlook of the people . . . rather they also serve above all the interests of the community, and the direct interests of the state.' However, the Empire collapsed before this draft could be submitted for parliamentary approval.

There was a further attempt to bolster the law in 1925 on the part of the conservative cabinet of the Roman Catholic Chancellor Wilhelm Marx. Minister of Justice Hergt from the German National People's Party was responsible for the new draft legislation. Although this no longer sought to criminalise female homosexuality, it did specify the nature of homosexual offences and sought to punish these with sentences of up to five years' hard labour. The author of the draft commented that, according to 'the German view of things', homosexuality was 'an aberration' which would lead to 'the degeneration of the nation and the collapse of its power'. Despite practical impediments to the law's implementation, Paragraph 175 nonetheless constituted a barrier 'which one could not remove without harm being done to the health and purity of our people's way of life'. There were already echoes in this of the terms and tone employed a few years later by the National Socialists. After 1933 these racial preoccupations would take over entirely.

Protests against these attempts to stiffen the penalties for homosexual activities largely came from the burgeoning homosexual civil rights movement, which since the late nineteenth century had campaigned for the abrogation of Paragraph 175 under the slogan that homosexuality was 'neither an illness nor a crime'. The best-known homosexual organisation was the Scientific-Humanitarian Committee (WhK), founded in 1897 by the doctor and sexual reformer Magnus Hirschfeld (1868–1935). In 1897 the Committee had submitted a petition to parliament calling for the abolition of Paragraph 175, and the signatories included August Bebel, the chairman of the Social Democratic Party. Moreover, from 1926 onwards, members of the Committee combined with other organisations promoting sexual reform to produce an alternative draft law, calling not only for the abrogation of Paragraph 175, but also for reforms in the entire field of sexual offences and the decriminalisation of abortion.

The rapid changes of government during the Weimar period also meant sudden shifts in attitudes towards Paragraph 175. In 1929, when the government was in the hands of the Social Democrat Hermann Müller, a parliamentary committee responsible for criminal law voted by a slim majority to decriminalise homosexual acts between two consenting adults. Those in favour included the Social Democrats, Communists and sections of the Liberals; those against included the Catholic Centre Party and the German National People's Party, which in 1933 entered a coalition government with the National Socialists (NSDAP). The NSDAP was not represented on the committee, however, their Party Press reacted to the decision to alter the law with predictable expressions of fury and outrage. On 2 August 1930, the *Völkischer Beobachter* warned the (Jewish) sexologist Magnus Hirschfeld 'Don't you believe that we Germans will allow such a law to exist for one day when we achieve power.' The Nazi paper described homosexuality as 'an evil lust of the Jewish soul', and vowed that it would be punished as a crime in the most severe fashion, 'with the noose and deportation'. The recommendations of the parliamentary committee were never put to the vote in the Reichstag. Paragraph 175 of the 1871 law continued in force until its modification by the Nazis in 1935.

If one views this period as a whole then two trends are apparent. Firstly, following the suppression of enlightened legal traditions in the various states in the interests of Prussia's hegemonic aspirations, the threat of punishment and exemplary application of Paragraph 175 was designed to contain homosexuality through a form of general prevention. Increasing nationalism resulted in attempts to extend the scope of the law. Phrases such as 'healthy instincts of the people', 'the strength of the nation', or 'the health and purity of the people's way of life' signalled the state's claims. The National Socialists would abandon the preventive aims of earlier legislation and policy in favour of a radical 'Final Solution'. Second, enlightened legal traditions which sought to decriminalise homosexuality were supported not only by homosexual civil rights activists, but also by Social Democrats, the Communists and some Liberals. The accession to power of the Nazis effectively terminated these traditions.

Following Hitler's appointment as Chancellor, the Nazis' immediate concern was to secure and consolidate their power. In this initial phase the Nazis' persecution of homosexuals had a spontaneous character. Marauding SA men and SS thugs, with a violent hatred of everything foreign, Leftist or 'un-German' were symptomatic of the Brown mob's intoxication with victory. The historical record reveals attacks on homosexual meeting-places, arrests, detention in 'wild', or *ad hoc*, concentration camps, violent attacks on individuals and the destruction of Magnus Hirschfeld's world-famous Institute for Sexual Studies. The homosexual rights movement quietly disappeared in a manner so far not investigated by modern historians. The centrally organised and systematic persecution of homosexuals only began in the wake of the 1934 Röhm affair.

As early as 1930 many people were aware of the homosexuality of the SA chief Ernst Röhm (1887–1934). At the time the Social Democratic Party (SPD) Press published private letters written by Röhm, which left no doubts as to his sexual orientation. The SPD traduced the 'intolerable hypocrisy' of the NSDAP's desire for a 'cleaner Germany' in view of its apparent tolerance of a homosexual in a very prominent position within a major Party formation. The purpose behind the SPD's resort to gutter-Press tactics of personal exposure was to weaken the NSDAP politically, or even to divide the Party. Whereas in 1930 leading Nazis, including Heinrich Himmler, had been fulsome in expressing support for their comrade, by 1934 the situation had altered drastically.

Once in power, the Nazis decided to make the discovery of Röhm's homosexuality their own exclusive property. The widely publicised revelations regarding Röhm and the simultaneous liquidation of the SA leadership contributed decisively towards the consolidation of the Nazi dictatorship. Tensions between Left and Right within the Party and, more significantly, between the para-military SA and the army, were resolved by spreading the rumour that Röhm was plotting a putsch in order to transfer power to a group of 'degenerates' and 'perverts'. As the historian Eugen Kogon noted, the Röhm affair also provided the 'window of opportunity' for the inauguration of the SS state. As far as homosexuality was concerned, what Hitler called the 'well-known unfortunate inclinations of Röhm' served to mobilise the 'healthy instincts of the nation' for the political aims of the NSDAP. In a radio broadcast, the propaganda chief Joseph Goebbels announced 'We want the co-operation of the entire nation, rich and poor, high or lowly ... bubonic plagues, dens of corruption, sickly symptoms of moral decay will be burned out, and moreover right down to the flesh'. The state-controlled media now embarked upon a systematic propaganda campaign against homosexuals.

In 1935, the year of the Nuremberg Racial Laws, the existing version of Paragraph 175 was amended. A legal commentary noted 'The new state, which is striving for a quantitatively and qualitatively strong, morally healthy people, must combat all unnatural instincts with vigour', thereby explicitly articulating the *völkisch* impetus behind the new legal thinking. An article in the journal *Deutsche Justiz* said that 'the principal deficiency in Paragraph 175 as it stands', was 'that it only encompasses activities resembling sexual intercourse, so that neither the prosecutors nor the police can intervene in cases of public intimacy between men'. By extending the scope of the law to include every instance of inter-masculine sexual contact, the Nazis simplified the business of proving it in courts of law. In 1938, the Reich Supreme Court decided that even evidence of physical contact was no longer essential: 'The purely optically arousing function of the male body is sufficient proof.'

In 1935 the lawyer Rudolf Klare took the opportunity presented by his dissertation to present a justification for the 'eradication' of homosexuals. In what became a standard work of National Socialist jurisprudence, Klare advocated a reversion to ancient Germanic legal customs, involving the killing of homosexuals as an expression of 'racial instinct'. He described homosexuality as 'a racially exterminatory manifestation of degeneracy', and called for the ceaseless 'cleansing' of homosexuals from the Reich, recommending that 'the courts make increased use of expert witnesses in order to achieve an increase in the number of cases resulting in custodial sentences'.

While anti-homosexual propaganda continued to run in the media, the Nazis quietly established a central organisation to gather data on homosexuals as a prelude to systematically persecuting them. On 1 November 1934 a special department responsible for homosexuality was established in the Berlin Gestapo headquarters; its first task was to centralise personal data on homosexuals throughout the Reich. The Gestapo was particularly interested in learning whether the police 'had knowledge of homosexual weaknesses on the part of political personalities', a turn of phrase which suggests that the object of the exercise was to blackmail political opponents into oblivion. Tactics such as these were later employed against Roman Catholic religious orders, the leadership of middle-class youth movements and against the relatively independent-minded General Werner von Fritsch, who was successfully 'framed' in a homosexual scandal by his opponents. On 10 October 1936 this special unit was taken over by the equally secret Reich Central Office for the Combating of Homosexuality and Abortion. The conflation of the two offences was not accidental. Both homosexuality and abortion signified the privatisation of sexuality and its products, thus flatly contradicting the *völkisch* view, whereby sexuality was construed in terms of collectivist biology. The decree that established the Reich Central Office made the connection explicit:

> The considerable dangers which the relatively high number of abortions still being performed present for population policy and the health of the nation, and which constitute a grave infringement of the ideological fundamentals of National Socialism, as well as the homosexual activities of a not inconsiderable proportion of the population, which constitute a serious threat to young people, demands more effective measures against these national diseases than has hitherto been the case.

In other words, persecution of homosexuals was a product of 'population policy and national health', rather than as is sometimes claimed, a defensive psychological reaction on the part of a Nazi 'male state' whose homophobia was driven by anxieties about its members' own 'latent' homosexuality.

According to the decree that established the Reich Central Office, its tasks were the central registration of homosexuals and instances of homosexuality, and the combating of the latter in accordance with systematised directives. This meant that the Reich Central Office became the clearing office for information from a host of agencies and for the results of medical research in this area. In the spring of 1937 Heinrich Himmler informed senior police officers of the necessity for the campaign against homosexuals, saying 'Homosexual men are enemies of the state and are to be treated accordingly. It is a question of purifying the body of the German nation and the maintenance and strengthening of the power of the German nation.' It was the task of the police to 'reduce all cases of homosexuality and abortion so that the demographic losses resulting from these offences will be kept to a minimum'. At the same time, police chiefs were given detailed instructions on how to avail themselves of the developing network of spies and informers operating in this area. The racial-biological imperatives that informed the *Reichführer*-SS's thinking were apparent in a secret speech he gave before SS leaders in 1937. Here he spoke of 'deficits in the sexual balance-sheet' of the nation, and estimated the number of homosexuals in Germany as being 'one or two million'. He continued:

> If you further take into account the facts ... that with a static number of women, we have two million men too few on account of those who fell in the war, then you can well imagine how this imbalance of two million homosexuals and two million war dead, or in other words a lack of about four million men capable of having sex, has upset the sexual balance-sheet of Germany, and will result in a catastrophe.

Later, in January 1942, when the German armed forces were suffering heavy casualties on the Eastern Front, Hitler observed, regarding the connection between the production of human beings and warfare, 'The child will be our salvation! Even if this war should cost us a quarter of a million dead and 100,000 crippled, the surplus of births which the German people has achieved since the seizure of power will give them back to us again.' In fact, there was no surplus of births and the casualty figures he mentioned were decidedly optimistic.

The creation of the Reich Central Office inaugurated the period of centralised and systematic persecution. If in 1934 there were 948 convictions, the number quickly rose to 5,320 in 1936, 8,271 in 1937 and 8,562 in 1938, falling off again following the outbreak of war. According to official statistics, between 1933 and 1945 some 50,000 persons were convicted. Most homosexuals ended up in the hands of the police either through denunciations by their fellow-citizens or through large-scale raids. A typical newspaper announcement on 28 August 1936 read:

> A special commando unit of the Berlin Gestapo was deployed in a cleansing operation in Berlin and many other towns. This resulted in raids within a short space of time on a large number of so-called sex joints. Some hundreds of people were detained ... a special bureau was created in Hamburg which brought charges before a special court of jurors. The accused were sentenced to between one year and twenty months imprisonment.

What this meant for those on the receiving-end can be gauged from an eyewitness account of persecution in Reinbek, at the time still a village on the outskirts of Hamburg:

> With one blow a wave of arrests of homosexuals began in our town. One of the first to be arrested was my friend, with whom I had had a relationship since I was twenty-three. One day people from the Gestapo came to his house and took him away. It was pointless to enquire where he might be. If anyone did that, they ran the risk of being similarly detained, because he knew them, and therefore they were also suspect. Following his arrest, his home was searched by Gestapo agents. Books were taken away, notebooks and address books were confiscated, questions were asked among the neighbours ... The address books were the worst. All those who figured in them, or had anything to do with him, were arrested and summoned by the Gestapo. Me too. For a whole year I was summoned by the Gestapo and interrogated at least once every fourteen days or three weeks ... After four weeks my friend was released from investigative custody. The fascists could not prove anything against him either. However, the effects of his arrest were terrifying. Hair shorn off, totally confused, he was no longer what he was before ... We had to be very careful with all contacts. I had to break off relations with my friend. We passed each other by on the street, because we did not want to put ourselves in danger.

Another eyewitness reported that in Hamburg there were systematic attempts to remove homosexuals from large concerns:

> At first they detained a few and then put them under pressure to reveal the names of other queers. When the Gestapo had enough names, they appeared in the personnel office one morning, got themselves taken through the individual departments and arrested the relevant persons. One raid alone on the Alsterhaus department store resulted in the arrest of about fifty queers. The same thing happened in the Hamburg power station.

In a 'strictly confidential! Official use only' situation report issued in 1941 by the Youth Leader of the German Reich the scale of these police activities was made explicit. Between 1936 and the first half of 1939 the police investigated 37,707 persons for infractions of Paragraph 175. Between 1937 and the first half of 1939 the Gestapo recorded the names of 77,990 persons in its records. In the following table these figures have been augmented with the number of persons convicted of homosexual offences.

YEAR	REGISTERED BY GESTAPO	INVESTIGATED BY POLICE	CONVICTED
1937	32,360	12,760	8,271
1938	28,882	10,638	8,562
1939	33,496	10,456	7,614
TOTAL	94,738	33,854	24,447

In a quantitative sense, the years between 1936 and the outbreak of war were the high-point of persecution of homosexuals. In this period alone, almost one hundred thousand people were registered by the Gestapo. About a third of them were then investigated by the police, with every fourth person being successfully convicted in accordance with the amended version of Paragraph 175.

Already in 1939, the Reich Central Office made a point of relaying the names of homosexuals of military age to the armed forces. Following the outbreak of war, when a large proportion of men 'capable of bearing arms' had been called up, persecution expanded within the military while the number of civilian arrests contracted. At the same time, persecution assumed a qualitatively different character. As early as 1935 the SS began demanding the death penalty for homosexuals. On 12 July 1940 Himmler ordered that 'in future all homosexuals who have seduced more than one partner are to be taken into police preventive custody following their release from prison'. Detention in a concentration camp was tantamount to a death sentence since the camps operated a programme of 'extermination through labour'. Homosexuals were also taken into preventive or protective custody throughout the Nazi period in order to protect the 'national community' from 'habitual and professional criminals', the 'asocial', 'community aliens' or 'parasites upon the people'. Already in 1933 the concentration camp at Hamburg-Fuhlsbüttel included a category designated homosexuals. On 15 November 1941 Hitler personally decreed the death penalty for homosexual members of the SS.

Although the SS managed to destroy a considerable proportion of records relating to concentration camps before the war ended, it is possible to find evidence for the presence of homosexuals in most of the camps. On the basis of an assessment of all of the available evidence, Rudiger Lautmann has estimated that about 10,000 men were forced to wear the degrading pink triangle in the camps, although 'it could have been 5,000 or 15,000'. Eugen Kogon, a political prisoner in Buchenwald until 1945, described their situation as 'deplorable'. Most of them simply died. They occupied the lowest rung in the prisoner hierarchy. In Buchenwald, according to Kogon, they made up the highest proportion of inmates transported to the extermination camps. According to R. Schnabel's eyewitness recollections of Dachau, the prisoners with the pink triangle 'never lived very long, and were rapidly and systematically eliminated by the SS'. A remarkable number of former political prisoners are in agreement that the SS treated homosexuals in a particularly brutal fashion. The writer Günther Weisenborn, who was sent to a concentration camp in 1942 on account of his activities in the Resistance, recalled that during his captivity he encountered 'many homosexuals who had been tortured', and that 'their sufferings were unspeakable; they were not sustained by any form of idea. They were absolutely defenceless and died rapidly because of this.'

The Nazis themselves were conscious that the terror they directed against homosexuals was ambivalent in character. Himmler himself remarked in 1936 that 'the great question of aberrant sexuality will never be regulated through policing'. In several scientific publications, the Nazi biologist and racial hygienicist Theo Lang cautioned against propelling homosexuals into marriage and 'normal' forms of sexuality. He wrote that one had to consider that 'the failure of homosexuals to reproduce had to be viewed not simply from the perspective of a quantitative, but also a qualitative population policy'. According to his theories, homosexuality was caused by chromosomatic disorders, from which he deduced 'that severe punishment and moral condemnation will drive homosexuals to at least attempt to marry and have children, or in other words [we will achieve] precisely the opposite of what harsh penalties are designed to prevent, namely the probable increase in the number of homosexuals in successive generations'.

These hypotheses reveal the fundamental dilemma the Nazis faced in combating homosexuality. As long as they were unable to satisfactorily answer the question 'What causes homosexuality?' the regime was effectively unable to embark upon a Final Solution in this area. Even if they succeeded in eliminating sections of the homosexual population, they would still be confronted with fresh generations of bisexuals and homosexuals. This made the situation of homosexuals rather different from that of other minorities persecuted during the Third Reich, for example Jews or Sinti and Roma, who were murdered regardless of whether they were eight or eighty years old, and thus for whom genocide meant the end of any possibility of reproduction. What connected the mostly Aryan homosexuals with these other groups, was that they were also categorised as being of 'lesser racial value' within the Nazis' programme of racial selective breeding. They shared this classification with those Aryan men and women who were compulsorily sterilised in order to inhibit their capacity to reproduce.

As far as homosexuals were concerned, from the mid-nineteenth century, science had been attempting to discover the causes of their 'illness'. Although the Nazis' research drew upon many of the resultant theories, an annual report by the Reich Criminal Main Office for the year 1939–40 suggested continued uncertainty on the facts of the matter: 'In order to discover further possibilities for the containment of this plague, and so as to leave no method unexplored, we will be examining the suggestions of various persons whose aim is to deepen scientific understanding of the problem of homosexuality.'

Science and research began to be employed more intensively, although precisely how remains largely unexplored. The most notorious example is of the hormonal experiments conducted in 1944 by the Danish SS doctor Carl Vaernet upon homosexual inmates in Buchenwald concentration camp. Himmler personally took a keen interest in Vaernet's work, supplying him with a secret letter of recommendation in November 1943: 'I request that you treat Dr V. with the utmost generosity. I myself also require a monthly report of between three to four sides in length since I am very interested in these questions.' According to Vaernet's correspondence with the SS, his experiments were designed 'to establish on a broad basis whether it is possible to implant an artificial sexual gland which will normalise abnormal sexual desires'. Should he be successful, Vaernet wanted to know 'whether one can normalise all homosexuals with these methods'. In the event that the experiments led to marketable offshoots, Vaernet agreed in advance to concede the SS exclusive rights both at home and abroad. Himmler's letter of recommendation indicated that the *Reichsführer*-SS and police had great expectations of these experiments. Himmler anticipated the mass application of Vaernet's future discoveries and planned to establish an institute where people would be treated with artificial gland implants. A few months before the collapse of the Third Reich he received information from Vaernet that a high dosage of the male hormone testosterone could obliterate any trace of homosexuality. On 10 February 1945, Vaernet dedicated his final report to Heinrich Himmler with gratitude 'for your lasting and generous support'. Apart from the suffering which these human experiments caused the 'subjects', two of whom died because of Vaernet's surgical incompetence, they are also an example of the process whereby a prejudice against a minority could be lent 'scientific' rationalisation.

It remains to note that the Nazis' modified version of Paragraph 175 remained on the statute books of the German Federal Republic until 1969. Between 1950 and 1965 about 50,000 people were convicted of homosexual offences. The highest Federal Court actually decided that the modifications to Paragraph 175 introduced in 1935 had been 'in order' and that they reflected 'no typically National Socialist way of thinking'. With a few exceptions, homosexuals received no compensation. Between 1 January 1958 and 31 December 1959 surviving homosexual concentration camp inmates were entitled to apply for compensation of DM150 for each month they had endured in a camp. On 20 December 1982 the statistical office of the Federal parliament responded to the question 'How many surviving homosexuals have received any compensation?' with the answer that it was impossible to say since 'no separate statistical data was kept concerning applications for compensation by homosexuals persecuted by the Nazis'. However, on 31 October 1986 the Federal government was able rapidly to provide the information that there had been twenty-three applications for compensation so far, with a further nine on the way as a result of a television programme shown in 1980 which drew attention to the compensation for hardship on offer. Even though funds have recently been made available for the so-called 'forgotten victims of National Socialism', the question of compensation for homosexuals persecuted by the National Socialists has largely been 'solved' simply by letting biology taking its course.

The Persecution of Homosexuals in Nazi Germany
Michael Burleigh and Wolfgang Wippermann, *The Racial State: Germany, 1933–1945* (Cambridge, 1991); Heinz Heger, *The Men with the Pink Triangle* (London, 1980); B. Jellonnek, *Homosexuelle unter dem Hakenkreuz. Die Verfolgung der Homosexuellen im Dritten Reich* (Paderborn, 1990); Rüdiger Lautmann, 'Gay Prisoners in Concentration Camps', in Michael Berenbaum (ed.), *A Mosaic of Victims: Non-Jews Persecuted and Murdered by the Nazis* (London, 1990), pp. 200–21; C. Limpricht, J. Müller and N. Oxenius (eds), *'Verführte' Manner. Das Leben der Kölner Homosexuellen im Dritten Reich* (Cologne, 1991); Richard Plant, *The Pink Triangle: The Nazi War against Homosexuals* (New York, 1986); Hans-Georg Stümke, *Homosexuelle in Deutschland.*

Eine politische Geschichte (Munich, 1989); Hans-Georg Stümke and Rudi Finkler, *Rosa Winkel, Rosa Listen. Homosexuelle und 'Gesundes Volksempfinden' von Auschwitz bis heute* (Reinbek, 1981); Günter Grau, *Hidden Holocaust? Gay and Lesbian Persecution in Germany 1933–45.* (London 1955).

CHAPTER XI

WOMEN, MOTHERHOOD AND THE FAMILY IN THE THIRD REICH

Jill Stephenson

Hitler's insistence on racial origin as the fundamental criterion for determining citizenship in the Third Reich affected all the inhabitants of Germany and also those of countries occupied by German forces during the Second World War. 'Racially desirable Aryans' had special duties as well as rights and were subjected to incessant propaganda and 'political education' campaigns, while the 'racially inferior' were outcasts from the 'people's community', suffering discrimination and often outright persecution and physical violence. Some whose racial credentials ostensibly entitled them to membership of the Aryan community were less valuable in Nazi eyes because of some actual or perceived physical or mental ailment — profound deafness, perhaps, or chronic illness, or the loosely-defined disorder of 'feeble-mindedness'. Also less valuable were Aryans who were, by Nazi criteria, delinquent or deviant, for example homosexuals or rebellious youth. Both men and women, and therefore also families, could be 'racially and hereditarily valuable', or 'worthless', regardless of social class or occupation. Almost all of the characteristics that indicated value in this sense were either inherent or involuntarily acquired: that is, most of those who manifested them had no power to control or alter them, and were therefore condemned at best to live on the margins of society in the Third Reich, with physical abuse and death either a palpable threat or grim reality.

The overwhelming emphasis on allegedly racial or inherited characteristics as criteria for belonging to the German nation meant that all aspects of reproduction and the nurturing of the young were regarded as being of paramount importance. By contrast with revolutionary Russia, where, at first at least, the aim was to diminish the influence of the 'bourgeois family', in the Nazi view the family was the 'germ cell' of the nation — its fundamentally important basic unit and a microcosm of the 'national community'. The family, claimed the Nazis, had been damaged and corrupted by a number of recent developments: effective birth-control methods, an increase in female aspirations and employment outside the home, and a materialistic ethos had together helped to promote the 'one- and two-child family' of the Weimar 'system'. The Nazi leadership aimed for a return to the large families of the later nineteenth century, but fecundity was to be encouraged and supported only among those who conformed to the Nazi criteria of 'racial and hereditary value'. These 'desirable' families were to submit to Nazi demands and to reorientate their attitudes, from being inward-looking self-interested collective entities to being the agents of Nazi policies, giving priority to the interests of the 'Aryan race' — as these were defined by the Nazi leadership.

The family was, then, to cease to be a private institution, becoming instead an instrument of Nazi policy, one partner in a triangular relationship, along with school and the Hitler Youth organisation of the National Socialists (NSDAP). These three agencies were to co-operate in the continual and unceasing indoctrination of the young. Further, the legitimacy of parental authority in the Third Reich depended on the subordination of private aspirations and gratification to the demands of the Nazi state. Disqualification from parental rights and responsibilities could follow if a child were encouraged to adopt a negative or hostile attitude towards the regime, its agencies and its policies. The fundamental duty of the family was to maintain and propagate itself as a 'racially and hereditarily desirable' unit, protecting the purity of its blood through the choice of equally 'desirable' marriage partners for all its members and promoting the strength of the 'Aryan race' through generous reproduction [see p. 169]. The emphasis on reproduction ensured that the roles fulfilled within the family by the two parents would be different and complementary. While father necessarily spent much time away from the family, earning the money to sustain it, mother was 'the first educator of children'. Men involved themselves in the world outside the family, which included their role in the armed forces in time of war, while 'the smaller world of the home' was women's preserve: but man remained the head of the household and guardian of his family, while woman was the homemaker within his domain.

> *'Marry! — but whom?'* — *Ten Commandments for choosing a spouse*
> 1. Remember that you are a German.
> 2. If you are hereditarily healthy, you should not remain single.
> 3. Keep your body pure!
> 4. You should keep your heart and mind pure.
> 5. As a German, choose only a spouse of the same or of Nordic blood.
> 6. When choosing your spouse, ask about his/her forebears.
> 7. Healthiness is also the precondition of physical beauty.
> 8. Marry only for love.
> 9. Seek out a partner for marriage, not a playmate.
> 10. You should hope to have as many children as possible.
> (*Der Deutsche*, 11 August 1934)

All of this affected policies and propaganda towards both Aryan and non-Aryan young and adult males, but to a much greater extent it conditioned Nazi attitudes towards women's nature and role in all aspects of life and society. To the Nazi leadership, the female of the species was, above all, an actual or potential mother. Thus, the 'racially desirable' woman, together with her equally 'desirable' partner, was to produce Aryan, 'hereditarily healthy' offspring — as many of them as possible, to counteract the 'pollution' that was alleged to have occurred in the past with non-Aryans and the 'diseased' and 'delinquent' breeding with each other, or even with Aryans, to produce 'less valuable' children. To reverse this perceived development, the Nazis embarked on a horrific and bizarre exercise in reproductive engineering, heavily influenced by two parallel developments. On the one hand, the evidence of a steadily declining birth-rate from around 1900 was a source of anxiety to many Germans, especially as it plummeted during the Depression years around 1930. Equally, scientific interest in human genetics and in the nature of inherited diseases, dating again from about the turn of the century, had created a climate (not only in Germany) in which manipulation of the quality of a population seemed not only possible but also desirable. The Nazis, then, in generating hysteria about the nation dying out, wanted Germans to produce not merely *more* children but specifically more 'racially and hereditarily valuable' children, born to families who had not demonstrated 'asocial' behaviour patterns. The grotesque corollary of this was that 'undesirable' persons were to be prevented from procreating.

Compulsory sterilisation of those judged to be less than valuable was inflicted on women as well as on men, with doctors, lawyers and administrators, among others, instrumental in the procedures to seek out and compel unwilling victims to undergo sterilisation and, if a pregnancy were under way, abortion as a preliminary to it.

These racial and 'eugenic' obsessions and practices formed the essential basis of Nazi policies involving women in the Third Reich. Valuable women were to be treated in ways that protected and promoted their reproductive capacity, with enhanced labour protection laws, for example, and to be constantly reminded of their personal responsibility for raising the birth-rate. But while the role of housewife and mother was the ideal state for all valuable women, it was recognised that some would work outside the home, certainly before marriage; this would preferably be in an area where they could express their 'womanly' or 'motherly' attributes — such as nursing or kindergarten teaching, or in agriculture or domestic service.

To instil in them an awareness of their responsibilities and an acceptance of their biological destiny, women were to be 'politicised'. In a state without conventional politics, this meant little more than indoctrination. But the regime's aim was not simply to suppress opposition and dissent: for valuable women, politicisation was to mean being informed of the regime's policies and requirements in all areas of life, enthusing about them, and implementing them in their daily life, under the guidance of the Nazi women's organisations. Above all, this meant safeguarding the future of the Aryan race, which would involve ostracising the less valuable, and ensuring that their children did the same. If they were employed in teaching, nursing or social work, for example, they might be expected to contribute to the exclusion, humiliation and even the physical abuse of individual adults or children who were labelled 'inferior', in Germany itself or, during the Second World War, in occupied countries.

It was in the realm of motherhood and family life that the women's organisations associated with the NSDAP found their niche. In reality, the élite Party formation, the NS-Frauenschaft (NSF — Nazi Women's Group), and its subordinate mass organisation, the Deutsches Frauenwerk (DFW — German Women's Enterprise), under the leadership of Gertrud Scholtz-Klink, herself a prolific mother, were politically impotent and generally insignificant in the male-dominated Nazi system. They were, however, entrusted with the sensitive task of indoctrinating the valuable female population and with supervision of individuals' child-care and household duties by approved visiting welfare workers, who were used to monitor pregnant women and therefore discourage resort to abortion. The NSF and DFW were also to instil a sense of 'social responsibility' in women, so that they would bring up their children to accept Nazi norms and requirements and to participate enthusiastically in the activities of the Nazi youth organisations. Nazi women's magazines ran articles reassuring mothers that the activities of the Hitler Youth were wholesome and healthy, and that the emphasis on physical endeavour was not taken to dangerous lengths. The NSF and DFW also had the task of trying to wean women away from the Christian Churches, both Evangelical (Protestant) and Roman Catholic, whose influence remained strong, especially in rural areas. But attempts to break the habit of church-going among women and, even more importantly, their children, proved to be virtually impossible, especially when the crises and tragedies of war brought an increase in Christian observance.

The other major activity of the NSF and DFW lay in the provision of courses on housekeeping, child-care and cookery, to try to ensure that valuable families were being nurtured in conditions of cleanliness with healthy (and thrifty) meals, and that the health and growth of infants and small children were being promoted. None of this was merely for the benefit of individual German Aryan families: all these efforts were geared singlemindedly to promoting the regime's racial and power-political objectives. For example, as housewives, women were to buy German goods and shun imports; to this end, they were to use second-hand goods, substitute foods and produce in season. Above all, they were to manifest restraint as consumers and to mend and recycle existing clothes and utensils instead of 'wastefully' demanding goods that were new. This drive for frugality, while thoroughly unpopular, was an integral part of the regime's quest for autarky, or self-sufficiency, in foodstuffs and other essential commodities, in preparation for the coming struggle to achieve the goal of Aryan domination of all of Europe. While the complementary policies of autarky and the damping down of consumer demand were intensified during the war, they were already being pursued before it, particularly after the introduction of the Four Year Plan for the economy in September 1936.

The full-time housewife and mother, caring for her children and providing domestic support for her husband, remained the Nazi ideal. Particularly once her children were of school age, much of her day was to be spent on careful shopping and thrifty housekeeping — mending and altering clothing, making jam and bottling fruit, washing clothes by hand and eschewing 'unnecessary' labour-saving devices. It was hoped that she would also throw herself into the DFW's recreational activities, attending sewing circles or learning about German folk customs and popular culture under the watchful guidance of a reliable NSF member, or learning new skills such as air-raid protection or first aid, allegedly in the spirit of community service. It soon emerged that DFW courses in practical skills, especially child-care and cookery, were quite popular, but there was consistently poor, even derisory, attendance at courses and events in which there was a high overt component of 'political education' and virtually no practical or entertainment value. Participation in the DFW's activities was, of course, restricted to valuable Aryans. But participation did not necessarily indicate enthusiasm for the regime, the Party or its women's organisations. The early *Gleichschaltung* (co-ordination) process, which had eliminated most independent social groups as well as political organisations, created a situation where, if women wanted some kind of associational life, there was little alternative to accepting Nazi structures and leadership. The major exceptions to this were the Christian Churches, because even where local Party zealots succeeded in closing down church social clubs, like women's guilds or youth clubs, regular church services still continued.

The activities of the Nazi women's organisations were geared to promoting Nazi values and aims, with special emphasis on reminding women constantly of their 'duty' not only to cherish existing children but to accept the need to have more. But although there was a rise in the birth-rate from 1934, after the extremely low levels of the Depression years, it soon became apparent that Germans were not prepared to reproduce themselves in sufficient numbers to provide a return to the large families of the later nineteenth century. This was hardly surprising, because German population development had followed the general modern demographic pattern of growth at a time of rapid industrialisation, followed by stabilisation and decline in mature urban society in the twentieth century. But beyond this, part of the problem for the Nazis was a self-inflicted handicap: because the aim was to achieve fewer births in the less valuable sections of the population, the valuable families would have to compensate for that shortfall and then, in addition, contribute extra children to raise the German birth-rate from its low level. This helps to explain the manic nature of large-scale Nazi campaigns to try to persuade the racially valuable to procreate and to add an element of coercion by banning abortion

— on pain of imprisonment — and endeavouring to make contraceptives unavailable. Nevertheless, illicit abortions continued at the rate of between half a million and a million a year during the 1930s, no doubt partly because of the greater difficulty in obtaining contraceptives.

There were also material incentives to propagate, to encourage the valuable to produce large families. These families were designated *kinderreich* (rich in children), whereas 'worthless' large families were simply *Grossfamilien* (big families) which were disqualified from receiving any of the benefits conferred on the *kinderreich*. Benefits took the form of recurrent children's allowances and one-off grants paid to the parents (in practice, to the father) of a large family, and were financed by taxing the childless. Beyond that, mothers of large families were to receive preferential treatment in public places: for example, in some towns they were given free seats at the theatre, while staff in government offices were ordered to give priority to a mother with several children before other people in a queue. To indicate the esteem in which the regime held valuable and prolific mothers, in 1938 the Honour Cross of the German Mother, for women with four or more children, was introduced, with a gold Mother's Cross awarded to those with at least eight children. But perhaps the most practical innovative incentive, was the Marriage Loan Scheme, introduced in June 1933, which provided a small grant for valuable couples intending to marry, on condition that the wife-to-be gave up her job. In reality, the grant was paid in vouchers which were to be redeemed for household goods from approved shops — that is, shops run by Aryans, not Jews. The carrot was that, on the birth of a valuable child, one quarter of the loan would be cancelled, with a year's moratorium on repayments to encourage a new pregnancy in order to have a further quarter of the repayments cancelled.

While encouragement to the valuable to procreate was primarily directed at married couples, with corresponding pressure on the single to marry, any valuable child was welcomed, even if its mother was unmarried. This led to an easing of official prejudice against unwed mothers and their illegitimate children which has given rise to popular rumours about positive encouragement being given by the Nazi leadership to young women to 'give the Führer a child' by a valuable consort, whether or not within the context of a stable relationship. Himmler's *Schutzstaffel* (SS) is particularly associated with this, given his obsession with all issues of population policy, which was extreme even by Nazi standards. Certainly, especially during the Second World War, the SS leadership was in the vanguard of those calling for equal treatment of married and unmarried valuable mothers, and its *Lebensborn* (Fount of Life) homes for expectant and nursing mothers welcomed both. Himmler had already declared, in 1938, that he, through the agency of *Lebensborn*, would assume guardianship of all valuable illegitimate children whose mothers were alone and vulnerable [see box below]. But, contrary to rumour, the *Lebensborn* homes were not established as 'stud farms' for the pro-creation of SS stock. If such things did exist, they were local initiatives by SS zealots. The reality was more sober: the illegitimacy rate in the 1930s was lower than it had been in the 1920s. But, during the war, Himmler was anxious that his men, having had to provide evidence of especially 'pure' ancestry as a condition of admission to the SS, should leave heirs for the future, and that a young woman left to carry an SS man's child after his death in battle should be cherished.

In future, each SS doctor, as a member of the *Schutzstaffel*, must stand up for the honour of the expectant mother, irrespective of whether she is preparing to give birth to a premarital or illegitimate child, to protect her from the possibility of social ostracism and to advise her in the fullest measure ... The present position of the unmarried expectant mother above all necessitates special *legal protection*, the particular safeguarding of her legal interests. The experience of our few months' work has taught us that the unmarried mother is more often than not in a completely helpless position, and since her financial means, too, are generally limited, she cannot call on the necessary legal assistance. Therefore to create a remedy once and for all, the *Reichsführer SS* [Himmler] has decided himself to assume the guardianship of all illegitimate children, through the association *Lebensborn* insofar as it seems necessary. He will therefore undertake the representation of mothers before both the courts dealing with matters of guardianship and the Youth Offices, and will supervise the payment of maintenance by the child's father.
(*Institut für Zeitgeschichte Archiv, MA 387, 5190/92 (?1936)*)

While illegitimate children were, therefore, not to be disparaged or dis-advantaged, the Nazi leadership felt that a better alternative to irregular relationships was the facilitating of marriage. Accordingly, a new Marriage Law was enacted in 1938 which unambiguously clarified the official Nazi view of the nature and purpose of marriage. This included an indication of what constituted an invalid marriage between otherwise 'desirable' couples: the new law made premature infertility in a childless union and also refusal by either partner to have children grounds for divorce. It also introduced the (then) radical principle of 'irretrievable breakdown' as grounds for divorce, without a 'guilty party' and after three years' separation. This, it was hoped, would enable those legally locked into a failed marriage either to enter a new relationship, which would be more likely to produce children, or to regularise an existing extra-marital relationship where there already were children. The new divorce law proved popular, with a sharp rise in both the divorce and marriage rates in 1939.

In addition to encouraging more pregnancies among the valuable, while (often forcibly) terminating those among the less valuable, the regime was anxious to get the best value from each conception, through a reduction in rates of miscarriage (spontaneous or contrived), dead births, infant and maternal mortality and childhood disease. Certainly, there was success in achieving a modest reduction in the infant and peri-natal mortality rates, continuing established trends. But, in spite of Nazi measures for incentives, coercion and surveillance, the rise in the marriage and birth-rates during the 1930s was modest, leaving the birth-rate still far short of pre-1914 levels. Whereas in 1910 there had been 128 live births per 1,000 women of child-bearing age, and 90 in 1922, the best that the Nazi regime could achieve was marked recovery from the Depression's nadir in 1933 of 59, with figures of 85 in 1939 and 84 in 1940. Thereafter, the Second World War saw a renewed decline in the marriage and birth-rates, with desperate attempts to combat this through such tactics as engineering postal romances between soldiers at the front and young women at home, using official 'letter centres' as supervisory match-making agencies [see box on page 176], and sanctioning weddings by proxy. Until the later stages of the war, efforts were made to allow husbands in the armed forces regular home-leave in the hope that this would stimulate conceptions.

The Nazi leadership thus seemed to have clear and ambitious objec-tives both for the control and manipulation of valuable women and their reproductive capacity, and for the marginalising of the less valuable. It was all too successful in the latter, pursuing a singleminded policy of dis-crimination against and persecution of the 'racially or hereditarily dis-eased', women and men alike. But its success in trying to persuade the valuable to procreate on a large scale was at best limited. Further, it soon

Letter Centre for the Marriageable in Gau Bayreuth

With the permission of the Party Chancellery, the Reich Association of German Families, in collaboration with the Racial Policy Office of the regional Leadership, a Letter Centre is opening in Bayreuth . . . The agency meets a need arising from the exigencies of war. For four, five and more years, young men of marriageable age have been in the forces. Many German girls are employed in war service, often far from home . . . The longing of the healthy German man and the healthy German woman for a happy marriage and the blessing of children is, however, unchanging. If even in peacetime not everyone finds a mate, the consequences of total war pose considerable new difficulties.

This is where the Letter Centre can and must play a role. The Letter Centre arranges introductions, gives young Germans who want to get married the chance to get to know each other by post and, if it is desired after this acquaintance through correspondence, to meet in person. The final choice of a partner, from several possibilities, is for the applicant to make . . . The nature of the Letter Centre's work carries the guarantee that applicants who are accepted for the scheme are hereditarily healthy, racially and personally unblemished fellow-citizens, who fulfil all the preconditions for a healthy and happy marriage . . .

The strictest confidence is guaranteed and also expected from all applicants. Thus anyone can take part in this project without regard to educational level, occupation, age, confession or property.

If someone is unwilling to take the first step in this, a relative or friend can get in touch with the Letter Centre as his/her sponsor. In accordance with the National Socialist conception of a German marriage, however, each applicant is expected to manifest a readiness to start a racially desirable, clean, child-loving and therefore also a happy family . . .

(*Völkischer Beobachter* (Süddeutsche Ausgabe), No. 238, 25 August 1944 in the Archives of the Wiener Library, London)

became clear that the regime's short-term power-political ambitions were vitiating its attempts to pursue a coherent policy towards valuable women. While the image of the full-time housewife and mother remained an ideal, it ceased to be unambiguously propagated as a goal from the mid-1930s because of a radical change in the employment market. Whereas in January 1933 there had been well over six million Germans unemployed, by 1938 there was a shortage of labour in key sectors of the economy; during the Second World War, German industry and agriculture suffered from acute labour shortages, even with the forced recruitment of prisoners-of-war and coerced civilians from occupied countries, to a total of over seven million in 1944. These foreigners, including in the end at least a million and a half women, had the advantage, as the Nazis saw it, of not requiring to be treated humanely: most came from Eastern Europe and were classed as 'racially inferior'. They could be deployed in areas where conditions were dangerous or insanitary, for long hours, in a way that might be (reproductively) hazardous for valuable Aryan women.

German women had, of course, figured in a wide variety of occupations long before 1933, including factory work, domestic service, clerical and other white-collar jobs and, especially, agriculture, where large numbers of wives and daughters of farmers worked as 'assisting family members' without a formal wage. A tiny number of well-educated women had breached male chauvinist professional bastions such as medicine and law, with larger numbers in school-teaching and the 'caring professions'. But in the shrunken jobs market of the Depression, prejudice against women in the workplace, especially if they were married, was strong before 1933 and the new Nazi government reflected a significant section of public opinion in calling for the return of women to home and family life. Restrictive legislation in 1933 against employing married women in the public service built on a pre-Nazi law of May 1932, while a quota system for female students was welcomed by many male professionals. Such measures gave the clear impression that the Nazis' aims in population development and employment policy would be compatible and mutually reinforcing. The Marriage Loan Scheme, after all, was introduced in a section of the Law to Reduce Unemployment of 1 June 1933, with the stipulation that the intending wife must relinquish her job on marriage as the crucial condition aimed at easing the straitened labour market.

While the Depression persisted, until the mid-1930s mass unemployment in all sectors of the economy and overcrowding of the universities seemed to provide double justification — over and above population policy considerations — for the Nazi policy of trying both to remove women, particularly married women, from jobs outside the home and to reduce the number of young women in higher education. These tactics were aimed at giving men (actual and potential 'fathers of families') priority in employment and educational opportunities, while recalling women to their 'natural sphere' of home, family and 'womanly work'. But the rapid revival of the economy meant that from the mid-1930s there were increasing shortages of labour in some sectors and later throughout the economy. With the exclusion of non-Aryans and political opponents of both genders from influential or promoted positions in thoroughgoing purges in 1933, German male labour and professional expertise were not alone sufficient for the regime's ambitions — which included the use of labour and expertise in programmes for compulsory sterilisation, 'euthanasia' and the extermination of the less valuable. Women were therefore encouraged to enter the employment market, even in areas that had previously been designated 'men's jobs'.

This contributed to an increase in women's presence in both higher education and the professions even before the war, once the graduate unemployment of the early 1930s had been absorbed, although women continued to figure overwhelmingly in the lower levels of the professions. While there were some new restrictions on women's employment and promotion prospects — from 1936, for example, women lawyers were excluded from participation in court-room work — the later 1930s provided increasing scope for individual women graduates. Some of this was due to the peculiar and pernicious nature of the Third Reich. For example, women doctors were in particular demand in the Nazi women's organisations, including the Bund deutscher Mädel (League of German Girls) and the Women's Labour Service, where not only the general health of young females, but also the detail of their reproductive development, was monitored. In addition, the involvement of doctors, lawyers and civil servants in the sterilisation and 'euthanasia' programmes created new jobs for those prepared to prostitute their professional training. There were also completely new occupations deemed to require graduate expertise, including work in the genealogical records offices, which were kept busy by the requirements of the 'racial and hereditary health' qualifications for both citizenship and the right to marry in the Third Reich.

By 1939 it was clear that the available *and willing* reserves of female labour had been exhausted, and that increasing recruitment in one sector meant a loss to another. In particular, young women in rural areas saw in the demand for labour in urban occupations an opportunity to escape from the long hours, low pay and physical exhaustion involved in farm work. It is an indictment of the harshness of life on the land that many viewed manual labour in a factory as preferable. By 1939, there were 50 per cent more women employed in industry than there had been in the depressed year of 1933, with increases in other sectors too, especially white-collar clerical work. Women industrial workers formed about half of the labour force in consumer goods industries throughout the 1930s, but only around 10 per cent in producer goods industries. They were much more likely to be found in textiles production than in armaments factories. Even so, by 1939 almost half of all German women classed as 'fit for work' were not employed, of whom the overwhelming majority were married: 36 per cent of married women, compared with almost 90 per cent of single women, were in work of some kind, whether as employees, proprietors or 'assisting family members' in small businesses, including farms. By the later 1930s, strenuous efforts were being made to attract more married women into work, with half-day shifts and the promise of more crèches — a promise never adequately fulfilled.

From the start of the war, the key labour problem that exercised the regime's leaders was how to mobilise more German women for the war effort without using outright coercion against these valuable citizens. The idea of labour conscription was repeatedly discussed but not enacted until January 1943; even then, it was imperfectly enforced. It has been argued that this was because Hitler was reluctant to risk women's reproductive health by forcing them into factory work, but it is clear that other factors were more important. Firstly, Hitler believed that unwilling and inexperienced female workers would be of little value, especially in compensating for skills shortages. And secondly, Hitler and some of his henchmen were reluctant to risk antagonising women and their families: middle-class women and their husbands, particularly, resisted appeals for more female labour in industry and found loopholes in the 1943 legislation. The regime had itself provided good reason for women's reluctance to go out to work in introducing an allowance to be paid to the wife of a serving soldier. The solution to the problem was the large-scale use of foreign forced labour, with skilled French workers and unskilled Soviet (and sometimes female) Ostarbeiter (literally, 'eastern workers'), under German supervision, providing some compensation for the loss of German male labour.

The foreign workers mostly lived and worked under oppressively segregated and policed control, especially in urban areas. Towards the end of the war, especially, many were close to starvation. But some foreigners — especially in the freer conditions of agrarian society — struck up relationships with Germans. While there were cases of foreign women workers becoming involved with German men or boys, more often the relationships were between German women and foreign men, especially, in rural areas, Poles. Sometimes this was the result of genuine affection, sometimes it was born of pure sexual need. A farmer's wife whose husband was at the front might voluntarily embark on a sexual liaison with a foreign male worker allocated to her as a replacement, or else she might accept it as the price to be paid for having a compliant worker without whose labour the farm could not function [see box below]. In the towns, too, a woman left on her own might strike up a friendship with a foreign worker, especially as he became more confident once the war turned against Germany. To the Nazi authorities these relationships were anathema, amounting to 'racial pollution'. The penalties for offenders, which were well-publicised, clearly demonstrated a gender-based double standard: a foreign woman and her German male lover often suffered little more than official disapproval, while a 'racially inferior' foreign man was hanged and his Aryan female lover sent to prison after being ritually physically abused by Nazi vigilantes, usually by having her head shaved in a public ceremony.

After the call-up of almost all able-bodied male workers, agricultural concerns were allocated, almost exclusively, Poles, Serbs and prisoners of war to work alongside the female workers already available. There are complaints about the rampant unruliness of these foreign elements which, one hears, leads not infrequently to the Germans actually being afraid of foreigners who at one and the same time make great demands and, in the face of stricter discipline and supervision, threaten to withdraw their labour. So the proprietors cut down on their own provisioning in order to please the foreigners, grant them various comforts, and, in spite of official prohibitions, let them eat at the same table, simply to prevent damage to their business ... Farmers' wives are afraid of them, especially because of frequent reports in the press of acts of violence and the murder of proprietors. The ever-increasing symptoms of prohibited contact with prisoners of war, especially pregnancies in German girls and women, are not least attributable to these circumstances. Frequently, women who are accused plead under questioning that they gave in to the prisoner of war so as not to lose his labour.

(*Bundesarchiv*, R22/3387, the Stuttgart Public Prosecutor to the Reich Minister of Justice, 31 May 1943)

The public humiliation and imprisonment of an Aryan German woman who had a sexual relationship with a foreigner indicates the ferocity with which even the valuable were punished when they violated Nazi racial prescriptions. There could be few sins greater than 'polluting

German blood', as a valuable woman was deemed to have done when she permitted the invasion of her body by a 'racial enemy', and the sanctions were accordingly draconian. Similarly, the death penalty was introduced in 1943 for anyone performing an abortion to terminate a valuable pregnancy, because this was 'racial sabotage', contributing to the 'dying out' of the German nation during the crisis of war. Beyond these specific sanctions, and those against overt political opponents, there was little direct brutality against valuable women, whose reproductive capacity had to be safeguarded at all costs. At the same time, the second half of the war saw an intensification of persecution of the Nazis' 'racial enemies' and the implementation of a systematic extermination programme in which they and the 'asocial' or 'deviant' were targeted with almost no discrimination between men and women. The chief exception was that male homosexuals were treated with appalling brutality, as 'racial saboteurs', while lesbians were seen as simply deviant, not as a racial threat. There were women villains as well as victims, including, most infamously, concentration camp guards. And a small band of committed NSF workers — regarded with contempt by large sections of the German population — not only tried to win valuable women's compliance with Nazi demands, but also assisted in the segregation of the valuable from the 'worthless', and in the dispossession of the latter, in occupied countries (see box below).

> *From the work of the NS-Frauenschaft in the Wartheland*
> The Border/Foreign Section [of the NSF/DFW] participates in the tasks associated with the German People's List, on the basis of which the division between Germans and Poles is strictly demarcated . . . The Wartheland [in occupied Poland] is a developing area. More and more Germans are flooding into this new region of the Reich . . . The task for all of them is to turn the Wartheland into a flourishing German territory . . . 136,000 women and girls are today in this community, inspired and imbued with the task of making a German homeland out of alien Polish territory.
> (Institut für Zeitgeschichte Archiv, MA 225, Gau Württemberg/ Hohenzollern, 2-408814/5, 29 April 1942)

Hitler's war did, nevertheless, create many hardships for valuable women, especially in its later stages, with increasing enemy bombing and then invasion, as well as material deprivation as rationing grew more stringent and everyday facilities and utilities were closed down or destroyed. The evacuation of women and children from urban bombing targets often led to hostility between them and their rural host families. Above all, during and sometimes also after the war, many women had to assume the role of breadwinner and head of the household, with a husband or father temporarily absent or never to return. With three million German men killed, and many others injured, maimed or taken prisoner, many 'valuable' young women would not find a husband. The long-term decline in the German birth-rate would continue, with Hitler able to suggest only one remedy for the post-war period: bigamy, to ensure that 'valuable' women would not be wasted reproductive assets. Nevertheless, while the 'racially valuable' woman was abused in the Third Reich by being subjected to Nazi control and manipulation, she – unlike the less 'valuable' — had some room for manoeuvre, even if that narrowed considerably under the pressures of war. Above all, a 'valuable' woman could not be forced to have more children, and strenuous attempts to deny her the means of birth control clearly failed. Particularly if she belonged to the middle classes, she was in a position to resist propaganda and direct appeals by Party or state functionaries to have larger families, to take paid employment during the war, to participate more in NSF and DFW activities, and to demand fewer consumer goods. 'Valuable' women who failed to comply with these appeals were certainly pestered with propaganda and pressure; but they were generally not subjected to coercion or brutality, because of their value and because these issues concerned mere policy objectives, not racial ideological imperatives.

Women, Motherhood and the Family

Stefan Bajohr, *Die Hälfte der Fabrik. Geschichte der Frauenarbeit in Deutschland 1914 bis 1945* (Marburg, 1979); Gisela Bock, *Zwangs-sterilisation im Nationalsozialismus. Studien zur Rassenpolitik und Frauenpolitik* (Opladen, 1986); Renate Bridenthal, Atina Grossman and Marion Kaplan (eds), *When Biology Became Destiny: Women in Weimar and Nazi Germany* (New York, 1984); Michael Burleigh and Wolfgang Wippermann, *The Racial State: Germany 1933–1945* (Cambridge, 1991); Frauengruppe Faschismusforschung (ed.), *Mutterkreuz und Arbeitsbuch*, (Frankfurt am Main, 1981); Ute Frevert, *Women in German History: From Bourgeois Emancipation to Sexual Liberation* (Oxford, Hamburg and New York, 1989); Clifford Kirkpatrick, *Woman in Nazi Germany* (London, 1939); Jacques R. Pauwels, *Women, Nazis, and Universities:*

Female University Students in the Third Reich, 1933–1945 (Westport, Conn., 1984); Jill Stephenson, *Women in Nazi Society* (London, 1975; New York, 1976); Jill Stephenson, *The Nazi Organisation of Women* (London and New York, 1981); Alison Owings, *Frauen. German Women Recall the Third Reich* (London 1993); Dörte Winkler, *Frauenarbeit im Dritten Reich* (Hamburg, 1977).

GLOSSARY

'Barbarossa': The German code-name for the attack on the Soviet Union on 22 June 1941.

Einsatzgruppen: The death squads of the SS and SD charged with killing Jews and Communists during the invasion of the Soviet Union.

'Final Solution': The Nazi euphemism for the mass murder of the Jews.

Führer: Leader, the title assumed by Hitler, first as leader of the Nazi party and later as leader of the Third Reich.

Gulags: The Soviet camps in which Stalin imprisoned alleged enemies of his regime along with criminals.

Herrenvolk: Master Race, the Nazi term used to describe the German, or Aryan race and its destiny as a ruler of humanity.

Historikerstreit: The name given to the German historians' controversy over the interpretation of the Nazi past which began in 1986.

Kampfgemeinschaft: Community of Struggle, the Nazi term which idealised the comradeship of soldiers in battle, as well as the `political fighters' of the Nazi Party before it came to power in Germany.

Lebensraum: Living Space, the Nazi term for the areas to be conquered in the East and to be colonised by the Germans.

Mein Kampf: My Struggle, the title of Hitler's book, in which he combined an autobiographical account of his early years with his ideas about history as an eternal struggle between races and his programme for German expansion and domination in Europe.

SS: *Schutzstaffel*, or Protection Squads, originally bodyguard units of the Nazi Party, later a vast organisation comprising military units, concentration and death camp administration, secret police (SD), and huge economic enterprises.

Untermenschen: Subhumans, the Nazi term for inferior races, of whom the Jews and the Slavs constituted the lowest species.

Vergangenheitsbewältigung: Overcoming the past, a term introduced in the postwar Federal Republic of Germany to describe the need to confront, or come to terms with, the Nazi past.

Vernichtungskrieg: War of extermination or destruction, the Nazi term for the war planned in the East.

Volksgemeinschaft: National Community, a Nazi term describing the ideal society of the future based on racial homogeneity and devoid of class tensions.

Weltanschauungskrieg: War of ideologies, the Nazi term for the war in the East as one conducted between two radically opposed world views, one of which would have to be totally annihilated before victory is achieved.

Organisations mentioned in the text (initial in brackets are those of author)

Abwehr, Military Intelligence (JN)
Aktion T-4 (MB)
AZR, Forced Labour Reich (WW)
Catholic Centre Party (PW, HGS)
Community Patients' Transport Service (MB)
Department for Twin and Hereditary Research (PW)
Deutsches Frauenwerk, DFW, German Women's Enterprise (JS)
Fascist Confederation of Industrial Labour (KJS)
Four Year Plan (UH, GA)
Free Corps (JN)
Generalgouvernement (GA, WW, MB)
Generalplan Ost (GA)
German Council of the Four Year Plan (GA)
German Labour Front, DAF (UH, AB, KJS)
German National Peoples' Party (HGS)
German Research Council (GA)
German Womanhood Association
German Women's Association
German Workers' Party (AB)
Gobineau Society (PW)
Hereditary Health Centre (MB)
Hitler Youth (AB, JS, OB)
Honour Cross of the German Mother (JS)
Hygiene Institute of the *Waffen*-SS (PW)
Institute for Deutsch Ostarbeit (GA)
Jewish Winter Aid (AB)
Kaiser Wilhelm Institute for Anthropology, Human Heredity and Eugenics (PW)
Law for the Combating of Gypsies, Travellers and the Workshy, 1926 (WW)

Law for the Confiscation of the Property of Enemies of the State and Nation (WW)
Law for the Protection of German Blood and Honour (AB)
Law for the Prevention of Hereditarily Diseased Progeny (MB)
Law for the Restoration of the Professional Civil Service (WW)
League of German Maidens
League for the Protection of Motherhood and Social Reform (PW)
Lebensraum (AB)
Main Trustees for the East (GA)
Marriage Health Law (WW)
Marriage Law, 1938 (JS)
Munich Racial Hygiene Society (PW)
National People's Party (JN)
National Socialist People's Welfare, NSV (AB)
National Socialist Workers' Party, NSDAP (UH, AB, WW)
NS-Frauenschaft, NSF, Nazi Women's Group (JS)
NSV (JN)
NS-Womanhood
Nuremberg Doctors' Trial (PW)
Nuremberg Laws, 1935 (PW, AB, WW, HGS)
Racial Hygiene Society (PW)
Racial Hygienic Research Bureau (WW)
Racial Political Office (*Rassepolitisches Amt*) (PW, WW)
Reich Central Office for the Combating of Gypsy Nuisance
Reich Central Office for the Combating of Homosexuality and Abortion (HGS)
Reich Commissariat for the Strengthening of Ethnic Germandom (GA)
Reich Committee for Economic Affairs (GA)
Reich Committee for the Scientific Registration of Serious Hereditary and Congenital Illnesses (MB)
Reich Labour Service (OB)
Reich Crystal Night (GA)
Reich Mother Service
Reich Office for Area Planning (GA)
Reichslandbund (JN)
Reichswehr (AB)
SA (UH, PW)
SAKK (JN)
Scientific-Humanitarian Committee, WhK (HGS)

SD, Nazi Security Service (JN)
socialist labour movement (UH)
`Sopade' (UH)
SPD (UH, HGS)
SS Marriage Order (JN)
SS Race and Settlement Main Office
Strength through Joy (UH, AB)
Travellers' Department of the Bavarian Regional Criminal Police (VW)
Vaterlandpartei (PW)
Vitalrasse
völkisch (UH)
Volksgemeinschaft (AB)
Wannsee Conference (OB)
Wehrmacht (UH, OB)
Well of Life association
Winter Aid Programme (JN)
Young Plan (JN)

LIST OF
CONTRIBUTORS

Götz Aly is a freelance journalist and historian living in Berlin. He is the author of several studies of the Nazi 'euthanasia' programme and the 'Final Solution', published in the series that he also edits, *Beiträge zur nationalsozialistische Sozial- und Gesundheitspolitik*. His books include (with Karl-Heinz Roth) *Die restlose Erfassung. Volkszählen, Identifizieren, Aussondern im Nationalsozialismus* (Berlin, 1984), *Aktion T-4, 1939–1945* (Berlin, 1987) (with Susanne Heim) *Vordenker der Vernichtung* (Berlin, 1991); (with Peter Chroustand Christian Pross) *Cleansing the Fatherland. Nazi Medicine and Racial Hygiene* (Baltimore and London (1994); *'Endlösung', Volkerverschie bung und der mord an den Europäischen Juden* (Frankfurt, 1995).

Avraham Barkai is a Research Fellow with the Institute for German History, University of Tel Aviv. His books include *Das Wirtschaftssystem des Nationalsozialismus* (Frankfurt, 1988), which has recently appeared in English as *Nazi Economics: Ideology, Theory, and Policy* (Oxford, 1990), and *From Boycott to Annihilation: The Economic Struggle of German Jews, 1933–1943* (Hanover, 1990).

Omer Bartov is Professor of History at Rutgers University and author of *The Eastern Front, 1941–1945: German Troops and the Barbarisation of Warfare* (London and New York, 1986) *Hitler's Army: Soldiers, Nazis, and War in the Third Reich* (Oxford and New York, 1991); and of *Murder in our Midst* (Oxford and New York, 1996).

Michael Burleigh is Distinguished Research Professor in Modern History at the University of Wales, Cardiff. His books include *Germany Turns Eastwards: A Study of 'Ostforschung' in the Third Reich* (Cambridge, 1988); (with Wolfgang Wippermann), *The Racial State: Germany 1933–1945* (Cambridge, 1991); and *Death and Deliverance: 'Euthanasia' in Germany, 1900–1945* (Cambridge, 1994). He wrote and researched 'Selling Murder' (Domino Films/Channel 4) on Nazi propaganda for the 'euthanasia' programme which has been shown in twenty countries and for which he won the 1991 British Film Institute Award for Archival Achievement. He was Programme Consultant to 'Master Race' in the BBC People's Century series.

Ulrich Herbert is Professor of History at the University of Freiburg. His books include *Fremdarbeiter. Politik und Praxis des 'Ausländer-Einsatzes' in der Kriegswirtschaft des Dritten Reiches* (Berlin and Bonn, 1985) which will shortly be published by Cambridge University Press; *A History of Foreign Labour in Germany* (London, 1990); *Arbeit, Volkstum, Weltanschauung* (Frankfurt, 1995) and *Best. Biographische Studien über Radikalismus, Weltanschauung und Vernunft* (Bonn, 1966).

Jeremy Noakes is Professor of History at the University of Exeter. He is the author of numerous articles on the Third Reich and of *The Nazi Party in Lower Saxony* (Oxford, 1971), *Government, Party and People in Nazi Germany* (Exeter, 1980), and (with G. Pridham) of *Nazism, 1919–1945. A Documentary Reader*, 3 vols (Exeter, 1986–9).

Klaus-Jörg Siegfried is an historian and head of the town archives in Wolfsburg. His books include *Universalismus und Faschismus. Das Gesellschaftsbild Othmar Spanns* (Vienna, 1974), *Rustungsproduktion und Zwangsarbeit im Volkswagenwerk, 1939–1945* (Frankfurt am Main, 1986) and *Das Leben der Zwangsarbeiter im Volkswagenwerk, 1939–1945* (Frankfurt am Main, 1988).

Jill Stephenson is a Reader in History at the University of Edinburgh. Her publications on women in twentieth-century Germany include *Women in Nazi Society* (London and New York, 1975) and *The Nazi Organisation of Women* (London and New York, 1981), and numerous essays and articles published between 1971–1992. Since 1985 she has also published essays and articles on her current research interest, society in Wurttemberg during the Second World War. She is joint editor of *German History: The Journal of the German History Society*.

Hans-Georg Stümke is a freelance writer and historian living in Hamburg. His books include (with Rudi Finkler), *Rosa Winkel, Rosa Listen. Homosexuelle und 'Gesundes Volksempfinden' von Auschwitz bis Heute* (Hamburg, 1981) and *Homosexuelle in Deutschland. Eine politische Geschichte* (Munich, 1989).

Paul Weindling is a Senior Research Officer at the Wellcome Unit for the

History of Medicine, University of Oxford. His books include *Darwinism and Social Darwinism in Imperial Germany* (Stuttgart, 1989), *Health, Race and German Politics Between National Unification and Nazism, 1870–1945* (Cambridge, 1989). He has edited *The Social History of Occupational Health* (London, 1985) and *International Health Organisations and Movements 1918–1939* (Cambridge, 1995). He is joint editor of *Social History of Medicine. The Journal of the Society for the Social History of Medicine.*

Wolfgang Wippermann is a Professor of Modern History at the Freie Universität Berlin. His books include *Europaische Faschismus im Vergleich, 1922–1988* (Frankfurt am Main, 1983), *Faschismustheorien* (5th edn, Darmstadt, 1988), *Das Leben in Frankfurt in der NS Zeit* (Frankfurt am Main, 1986), vols 1–4, *Der Deutsche 'Drang nach Osten'* (Darmstadt, 1981) and (with Michael Burleigh) *The Racial State: Germany, 1933–1945* (Cambridge, 1991).

INDEX

Page locations in **bold**
denote main sections.
Chronological order is
introduced in sub-headings
where appropriate.

abortion 67, 72, 159, 172–3,
   175, 181
'Aktion Reinhard' 109
Aktion T–4 see T–4
Aly, Götz 12, 14–16, 80,
   140–53, 188
anthropologists: role in
   racial policies 66, 75, 80,
   151
Arendt, Hannah 140, 152
'asocial' concept 67, 114,
   118–19, 162, 181
Astel, Karl 82
asylums see psychiatry
August-Wilhelm of Prussia,
   Prince 55, 56
Auschwitz camp 19, 40, 46,
   109
   'Gypsy camp' 114–15,
      116, 118, 123
Auschwitz Decree (1943) 7
Austria
   'Aryanisation' of Jewish
      business 141, 142, 144
   recruitment of workers
      38

Badoglio, Marshal Pietro
   39 43
Barbarossa, Operation see
   Soviet Union
Barkai, Avraham 12, 20,
   84–97, 188
Bartov, Omer 12, 17,
   125–39, 188
Bayerische Motorwerke
   (BMW) 38

Bebel, August 69–70, 156
Bechstein family 53
Belgium: 'foreign labour' in
   Germany 39, 41, 43, 44
Belzec camp 109
Berlin
   Horchers Restaurant
      61, 63, 64
   pre-war 'spartanic' life
      31
   role in high society 53
Bernburg extermination
   centre 107
Binding, Karl 98–9, 104
Bini, 103
biology
   19th–20th C. view of
      69, 71
   National Socialism as
      applied b. 76
   role in racial policies 66,
      68, 70, 73, 151
Bismarck, Prince Otto von
   25, 69
Bismarck-Schönhausen,
   Count Gottfried von
   62, 63
Blaichach camp 118
Boepple, Ernst 53
bombing raids 33–4, 36,
   138, 182
Bormann, Martin 65
Borsig, Ernst von 54
Bouhler, Philipp 105, 109
Brack, Viktor 109, 142
Brandenburg extermination
   centre 107
Brandt, Karl 105
Britain: Hitler's wish for
   settlement with 126–7
Broszat, Martin 2–3, 14, 18
Browning, Christopher 17,
   79

Bruckmann family 53
Brüning, Chancellor
   Heinrich 52
Brunswick: factory training
   school 38
Buchenwald camp 78,
   162–3, 164
Bund deutscher Ma["]del
   (League of German
   Girls) 178
Burleigh, Michael **1–22**, 73,
   98–111, 188

Carnap, Helen von 56
Catholic Centre Party 72,
   156
Cerletti, 103
Chamberlain, Houston
   Stewart 53
children see women and
   children
Christof of Hesse, Prince
   55
Christoph, Franz 9
Churches and religion
   107–8, 171, 172
Cianetti, Tullio 41
civil servants: part in racial
   policies 140–1, 151–2,
   178
class issues see high society;
   middle class; work force
Communists
   in pre-war Germany 25,
      31, 156, 157
   in Russia 127, 128
Community
   Patients'Transport
   Service 107
concentration and
   extermination camps,
   see also *individual
   camps*

conversion of asylums
107–9
forced labour 39–45, see
also work force
'Gypsy' camps 113,
115–18
medical procedures
77–8
'police preventive
custody' 115, 118
Soviet post-war camps
1–2
Conze, Werner 141
cremation movement 79
Czechoslovakia:
'Aryanisation' of Jewish
business 144

Dachau camp 118, 163
DAF see German Labour
Front
Dahrendorf, Ralf 13
Daimler-Benz 6, 46
Darré, Richard 76
Denmark
'foreign workers' in
Germany 32, 39
self-sufficiency in food
148
Der Stürmer 92
Deutsche Justiz 158
Deutsches Frauenwerk
(DFW; German
Women's Enterprise)
170–1, 172, 181, 183
Deutschvölkische Schutz
und Trutzbund 53
diplomatic corps 51–2, 60,
61
Dirksen, Viktoria and
Willibald von 56
doctors, see also medicine
and health
Jews 91
role in racial policies 66,
67, 70, 74, 78–80, 81,
151, 164–5, 170
in psychiatric asylums
101, 107, 109–11
women 178
Dodd, Martha 51, 52

Dressen, Willy 19

Eberl, Irmfried 109
Eberstein, Karl Freiherr
von 55
Ebert, President Friedrich
51
Eckart, Dietrich 53
economy, see also financial
matters; Four Year
Plan; work force
industrial capacity 26,
38, 45–7, 151
Jewish contribution and
its elimination 88–9,
90–2, 95, 97, 149–51
NSDAP policy
successes 26, 29, 35,
133, 178
of Poland 145, 146–7
social/biological
concepts 73, 80, 99,
100, 143–52
1946 UN report on
Europe 153
Eduard of Saxe-Coburg,
Duke 55
Eglfing-Haar asylum 99,
100–1, 103–4, 105–6
Ehrenfels, Christian von 71
Eichberg asylum 101
Eichmann, Adolf 144
Eimann, Kurt 106
Escherich, Karl 53
The Eternal Jew (film) 93,
96
eugenics
history of in Germany
68–71
seen as legitimate
science 66, 68, 72–5
part in racial cleansing
75, 76, 79, 100, 170
euthanasia programme
9–11, 75, 99, 104–11,
142–3, 178

Fallersleben factory 37–49
Fallingbostel camp 46
Fallnbigl, Pte Fred 132
Fascist Confederation of

Industrial Labour 39, 41
Faulhaber, Cardinal
Michael von 92–3
Federal Republic
compensation issues
4–8, 21, 165
post-war society 135
Supreme Court ruling
on Sinti and Roma
7–8, 118–19, 122–3
Fetscher, Eugen 72
Fichte, Werner von 55
financial matters
cost of Depression 146
Marriage Loan Scheme
173
support from social
élite 53–4
workers' wages 4, 26, 30,
31
post–war compensation
claims 4–8, 21, 165
First World War
socio-political conflicts
30, 71–2, 128
psychiatric abuse 98
reparations 54
Fischbock, Hans 144
Fischer, Eugen 71
food
in asylums 108, 110
shortages 26, 31, 33,
148, 151, 171
Ukraine as
'breadbasket' plan
141, 147
forced labour see work
force
Four Year Plan 28, 141,
144–5, 148, 171
France
Dreyfus Affair 17, 84
Imperial Germany's
view of 17–18
Nazi view of 126–7
Hitler's invasion 126
forced labour in
Germany 31, 39, 41,
42, 43, 44, 179
prisoners of war 39
Vichy France 41

Franz, Kurt 109
Free Corps 55, 56
Frick, Wilhelm 61
Friedländer, Saul 3
Friedrich-Christian of
    Schaumburg-Lippe,
    Prince 55
Fritsch, Gen Werner von
    159
Fromm, Bella 56, 59–60,
    60–1
Fuhlsbüttel camp 162

Galton, Francis 70
Gansser, Dr Emil 54
Generalplan Ost 148–9
genetic theory 68, 70, 74,
    75, 80, 169
German Democratic
    Republic: post-war
    reparations 4–5
German Labour Front
    (DAF) 3–4, 37–8, 39,
    40, 87, 88
German National People's
    Party 54, 156
German Workers' Party 85
Gestapo
    pre-war suppression of
        working class 28, 29,
        86
    harassment of
        homosexuals 158–9,
        160–2
    persecution of Jews 91,
        95
    at Fallersleben factory
        40, 44
    forced labour camps 117
    attempts to suppress
        black market 33
Geyer, George 119–20
Gierek, Edward 5
Gigli, Benjamino 60
Globocnik, Odilo 109, 110
Gobineau Society 71
Goebbels, Josef 61, 64, 94,
    143, 158
Goebbels, Magda 57
Goering, Hermann 56–7, 61,
    64, 95, 140, 143–4, 148

Grafeneck extermination
    centre 107
Grynszpan, Hershel 94
Günther, H.F.K. 'Rassen'
    68, 76
'Gypsies' see concentration
    camps; Roma and Sinti
    people

Habermas, Jürgen 16
Hackenholt, Lorenz 109
Hadamar extermination
    centre 107
Haecker, Walther 72
Haina asylum 101
Hallendorf Camp 21 40
Hamann, Matthias 14–16
Hamburg University
    Hospital: Twin and
    Hereditary Research 75
Hanfstängl, Erna and
    'Putzi' 53
Harmsen, Hans 107–8
Hartheim extermination
    centre 107, 108
health see medicine and
    health
Heim, Susanne 14–16, 80
Heinrich, Wolf, Count von
    Helldorf 55
Henckell (later Ribbentrop),
    Annette von 57
Herbert, Ulrich 13, 23–36,
    189
Hereditary Health Courts
    102, 106
Hermann Göring-Werk,
    Salzgitter 38
Hess, Rudolf 61, 76
Heyde, Werner 106
Heydecker, Joe 19–20
Heydrich, Reinhard 16,
    143, 144
high society 51–65
    and political élite 13,
        51–4, 56–7, 60–1
    attempts to measure
        'good blood' 59
    enrolment of nobility in
        NSDAP and SS 13,
        54–6, 57–60, 62–3

marriage of Princess
    Maria-Adelgunde
    and Prince
    Konstantin 63–4
Hill, Müller 74–5, 76
Hillgruber, Andreas 3, 16,
    136–7
Himmler, Heinrich
    leader of SS 55, 58–9
    SS procreation policy
        174
    society figure 55, 61
    Lebensborn homes 174
    Solution of the Gypsy
        Question (1938)
        113, 118
    concentration camp
        empire 46, 117
    deal with Porsche 46–7
    homosexuality decree
        162
    part in eugenics
        programme 68, 72,
        74, 157, 159–60, 163,
        164
    part in Holocaust 16,
        109, 151
Hindenburg, President
    Paul von 51, 54, 60, 91
Hirschfeld, Dr Magnus 71,
    156, 157
Historikerstreit 1–4, 14, 16,
    18, 135–6, 140, 184
Hitler, Adolf, see also Mein
    Kampf
    psychopathic make-up
        67, 74
    rise to power 85–6
    aim of egalitarian
        community 14
    society figure 52–3,
        53–4, 54, 60–1, 65
    SS and the 'blood
        banner' 55
    racial purity policies 68,
        73–4, 89, 105, 106,
        125–6, 142–3, 157–8,
        162, 167
    view of Anglo-Saxon
        race 126–7
    laying of Fallersleben

foundation stone (1938) 37
concept of war 125–6, 160
pre-war conquests 31
pact with Stalin (1939) 31, 126
diktat to Army in Russia 131, 140
role in Holocaust 76, 109, 136
deal with Porsche 46
women and reproductive policies 179, 182
Hitler Youth 92, 132, 134, 168, 171
Hoche, Alfred 98–9, 104
Hoess, Rudolf 109
Hohenzollern, Princess Maria-Adelgunde of 63–4
Holocaust see Jews
Hölzel, Dr Friedrich 105–6
homosexuality 20–1, 67, 71, 87, 154–66, 181
Hoth, Col-Gen Hermann 130
Hugenberg, Alfred 54, 90
Hygiene Institute of the Waffen-SS 72, 78–9

Idstein reformatory 101
Imperial Germany
anti-semitism 84
genetics 70
industrialisation 69
psychiatry 98
treatment of 'Gypsies' 7
Institut für Deutsche Ostarbeit 148
Institut für Zeitgeschichte 1
Institute for Psychiatry 76
Institute for Sexual Studies 157
Israel: post–war compensation agreements 4, 5
Italy
Fascist social policies 35
forced labour and

killings in Germany 39, 41, 43, 45, 110
low racial concepts 68

Jagow, Dietrich von 55
Japan: record of brutality 138–9
Jews
history of anti-semitism 84–5, 88–9, 92
'racial degeneracy' concept 67, 76, 77, 87–8, 126
'responsibility' for disease 21, 77
eugenic programme link 76, 78, 80, 81
persecution 18–20, 28, 88–97, 109–10, 149, 156, 163
1938 pogrom 20, 94–5, 144
'Aryanisation' 91–2, 95, 97, 141–2, 143–4, 150
in Auschwitz 40, 46, 110
cheap labour force 151
deportation 95, 149–50
'Final Solution of the Jewish Question' 15–16, 19–20, 76, 79–80, 89, 128, 136–7, 139, **140–53**
fate of Russian Jews 127, 129–30, 132, 149
post-war Jewish Claims Conference 4–5
Justin, Eva 120–1, 122

Kaiser Wilhelm Institute for Anthropology, Human Heredity and Eugenics 66, 73
Kampfgemeinschaft 126, 134–5, 184
Karsten, Leo 122, 123
Kater, Michael 18–19
Katharinenhof asylum 104
Kautsky, Karl 70

Kershaw, Ian 18–19
Killinger, Cdr Manfred von 55
Kirdorf, Emil 54
Klare, Rudolf 158
Klee, Ernst 19
Kneissler, Pauline 110
Kogon, Eugen 157, 162–3
Kolb, Gustav 99
Konstantin of Bavaria, King 63–4
Köppke, Gustav 134
Körbel, Dr Hans 42, 49
Krosigk, Schwerin von 144
Kübelwagen ('bucket car') 38, 46
Kulka, Otto Dov 19
Kulmhof extermination camp 109

Lafferentz, Dr Bodo 46
Lang, Theo 163
Lange, Herbert 106, 109
Lanzmann, Claude: Shoah 19
Lautmann, Rudiger 162
Laws
for the Combating of Gypsies, Travellers and the Workshy (1926) 113
Sterilisation Laws (1931) 76
for the Confiscation of the Property of Enemies of the State (1933) 121
for the Prevention of Hereditary Diseased Progeny (1933) 8, 101–2
to Reduce Unemployment (1933) 177
for the Restoration of the Professional Civil Service (1933) 113
Marriage Health Law (1935) 113
Nuremberg Laws

(1935) 8, 73–4, 87,
93–4, 113, 158
for the Protection of
the German Blood
and Honour (1935)
94, 113
Marriage Law (1938)
174–5
League of German Girls
178
League for the Protection
of Motherhood and
Social Reform 71
Lebensborn (Fount of Life)
homes 174
Lebensraum 72–3, 78, 80,
89, 126, 128, 184
Leffert, Karl August von 56
Lehmann, Christine, and
family 112, 113–16, 122
Lehmann, Julius 53
Lenz, Fritz 80
Ley, Robert 14, 37–8, 41,
61
Linden, Herbert 106–7
Lithuania: epidemic threat
79
Lorenz, Konrad 74

Maelicke, Alfred 150
Main Trustees for the East
150
Manstein, Gen Erich von
129
marriage
Weimar policy 72
homosexuals and
marriage 163
Marriage Laws 74, 94, 113,
169, 174–5
Marriage Loan Scheme 173,
177
Letter Centre 176
Marx, Chancellor Wilhelm
155
Marzahn 'Gypsy camp'
116–17, 118
Mason, Tim 13, 24, 29
Mecklenburg, Grand Duke
of 56
medicine and health, see

also doctors; eugenics;
euthanasia; genetics;
psychiatry
19th–20th C. views
69–71
Nazi concept 73–5,
79–81
Hereditary Health
Courts 102, 106
genocidal role 21, 66–7,
76–9, 117, 159
concentration camp
procedures 77–8
Meduna, Ladislaus von 103
Mein Kampf 60, 73, 76,
125, 184
Meissner, Frau 59
Meissner, Otto 52
Meltzer, Ewald 104–5
Mengele, Josef 74, 76
Mennecke, Friedrich and
Eva 110
Meyer, Adolf 80
middle class
place in Nazi ideology
81, 170
persecution of Jewish
professionals 90–1
role in racial policies
14–15, 19–20, 140–1,
146, 151–2, 178
Mombert, Paul, and the
Mombert Formula
145–6
Mommsen, Hans 5–6, 20,
47, 48, 79, 142
Moravek, Dr Karl 120
Mrugowsky, Joachim 72,
78, 79, 80
Müller, Hermann 156
Müller, Karl Alexander von
53
Munich: role in high
society 52–3, 54
Munich Putsch (1923) 52,
53, 54, 55, 73, 98

1919 National Club 54
National Socialist People's
Welfare (NSV) 60, 87
Netherlands

'Aryanisation' of Jewish
business 144
'foreign workers' in
Germany 32, 39, 41,
43, 44
post-war euthanasia
issue 9
Neuengamme camp 40
Neumann, Erich 145
Neurath, Konstantin and
Frau von 59–60
Nitsche, Paul 111
Noakes, Jeremy 12, 13,
51–65, 189
Nolte, Ernst 3, 16, 17, 136
Norway: 'foreign workers'
in Germany 39
NS-Frauenschaft (NSF;
Nazi Women's Group)
170–1, 172, 181, 183
Nuremberg Laws (1935) 8,
73–4, 87, 93–4, 113, 158

Oberhauser, Josef 109
Oberländer, Theodor 145,
147
Obernitz, Hanns Günter
von 55
Olympic Games (1936) 8,
117
Opel company 37
Overy, Richard 31

Papen, Franz von 52, 60
Pfannmüller, Hermann
102, 103–4, 105–6
Pfeffer, Captain von 55
Philipp of Hesse, Prince 55
Ploetz, Alfred 69, 70, 71
Pohl, Gisberg 134
Poland
Hitler's invasion 126,
145
'Gypsy' deportations
from Germany
113–14
dispossession of
'Aryan' Poles 142,
150, 181
population 'problem'
145–7, 148, 150

forced labour in
Germany 4–5, 31,
32, 39, 41, 180
Volkswagen factory 39,
41, 42, 43, 45
persecution and murder
of Jews 94, 109, 144
post-war reparations
4–5
police, see also Gestapo
pursuit of 'shirkers',
'Gypsies', etc 28,
113–22 passim,
160–2
population
optimum population
theory 145–6
birthrate decline 71–2,
88, 169, 172, 175,
182
Nazi reproductive
engineering 67, 159,
160, 169–79
Poland, Russia, and
'overpopulation'
145, 146–50
Stalinist policy 152
Porsche, Ferdinand 6, 37,
46–8
prisoners of war
forced labour 31, 39,
42–3, 46, 48
Soviet see Soviet Union
Proctor, Robert 75
psychiatry, see also
euthanasia
historical background
98–100
fate of patients 76,
100–11, 140
asylums 99–101, 106–8,
110, 142–3
Pückler-Burghaus, Count
Carl-Friedrich von 63

Racial Hygiene Society 70,
71, 72, 82
Racial Hygienic Research
Bureau 123, see also
Hygiene Institute
racial policies, see also

eugenics; euthanasia;
genetics; Jews; medicine
and health; Roma and
Sinti
19th–20th C.
background 69–73
among workers 27–8,
35, 41
indoctrination of
children 92, 102,
132, 168
Nazi ideology 47, 66–83
126, 156–7, 164,
167–71, 181, see also
Nuremberg Laws;
Volksgemeinschaft
overpopulation theory
143–7
Racial Political Office 81,
116, 120
Ratibor-Corvey, Prince 61
Reagan, President Ronald
137
Reich Central Office for
the Combating of the
Gypsy Nuisance 120
Reich Central Office for
the Combating of
Homosexuality and
Abortion 159, 160, 162
Reich Commissariat for the
Strengthening of Ethnic
Germandom 141, 142
Reich Committee for
Economic Affairs 141,
144
Reich Criminal Main
Office 164
Reich Criminal Police
Office 115
Reich Crystal Night (1938)
20, 94–5, 143, 144
Reich Labour Service 132
Reich Main Security Office
16, 115, 145
Reich Office for Area
Planning 141
Reichenau, Gen Walthar
von 129
Reichslandbund 54
Rentzsch, L/Cpl O. 132

Research Council 80
Ressovsky, Timoféef 74
Ribbentrop, Annette von
57
Ribbentrop, Joachim von
56–7, 61
Ritter, Dr Robert 119, 120,
121
Rodrigue, Aron 19
Röhm, Ernst 61, 157–8
Roma and Sinti people
('Gypsies') 6–8, 28, 67,
87, 112–24, 163
Rose, Georg 123
Rose, Mazurka and family
116–23
Rosenberg, Alfred 61
Roth, Karl-Heinz 14, 73,
80
Rovan, Joseph 6
Rüdin, Ernst 70, 74, 76

SA (Stormtroopers) 25, 55,
87, 90, 157
Saarland: recruitment of
workers 38
Sachsen-Meiningen,
Princess Luise and
Prince George von 61
Sachsen-Weimar, Grand
Duchess of 61
Sachsenhausen camp 2,
117–18
Sakel, Manfred 102–3
Schacht, Hjalmar 93, 144
Schallmayer, Wilhelm 70,
71
Scheubner-Richter, Max
Erwin 54
Schieder, Theodor 141
Schleicher, Kurt von 52
Schmidt, Helmut 5
Schnabel, R. 163
Schneider, Carl 111
Schneider, Richard 93
Schoenbaum, David 13
Scholtz-Klink, Gertrud 170
Schreck, Josef 107
Schulenburg, Fritz-Dietlof
von 63
Schulte, Theo 17

Schultze, Walter 'Bubi' 106–7
Schumacher, Kurt 25
Schwarze Korps 101
Scientific-Humanitarian Committee (WhK) 156
SD (Nazi Security Service) 64
Shoah (film) 19
Siegfried, Klaus-Jörg 5, 37–50, 189
Siemens, Werner von 52
Silesia: recruitment of workers 38
Simon, Hermann 99
Singer, Peter 9, 10–11
Sinti people *see* Roma and Sinti
Slavs 67, 77, 79, 126, 149
Sobibor extermination camp 109
Social Democratic Party (SPD) 156, 157
in exile (Sopade) 23–4
Sonnenstein extermination centre 107
Sopade *see* Social Democratic Party in exile
Soviet Union, *see also* Stalin
social model for Hitler 14
epidemic threat from 79
forced labour in Germany 4–5, 31–2, 39, 42, 43, 45, 179
prisoners of war 17, 78, 125, 131, 148
in Volkswagen factory 39, 42–3, 46, 48
German invasion ('Barbarossa') and mass murder policy 77, 89, 125, 127–38, 140, 141, 147–8
defeat at Moscow (1941) and Soviet counter offensive 32, 131
dictatorships in

conquered countries 138
post-war reparations 4
Speer, Albert 46, 151
Sprauer, Ludwig 106
SS (Schutzstaffel)
origin and élitism 55–6, 57–9, 87, 184
Marriage Order (1931) 59
part in eugenics and euthanasia programmes 74, 76, 78, 80, 101, 106, 107, 109, 157, 160
oppression of homosexuals 157, 160, 162, 163
persecution of Jews 90, 127, 144
part in Final Solution 76, 77–8, 128, 144–5
concentration camp brutality 39, 77–8
at Eglfing–Haar asylum 100–1
at Fallersleben factory 40, 43, 45, 46
genocide policy in Soviet Union/Eastern countries 76, 127, 140
procreation policy 173–4
Waffen-SS 38, 46
Hygiene Institute 72, 78–9
Stahlhelm 54
Stalin, Joseph 31, 126
Stangl, Franz 109
Stephenson, Jill 21, 167–83, 189
Stöcker, Adolf 98
Stöcker, Helene 71
Streicher, Julius 92
'Strength through Joy' organisation 28–9, 37, 41, 87
Stümke, Hans-Georg 20–1, **154–66**, 189

Sudentenland: recruitment of workers 38
suicide 99, 102

T–4 (Tiergartenstrasse 4; Aktion T–4) 75, 104, 107–11
Thule Society 53
Tiergartenstrasse 4 (Aktion T–4) *see* T–4
Treblinka camp 109
Trott zu Solz, Adam von 62
Tschammer und Osten, Hans von 55

Ullrich, Völker 19
Ulrich, Lt–Col Kurt von 55
unemployment 84–5, 86, 88, 177
United Nations: 1946 report on Europe 153
Untermenschen 126, 131, 184, *see also* Jews; Slavs
USA
social model for Hitler 14
post–war euthanasia issue 9
Vietnam war and conduct of Army 138

V–1 bomb manufacture 38, 46
Vaernet, Dr Carl 164–5
Vassilitchikov, Marie: *Berlin Diaries* 62–3
Vergangenheitsbewältigung 135, 184
Vernichtungskrieg 127, 184
Vichy France 41
Vichy youth organisation 39
Vienna: 'Aryanisation' of 141, 142
Vietnam War: conduct of US Army 138
Vitalrasse 70
völkisch concept 30, 76, 85–6, 158, 159

Völkischer Beobachter 101, 156, 176
Volksgemeinschaft notion 67, **84–97**, 86, 126, 133, 134, 184–5
Volkswagen, *see also* Porsche, Ferdinand
  Fallersleben factory 37–49
  post-war compensation 5–6
Volkswagen Foundation 1

Waffen-SS *see* SS (Schutzstaffel)
Wagner, Gerhard 74
Wagner, Richard and Winifred 53
Waldeck and Pyrmont, Prince of 56
Wann*see* Conference (1942) 128
Warsaw Ghetto 79
Wehrmacht
  Abwehr 62
  mass murder policy in Russia 16–17, **126–38**
  conduct in other theatres 127, 138
  involvement in Final Solution 138, 139
Weimar Republic
  family value ethos 168
  origins of racist policies 11, 72, 85
  political and social problems 85, 87
  psychiatric reform movement 98–9
  treatment of 'Gypsies' 7

Weinberg, Wilhelm 70, 71
Weindling, Paul 12, **66–83**, 189
Weitz, Wilhelm 75
Weltanschauungskrieg 127, 185
Werlin, Jakob 46
'Westwall' fortification project 38–9
Wienken, Bishop Heinrich 108
Wilhelm II, Kaiser 57
Wilhelm of Hesse, Prince 55
Winter Aid Programme 60, 87, 88
Winterfeld, Manna von 56
Wippermann, Wolfgang 8, 73, **112–24**, 190
Wirth, Christian 109
Woltmann, Ludwig 70
women and children 21, **167–83**
  Weimar policies 71, 72
  birthrate policies *see* abortion; population
  children's homes 42, 48, 174
  compulsory sterilisation 100, 102, 170
  female homosexuality 154, 155, 181
  Nazi view of the family 167–9, 171–3, 178, *see also* marriage
  Honour Cross of the German Mother 173
  paediatric 'clinics' 105–6
  women doctors 178
  women in high society

53, 60, 61
women in workforce 30–1, 39, 40, 42, 48, 177–9
  relations with foreign workers 179–81
Women's Labour Service 178
work force
  foreign labour 4–7, 31–2, 34, 35–6, 110, 179–81
  in Volkswagen factory 38–45
  shortage of labour and use of women 30–1, 39, 40, 42, 48, 177–9
  treatment of 'rejects', etc 27–9, 32, 35, 39, 100, 113, 117, 119
working class **23–36**
  acceptance of Nazi regime 13, 23–6, 29–30, 31, 34–6, 133–4
  dismissal of Jewish workers 88
working conditions and living standards 26, 28–31, 32–3, 37, 41–4, 87
Wuhlheide 'work training' camp 117, 118

Young Plan 54
Yugoslavia: murder of workers in Germany 110

Zitelmann, Rainer 14

ILLUSTRATION
ACKNOWLEDGEMENTS

The illustrations in the plate section have been supplied or reproduced by kind permission of the following: Bayerische Staatsbibliothek, München 24; Berlin Document Center 9; Collection Bouqueret 23; Hessisches Hauptstaatsarchiv 2, 12, 13, 14, 15, 16, 17; Public Record Office, Kew 5; Stadt Archiv, Wolfsburg 4; Transit Buchverlag, Berlin 25; Ullstein Bilderdienst 6, 8, 19, 20, 21; US Army Centre of Military History 18.

The publishers have made every effort to clear all permissions, but in certain cases this has not been possible and the publishers would like to apologise for any inconvenience this may cause.